TRIA

AND

TRIBULATIONS

OF LIFE

All inquirers should be addressed to:

Book Savvy International Inc.
PMB 428 1751 Colorado Blvd. Los Angeles, CA 90041

Hotline: (213) 855-4299
https://booksavvyinternationalinc.com/

Ordering Information:
Amount Deals. Special rebates are accessible on the amount bought by corporations, associations, and others. For points of interest, contact the distributor at the address above.

Printed in the United States of America.

ISBN-13 Paperback 979-8-89190-215-2
eBook 979-8-89190-214-5

Library of Congress Control Number: 2024917793

TRIALS AND TRIBULATIONS OF LIFE

AL WYNN ROSS

PREFACE

This book *Trials and Tribulations of Life* is a direct picture of the life I have lived thus far. It shows all my good, bad, and hard times. It began in West Point, Georgia, and my journey to Chicago where at eight years old, I began to see a whole new view of the world. In this book, I included my experience of having sex at the early age of twelve. I witnessed drug users, pimps, hustlers, and con artists, and through it all, I learned life for what it is. "What is life?" Life is a school of good and bad breaks, where "lessons are hard learned" and reach the soul and leave an imprint, and that imprint is an experience!" I have rubbed with aldermen, congressmen, judges, and top-notch gangsters of Chicago. Most of whom were head gang lords in the late sixties. I have lived through several narrow escapes in my life. This book, I hope will make you laugh, cry, and learn "lessons hard learned." I believe that if not for the grace of God, I wouldn't be here, I want to believe that all these children, dope dealers, street-walkers, and night people's lives are so short-lived because it is written to honor thy father and thy mother, and thy days will be long on this earth." They have forgotten these words and no longer listen to their elders. The people of this time and era are not reaching their children anymore. I want to believe that God is speaking to them through me and my experiences, and maybe this is why God has spared me. Who knows?

Enjoy!

Errata:

I hope this book will make you laugh, cry,

and

learn from my past mistakes.

PROLOGUE

The four (4) main things that I think hinder the growth of our children are:

1. Environment

   The environment is where one is raised; the life standards that have not been set for them.

2. Level of Respect

   They do not respect nor accept the teachings of their parents or elders they encounter each day.

3. Religion

   Taking religious teachings and prayers out of schools.

4. Authority

The loss of authority of the individual parents, not being able to raise our children with reasonable force. (Spare not the rod, spoils the child.) The Bible teaches us when this is absent, there is no guidance. It is easy to speak out on a problem or bad situation but is harder to come up with a solution to the problem. My part of the solution, I hope, can be my book, Trials, and Tribulations of Life. I would like it to be a testimony of the life I have lived, the mistakes I have made, the "lessons hard learned," and the blessings I have received from God. Your part—meaning the church, parents, and elders—in my opinion, is to focus on our youths and put the four things we can see are missing in their lives.

We need to start today!

A thought, whether right or wrong, if meditated on, will manifest, and turn into reality. That is why you must watch what you read. The subconscious mind is like a tape recorder listening to the negativity and recording it. If your thoughts are negative, sooner or later, your actions will be negative. Negativity begat negativity. Use this, for example, if you desire a certain woman, you see and keep feeling that thought and don't dismiss it from your mind, you will find that it will manifest itself into reality and that first seed that you didn't dismiss will manifest her into your life.

What you thought about and kept desiring in your heart manifested itself into a reality. Remember, the hearts of all men are treacherous. So, therefore, you need God's knowledge to feed your mind and your thoughts to holiness and righteousness, and you will reap the benefits of those efforts.

Knowledge is power. When you learn to mix wisdom, knowledge, and patience together, you can achieve success. Along with communication, there must be consideration and cooperation.

Communication is the key to understanding.

Consideration is the compensation for something, when you buy a TV, you give monetary consideration When raising a child, the consideration you give is love, patience, and knowledge to the child, and the payment that you expect to receive is that the child becomes a successful adult with moral traits.

Cooperation is explained as two or more moving and grooving in the same direction—two or more minds on the same plane, working together. When something or someone is said to be cooperative, they are doing the right thing, or what is expected of them in any given situation.

Children are like a blank page of a book. You must teach them and mold them into adults; they will become whatever you mold them to be. The saying goes that whatever you put in affects what you will get out and that you are what you eat. Character and character traits are the effects of the motivation given to you by your upbringing. So, look at your baby as a putty, shaping the infant from birth. It may be a hard struggle, but in the end, what you have manifested in them, you will see that your molding will become a reality. Without guidance and teaching, many kids take the wrong direction and end up lost and affected by their environment.

I don't claim to be a doctor of anything, but through seventy-three years of living, these things of which I speak have proven to be true through my own experiences of "lessons hard learned."

These words are very serious about our children. These words can come alive with one movement from you. Look down through the pages of my life and look at the environment.

Maybe if I had a proper upbringing, love, and guidance at that time, I would be sitting behind a judge's podium or standing in front of it as a lawyer or in front of a pulpit as a preacher—these were my desires. It is written that whatever your mind can believe you can achieve with help and guidance.

You can raise a better generation if you just believe and make the necessary efforts for the bible says that one generation comes, and the others ass away. It would be a shame if we couldn't learn from our elders and the generations that just passed away.

It was said by a modern Muslim Iman that it takes a man seventy-five years to learn how to live. I only have two more years to go. I am a witness that he is telling the truth, and I am still learning at seventy-three. As I have stated in the book, if you take this book as being the truth, then you will have seventy-three years added to your years to come.

CHAPTER 1

I sat there listening to the muttering sound of the tongue-tied woman going on and on about the money she won from a lottery ticket. She reached into her pocket and looked at me for a long time. Slowly bringing her hand out of her pocket, she showed me a roll of play money (dollar bills) in the sum of one thousand dollars.

"See what you could have, but no! You don't want to go get our dead kids that they have stolen from me in the hospital. You are just like my husband. You want all the money, but you don't like our kids. No, I am not going to give you a dime until we go and find them." She sat across from me in my car at Tom's and Red's Hardware, a Tripler store of Monterey Hardware, Illinois Lottery, and Currency Exchange.

It was a big lot, and we sat there. She talked on and on about the babies. I sat there and listened to the noise. I knew the drill; she goes through this every time she runs out of her "Stay Cool Medicine." I leaned back in my seat and enjoyed the scenery.

On the northwest side of 112th and Vincennes was Morgan Park High School, with a huge running and walking track. On the south side was Morgan Park Professional Center and on the southeast corner was Monterey Hardware. Behind the Monterey Hardware, across the alley going east, was the Morgan Park Church. Across the street, the Amoco food shop sat on the northeast corner. Houses stretched out, going east for the next block to Ashland

Avenue. It was the year 2000, and most of the houses were being torn down, going east of the church for a small plaza to be built in their places. I saw the young ladies going to school with their skirts up over their thighs, and the young men with their baggy pants hanging down around their hips, showing their asses.

This was the beginning of the new millennium, and I was sixty-six years old. Still hustling, I looked over at the woman who was still talking. She was forty-six years old. The Westside Street corner (Ked Vale Street), where she grew up had taken its toll on her. She wore her hair very short, making her look more like a boy than a girl. She was stout and had a pleasing smile, but somewhere between the ages of twenty-five and thirty-five years old, something or someone had tampered with her elevator, and today she was stuck somewhere between the first floor and the basement. Sue Ann lit a cigarette and went on talking. "You know, Al, I think I saw the twins of mine on television. They look like my husband, me, and you." I could see the tears in her eyes as she whispered, "I'm going to get my kids. 'They can't hide them forever."

I felt sorry for her each time she missed taking her medicine. I was her landlord, not her man. I was her friend, not her doctor. I knew one thing for sure and that was I was getting too old to keep going through this bullshit each month for five hundred dollars. I turned on the ignition of the blue 98 Chevrolet Ventura van and headed east for I-57 going southbound. At 147th Street, the exit sign that read Dixie Highway headed for 159th Street. I pulled into the rear of the sixteen-flat building driveway that sat on the west side of Dixie Highway. I backed out of the driveway and headed for Dixie Highway. I pulled behind the stop sign facing east and parked with the side of the car on the sidewalk grass. She went on talking. "I don't care for my husband anymore. After I found out about the babies he had with my best friend and put me out of my own house for that twenty-year-old slut, I could just kill him. That's why I tell you that he might come here when you are away and kidnap me for my check. He takes my money and locks me up in a room in his house in Kankakee, and when all the money is gone, he puts me out. I am getting damn tired of it. So, if I get kidnapped, you come and get me when I call." Hearing the word *"kidnapped,"* repeated in my mind, took me back in time and into another era on the south side of Chicago.

CHAPTER 2

It was a cold November evening of Thirty-First Street. The wind howled as bits of paper flew from one side of the street to the other. A middle-aged woman got out of the cab before me. As I stepped onto the sidewalk, she smiled at me admiringly, then turned and walked eastwards to the Glass Bar Lounge. I, on the other hand, walked straight ahead to the 114 Club, about six doors down from the corner.

The club was crowded. There was one empty stool at the far end of the bar. As I passed the drunken customers, I recognized the faggot and the whore seated at the bar. They gave me a slight smile of recognition, and I returned the gesture with a nod as I seated myself on the stool.

A loud voice came from across the room. "Hey, Al, get a drink on me!" It was Smitty at the pinball machine and he boasted "This machine is on fire tonight!"

I thanked him and turned back to face the bar. I glanced into the mirror, admiring the nineteen-year-old boy who stared back at me. He was dressed very slickly. The Dunlap waxed, beaver hat that matched the brown coat complemented his tan, youthful face. I smiled in the mirror to show off my gold tooth and thought to myself, "*Damn, I'm a nice-looking guy.*"

"What's it going to be, Al, gin and water?" Joe, the bartender asked. "Yes, a double," I answered. "The drink is on the Smitty."

"Yeah, I heard." He said as he went to get my drink. The noise of the crowd softened, only the pinball machines could be heard. Finally, someone dropped a dime into the jukebox, playing a record by Johnny Ace. The bartender came back with my drink, and I took a sip from the glass.

"Oh, by the way, Al, your girl Maxine called about nine o'clock tonight. She seems to have been in trouble. She said she had four hundred dollars for you, but two guys won't let her leave the lounge. She is at the Pitch Pub Lounge on Thirty-Ninth Street and Drexel. Avenue, she wants you to come and get her."

I glanced up at the clock in front of me on the wall. The time was 12:05 a.m., and three hours had passed. My blood rushed to my head. I felt like I was going to pass out. Joe could see the fear in my eyes and hear it in my voice as I asked for another drink. I stared into the mirror once again, but this time, I saw a frightened child with no gun, big brother, or anyone who would be willing to go help me fight this battle. I never had a woman to take care of me like Loraine. She bought me clothes and shoes, and she paid for my apartment. I knew in my heart that if I wanted to keep her, I had to go get her.

"Look, Al, I know that you are only nineteen. I let you in here because you spend good money, and you are a nice fellah. Besides, you never give me any trouble. I can see that you are scared and confused about what your next step should be. You don't know—"

"No" I interrupted, 'I really don't know what to do." I looked around the room to search for a Superman, a gunfighter, a gangster; any help was welcome at this point. I looked around for Smitty at the pinball machine, but he was nowhere to be found. The lounge was empty except for the company of four or five other people. "I'll see you later, Joe," I said while heading for the door. When the cab reached Twenty-Ninth Street, I looked over at the auto light factory that stretched out a half black in each direction. The factory was dark and deserted. I walked back into Sam's Lounge, where Henry was the bartender. As I arrived at the bar, I spoke to Henry, but seeing Lois at the jukebox, I walked over to her. Nat King Cole was singing "Walking My Baby Back Home."

"Hello, Lois," I said. "Oh, hi, Al," she answered as she placed the dimes into the vendor. Where is everyone?" I asked, "Terrell, Tony, and Seal are agone with Rabbit and two other fellas to Boots and Saddles to gamble. Joe, Lewis, and Tuck are gone to twenty-Fourth Street to the big building Lounge. Tuck had met a new girl. He's gone to see how much money she brought back from Milwaukee. Josephine, a new girl, went with Little Daddy and his woman, Pretty," she informed me.

I left, heading for Twenty-Fourth Street where the cab drove swiftly down Indiana Avenue. The Victorian buildings stood side by side like marching soldiers lining both sides of the street. Every now and then, you could glance at a person sitting in front of the window on the first, second, and third floors of the buildings. The cab stopped on Twenty-Sixth Street, picking up a passenger and continuing to Twenty-Fourth Street.

As I entered the big building tavern, everything was quiet, and no one was around. I caught a cab back to the 114 Club on Thirty-First Street. The 114 Club was white-owned, but it was a black hangout. Joe was one of the owners and tonight, my only contact with Loraine, I wondered if she had called again. I ordered a double gin and asked if he had heard from her.

"No, I thought you were on your way to get her when you left," he answered while wiping off the bar. He further reminded me that the bar closes at two and they close at four and that I had better be on my way. I interrupted him, "Okay, but one more for the road" I muttered regretfully. "No, Al, I don't think you need another drink." You need to be sober while taking care of your business," he advised.

I took his advice and left. As I entered the cab, I asked the cab driver if he'd turned off the line. He replied jokingly "Sure, Buddy, if you got the money, I'll take you to New York!" "I asked because most cabs run the line from Twenty-Fourth and Indiana to Sixty-Fifth and Indiana" I explained.

Well, it's like I said before, if you want to go, I'll take you." (jitney cab passengers sharing the cab), The cab stopped at Thirty-Fifth Street. "You know the tavern by Two-Gun Pete's place?" "Sure, I know the place. That will be $1.50." "Good, let's go," I said. The cab driver was a young-looking fella wearing a white shirt and a black cloth tam. He had a way about him that gave people the impression that he was some type of street hustler. I felt comfortable with him. Although my heart was like a lump in my throat from fear, I started a conversation with him to relieve my stress.

"Say, my man, what would do if you had a woman that had four to five hundred dollars for you, and she's been kidnapped by two men who are holding her in a raven? How would you play your hand if you were her man?"

The cab driver came to an abrupt stop. "Look, my man, he shouted, 'I'm a damn cab driver, not a policeman. If you're looking for trouble, I can let you out right here!!!" I replied, "No problem my man, but I do want you to wait for me for about five minutes. If you stay and wait, I'll pay you $20.00," I pleaded and handed him the money and he agreed to wait for me.

The cab pulled to the curb. The lounge looked dark with only a dim light that could be seen from the rear. My first impression was that the lounge was closed for the night. But as I moved closer to the plate glass window and peeped in, I could see one man seated at the far end of the bar with his back facing the window. Loraine was seated on the other side of him with her back to the bar. The second man stood on the other side of Loraine facing her and they seemed to be in a deep conversation.

Suddenly, from the corner of my eye, I could see a man coming from the left of me inside the lounge with a flashlight heading my way. I swiftly moved from the window to the door, not really noticing my movements, I muttered softly, "Help me, God!" With these words, my left hand went into the patch coat pocket and my right hand knocked on the door like a log of wood. The man shone the flashlight towards me and said in a low voice "We're closed." I replied, "I came for Loraine," and he asked, "What?' I shouted "LORAINE!" The door came ajar, and the man asked me "Who did you say? "At a young age, I could always act in a role that should be acted in any given situation.

Now, tonight, without noticing my own movements, I was once again on a stage playing a role. With my left hand still in my pocket, I stepped with my right foot, blacking the door, and with the same movement, my right hand pushed the door open, and I said, "I came for my woman, Loraine!" Everyone at the bar faced me. The old man stood there in shock watching my face and left-hand pocket. "Bitch," I screamed at her. "Get your ass off that stool and let's go!" She rose to obey, but the guy who was standing in front of her pushed her back onto the stool. I heard a guy who was sitting say to his friend, "Be careful, man, that niggger might have a gun." The voice was a whispering sound, but I heard it and acted accordingly. I took two steps and asked, "Did you hear me, bitch?" Get off that damn stool before I kill every motherfucker in here!" She rushed to me and with my right hand I slapped her hard across her face. Then with the same hand, I grabbed a handful of her hair and pulled her slowly out of the door.

The jitney pulled out from the curb and headed back to Thirty-First Street. Loraine was still crying and wiping tears from her eyes. “I don’t know why you hit me I called you all night to come and get me.” The crying continued loudly. “Shut up, bitch, ‘and you better have all my money,” I said while giving her a long stern stare. My heart quivered, and I relaxed after I had checked the rear window to see if we were being followed. Loraine went into her brassiere and came out with a roll of bills that made a knot. The cab driver’s eyes seemed to come through the rearview mirror as she handed me the knot. I counted it with the cab driver as a witness; it was $480.00, one and a half days’ work.

I don’t blame you, my man. As fine as this lady is I would go to the moon to get her,” he said with his teeth showing in the mirror. “You can ice all that bullshit” I answered. “You got your tip from the get-go. If you want to turn a trick with that twenty-dollar bill I gave you then say so” I said while getting braver by the minute in front of my woman, Loraine. I glanced over at Loraine as she was matching the stare of the cab driver in the rearview mirror. She was a smooth black woman with thick black hair that hung in a curl roll at the top of her shoulders. She had perfect white teeth that sparkled when she smiled. Her legs and shape gave authority to her being a woman. Yes, she was beautiful, I thought as I leaned back and enjoyed the ride to Thirty-First Street.

CHAPTER 3

Estell Wynn was a whiskey runner. He had fifteen gallons of moonshine liquor in boxes on the back of his T-model Ford truck. The truck turned into his backyard where several people were waiting for the distribution of the liquor. He lived in a duplex on the corner of Mountain Spring Highway in West Point, Georgia. At the other end of the house, lived his cousin Callie Davidson, her husband John, son Forest, and younger girl, Mary Joe Davidson. Estell turned off his headlights and got out of his truck.

Elsie looked up at him and asked, "How did it go?" She continued, "I mean with Rass being sick and all, how was it in the woods by yourself?" He looked hard at her and gave his slight smile saying, "I'm here." She smiled happily. The people came out of Callie's house to get their liquor. Estell collected $30.00 that Saturday night in 1940. $30.00 was a lot of money in those days. He took the money and put $6,00 in his pocket and the rest of the money went into the jar where the rest of the money went for the long-awaited trip north to Chicago, Illinois where his sister, Zora, and her husband John, and his cousin, Elsie's brother Heard was waiting their arrival.

In the next year, 1941, Estell hustled harder than ever and kept filling the jar with the whiskey money. For some time now, Rass and Estell had been having second thoughts on continuing their won whiskey distillery business. Then there was a long wait for the making of the whiskey. Lawmen and thieves were out in the woods with them waiting to arrest, steal, and kill anyone who was bondable. The whiskey hustle was getting harder and harder to deal with. Rass could see the restlessness in his partner Estell's eyes. He knew in his heart that Estell wanted to take off to the north, Chicago, Illinois.

Estell was about nine years younger than Rass. When Estell was eighteen years old, Rass took him under his wing after the death of Estell's parents. His mother and father left behind five young children. Estell, being the oldest, had three young sisters—Zora, Queen, and Emma, and a younger brother, Prince. Estell had an older brother, Gus, who preceded his parents in death, drowning in a tragic swimming accident where he got caught in a whirlpool. There was also an older half-brother, who lived in Lagrange, Georgia, whom neither of the children ever saw. There was talk that he was a chip off their father, Marshall's block.

Marshall was a nice-looking fellow. He was short, about five feet six inches, loved chasing women, and was a drunkard on Fridays and Saturdays. Marshall was medium tanned, and his wife, Mary was about five feet eight inches and 98 percent white in color. She was a slim, nearly shaped woman with reddish-brown hair that hung down her back. She had a friendly way of greeting people with a slight smile that was captivating to all the listeners.

After Estell's father and mother died, he and his three sisters went to live with his cousin, Callie. The girls were old enough to help clean and wash clothes. Estell was also sickly like his mother. They both suffered from severe stomach ailments which was the cause of his mother's death. His father was poisoned by a woman three months before the death of his grief-stricken wife. Estell was too sickly to go to the fields to pick cotton, so he stayed around the house and cut wood for the fire, fed the chickens, and slopped the hogs. For two or three weeks, he noticed Rass Thomas going down the pass road, heading for the creek with a sugarcane fishing pole. After two or three hours, he would come back up the pass with two potato sacks. He would come out of the woods on Mountain Springs Highway, heading for River Road where he lived.

One day while slopping hogs, Estell heard his cousin, Callie talking to her son on the front porch saying "Here comes that old roguish Rass Thomas. I wonder what in God's name has he stolen today." "I don't know, Mom, but he's got something in his bags," her son Forest Davidson answered. "He sure does take care of his wife and kids. So, whatever it be, it's his business," Callie said. Estell moved closer to the house to watch Rass as he turned the corner of River Road and headed home.

Estell had made up his mind he was going to find out what might be in the bags. Rass came by every day at about 11:30 a.m. So, the next day Estell, without telling anyone of his plans had awakened early and cut the wood, fed the chickens, and made a fire in the fireplace and the stove so Cousin Callie could be warm when she got up to put on them buttermilk biscuits, sorghum syrup, and fatback meat. He wouldn't be there to enjoy the meal because he had told her the night before that he was going hunting for rabbits and wouldn't be back until suppertime.

It was about eight o'clock when he got half a mile into the woods with the single-barrel shotgun slung across his shoulder. He walked very slowly through the bushes and trees. Estell had been on many hunts with his brother Gus, and father, Marshall. He was walking up a slope when out of a pile of dead branches and leaves jumped his first rabbit. With his gun in hand, he took aim at the rabbit. The rabbit stopped, hesitated for a moment, and then made a swift dash. Nevertheless, before ten-thirty that morning he had killed four rabbits, taken the cord from his pocket, and tied the feet of the rabbits. He hung them over his shoulders, two in front and two behind.

Satisfied with the kill, he made his way across the creek to a hiss that looked like a mountain to him. Maybe it was a mountain. Maybe this is why they named the road Mountain Spring Highway.

He went up so high he could see the path that led into the woods. Ras was right on time. It was about eleven fifteen when Estell saw him walking from the road to the path leading into the woods. Today, he had his shotgun and not his cane fishing pole. He walked swiftly past about two or three miles, over the creek, heading in the direction of Mr. Burdock's farms. Estell walked the bank, keeping the trees between him and Rass. He looked down into the field where Rass was walking. The light from the burning sun illuminated the sunflowers and lilies, the blueberries and blackberries hung in a big bunch on both sides of the pass to Burdock's place. The plum and apple trees beautified the entire country's scenery. Every now and then, you could see a rabbit spring up and just as quickly, they would disappear. The squirrels jumped from limb to limb, and butterflies danced from follower to flower.

Rass stopped in the bushes to use it as Estell watched from the hill. As Estell stood high on the hill looking down, he saw Mr. Burdock and his nephew, Horse, a big log carrying "peckerwood." They both had rifles. Estell moved very slowly as he got closer to them. They were hiding behind a tall weeping willow tree. Burdock said to his nephew "I just wanna make sure we got the right niggah, cuz if he ain't, we gonna have to do this all over again. I'm getting damn tired of my cows, pigs, and chickens getting taken away from me. We let him get through shitting, and if he gets to my cows, I'm gonna blow his damn brains out." "Hell, all dem dar higgahs say he's a roguish bastard, so why wait?" "I just wanna make sure, damn it. I just want to make sure!"

Estell almost slipped while trying to get away before they saw him. He managed to crawl out of their sight and then took off running as fast as he could back to the pass which Rass had come, stumbling, and falling down the hill. He reached the path and crossed to the other side to the wood section. As he rushed through the trees, he wondered "Am I too late?" He looked across from his hiding place and saw the weeping willow tree that hid Burdock and Horse. He came out of the path singing loudly, "Going down to the station, up in the yard, gonna catch me a freight train, times dun got hard. Cause she's gone, and I ain't gonna worry 'cause I am sitting on top of the world."

Estell didn't see Rass but he knew he was close by, so in a loud voice he shouted, shifting the rabbits from one shoulder to the other shoulder, "Hey Rass, where you at?" Now, Burdock and Horse had seen Estell come from the bushes and trees. Horse asked Burdock, "Ain't that Aunt Callie's cousin?" "Yeah, what is that he got hung on his shoulder?" "Look like rabbits to me," replied Horse. Estell shouted again, "Hey Rass, where you at? I think we got enough rabbits, and I'm getting hungry." "We are too close to Mr. Burdock's place. We don't want him to think we tried to steal something. Hell, cousin Callie says that he is the best white man in this country, and as long as she has worked for them, she never took anything from them, 'cus they are good white folks, we better go before he finds us here and think something funny."

Rass almost scared the shit out of Estell as he stepped past behind him as close as touching distance. "What you say, boy?" Estell jumped and turned to face him. Rass was pulling his pants strap over his shoulder. The sound of Rass's voice could not be heard by the observers. Estell whispered softly, "Don't run…just be calm, Mr. burdock and Horse got two rifles on you." Then, thinking very quickly he took two rabbits from his shoulder and handed them to Rass and turned for home. "You can carry your won rabbits, cuz I'm done hunting." Rass took the rabbits, threw them across his shoulder, lifted his shotgun, and followed Estell down the road.

They were almost home before a word was spoken. Rass broke the silence. "What about over there under the shade of a tree, Stell?" Estell responded, "My name is spelled 'E-S-T-E-L-L,' Estell!" They laid their shotguns and rabbits on the ground and seated themselves. Rass said, "You be Gus's brother and Aunt Callie's cousin?" "Yes, I am Gus's brother. Did you know him?" "Yes, I met him over to Aunt Callie's when your father would send him to get whiskey and he would go to town for your daddy. I talked to him a few times. He was a nice boy. I am the one who give him them black and brown brogan shoes." "Oh! You are the one he would talk to me about. You're the one that kept Mr. T.C. Nichols from whipping him?" "Yeah, I am him. You see, Gus had come out of Pluke Smith's store with an ice cream cone, almost falling over a piece of wood. He buried that ice cream all over that Peckerwood's coat and shirt. Mr. Nichols slapped him down and said, "Boy, you black bastard? "I'm gonna whip your black ass!" I had got some fat back for my beans and was coming out the door behind Gus. I saw the look in that honky's face and knew he was gonna hurt him bad, really bad! I said, "Please, oh please such! Mr. Nichols, this, here, be a cousin of mine, and he ain't got right good sense, please!! I got a gallon of the best whiskey you ever tasted. Yes, so much better than that last whiskey you got from Aunt Callie."

I had sold Aunt Callie three gallons before I went to the store, and now, I was her first customer to come back with Mr. Nichols. So, Stell— "Estell cut him short, "Estell, I told you!" "I know you did, but you see, I used to court a girl named Estelle, and I know you ain't her, but I feel better calling you "Stell" if you don't mind. Estell gave a nod of approval. Rass continued talking, "Your brother would tell me how sick you and your mother used to be, and I hear that you are too sick to work in the fields now. So, since you saved my life today, maybe I can help save yours and help you care for them sisters of yours." "How would you do that?" "Do you know anything at all about whiskey and mash?" Estell replied, "Yes, I know a little about whiskey…how to make it, but Cousin Callie is the home-brew maker, she knows it from head to toe." Rass responded, "Yes, I know, but I am the whiskey maker and I know it from head to toe! I need a buddy who will listen and do as I say. We will roll in money. Have you heard of jab-bo, the whiskey maker?" "Yes, the one the Klu Klux Klan hung and set on fire because they said he was going with a white woman."

"That be my daddy, my stepdaddy. He told me about whiskey in every detail. Mr. Bull Durham, as you call him, he is my real daddy. He kicked my mama off his farm when she got with me." "I am," Estell said. "Is this why you look so white, with green eyes and red hair?" Ras retorts. "Don't talk about eyes. Yours is grayish green, didn't you know that?" Estell dropped his head and looked into the field. "Want a roll?" Rass asked, handing him the "making" of a cigarette. For the next three months, Rass taught Estell all he knew about stealing other people's goods. "In order to keep money in your pocket you got to give the folks what they want, whether it be chickens, pigs, or cow meat, potatoes, corn, or greens. You get yourself a list of folks and meet their needs." He would pound this into Estell every day. "Give the folks what they need."

Rass and Estell had done well for six months. They hustled together. At first, Cousin Callin had said, "No! I don't want you running around with that Rass. He will get you dead." But after Estell had told her that they only hunt together, he reached into his pocket and handed her $2.00, then told her he would give this every week, she stopped questioning him about Rass and what he was doing in the woods. "Well, Stell," Rass said, throwing his shotgun across his shoulder at the path leading into the woods. Estell stood there looking at him. He raised the stock of his gun as they walked down the pass, Rass continued, "I have given you everything I have to give, now you can beat me in making whiskey. 'Tonight, we will jug twenty gallons. You know how much that be?" "Yes, forty dollars" Estell answered.

"Did you tell Little Boy where to pick up the whiskey?" "Yes, I told him to come to the flat by Leroy's place and wait for the signal from my light." "Hell," Rass said, "Let's sit here by this apple tree." There they sat. "How many rabbits do we need?" "Eleven rabbits, six squirrels, and three geese," Estell replied. "Let's see here…eleven rabbits at a quarter apiece are $2.75, six squirrels at 40 cents each is $240, and $1.50 for the geese come in all to $6,65, Okay, Stell, you are good at rabbits, I'll get the squirrels and geese." Five hours had passed, the sun was down, and the moon shined brightly on the gallons of whiskey that Rass and Estell hid in some of the bushes in the flat by Leroy's farm. They had the geese and rabbits tied on a string just in case they were stopped by the sheriff, but now they were on their alibi for being in the woods at night.

Fourteen minutes had passed when they saw Little Boy's truck coming to the flat, Estell gave a signal with a small flashlight, one long flash, and two short flashes. The truck stopped, and two guys jumped from the bed and headed their way. After carrying the whiskey to the truck and hiding it in the false bed of the truck, Rass turned to Estell and said, "This is your big night. You're riding to Alabama with Little Boy. You know he lives in Alabama. So, you will get to meet Mr. Charlie, a farmer who takes every gallon of whiskey that we can get to him; cows, or any other items we might have that he needs, but we are not in the cow business any longer. We are now whiskey men. So, Little Boy will stay in Alabama, and you will drive your truck home." My truck?" Estell asked with joy. "Yes, your truck," Rass answered. "You earned it. You learn fast, and I have another surprise for you, Stell, you know that Little Boy works for Mr. Clark at the Kroger Grocery store, well, he is sick with the shaking disease, so he told Mr. Clark that you were the man for the job. It just fits you. You don't have to lift anything. They load you up at the grocery store, and they unload you at your stops."

Estell began shaking his head; "No man, I like the truck and all that, but I want to be with you in the woods." Rass could see the sadness in his face. He liked Estell very much. He was brave, could shoot, and wasn't afraid of the sheriff or any other peckerwood. And when they were making whiskey, he didn't talk or sing like most guys would, singing and talking will bring the sheriff right upon your still. Estell was closed-minded, but on the other hand, he was sickly, and those damp woods were no place for him in the long run. "Listen, Stell. We are still partners. You, in the delivery business, and me in the making whiskey business. Together we get money, money, and more money. With this job, you can get to Alabama every Wednesday, seeing Mr. Charlie when you deliver groceries. Then if you are as smart as I think you are when you deliver supplies to LaGrange, Georgia, you can find other whiskey buyers. Little Boy has been working for Kroger's for ten long years and has been working for me for three years right up under the white folks, and they never noticed him. You can play a much better role than Little Boy. You see Mr. Len Clark tomorrow at 12:00 O'clock with your truck. The main thing is for you to make that cracker like you. Be the good nigger for him, and if he likes you and keeps you on working, no sheriff in these counties is going to mess with you. You will be the man on the road."

After the whiskey was loaded, Estell got into the truck with Little Boy. Rass threw rabbits and geese over his shoulders and handed the squirrel to one of the other two men and the three of them took off into the woods Estell rolled a cigarette as they headed for Linner, Georgia downtown where most of the whites lived except for the big ranchers and farmers. They lived out in Harris County, where the blacks lived. Fifteen minutes later, they were downtown. He looked over at the movie house on his right side. He and Gus had only been there twice. "Hey! Look straight ahead to the left, that's Kroger's Grocery store where you will be working. Hell," Little Boy said, "you are going to be alright just keep your mouth closed and do what them white folks say, and you will be there as long as me."

Little Boy looked over at Estell. "Now this is how this thing goes. You will be working and there will be no need for you to see Rass until he comes to get you to go hunting or night fishing, you understand?" "Yes," answered Estell. They reached the bridge that would put them on the Alabama side. Estell looked closely at the signs and marked the route. Little Boy went on talking. "There is no need for those white folks here to see you and Rass together every day. Now that you'll be driving the truck, they might speck something." As they rode, Estell observed the cornfield, the soybeans, the cows and horses scattered here and there. He looked over at Little Boy, he was slim with a long neck and an old straw hat sat on his head and he wore a plaid shirt and strapped overhauls. His head would shake a little when he talked, and he would have a slight stutter in his voice.

"So, how's the business been going, and what do you think I should know to be on the job as long as you?" Estell asked. "What I just said." Little Boy snapped back at him, "Just pay attention to your own business. White folks' business is their business, and Rass' business is your business, and you take heed to what he says, and you will be fine. "Hell, a lot of whites spend time on Rass, and a lot of them crackers like him too! Even ole peckerwood daddy of his. Oh, Mr. Bull Burnham doesn't act like he likes him in front of his face, but the word came down a long time ago that he doesn't want any white folks or sheriff to hurt a hair on Rass' head. 'If you can prove to me that he did something wrong, then bring him to me. He is my nigger and only me whips my niggers.' These are the words that Mr. Burdock said to the Alabama sheriff and the West Point Sheriff. Them white folks, they know who had been stealing cows, pigs, horses, and so on. They know, but they can't catch him. Rass had this false bed built in Atlanta, Georgia and brought this truck to my house and told me that the truck was mine. Told me to sell my old truck and gave me the papers for this truck. Said that he wanted me to be his runner. He said that Mr. Charlie had told him that I was a damn good driver and a good worker. He, Mr. Charlie recommended me for this here job, I tell you, Estell, if white folks are for you, you can't lose."

Little Boy looked out the window, then looked back to Estell, "I have the papers here." He parted his shirt pocket. "Take care of this truck, and it will be your best friend. In the dark at night, it will bring you home." Little Boy made a sharp left turn off the highway through an eight-foot gate that was hanging loose from its pole". A half mile down the road Little Boy parked his truck at the back yard of Mr. Charlie's house. "By the way, Mr. Charlie got me the job at Kroger's Grocery store from Mr. Len. They are brother-in-law. But they don't know about each other's business, they say." I stay here with my family down yonder on the other side of that peach orchard. My daddy, his daddy was born on this farm." Estell met Mr. Charlie on that April night, two days after his nineteenth birthday. Mr. Charlie was a big lumberjack man, portly built in the middle with a small face that sat under a huge forehead. He seemed pleasant. As they finished unloading the liquor and placed it in the corner of the barn, Mr. Charlie said, "Well, one thing I can see right off, you don't talk much, do you?" "No, sir, nothing to talk about." Answered Estell, "I like that. You will see Mr. Len about that job tomorrow and Rass will be here to go hunting with you Wednesday night. He will let you know what to do then." Estell turned the truck around and headed for West Point, Georgia. The night was cool, and he thanked God for letting him meet Rass Thomas. Maybe now he could help his sisters and his baby brother up there in Chattanooga, Tennessee with his cousin Mattie Houston.

The year was 1928, and Estell still saved a little money after helping Cousin Callie, his sisters, and his brother Prince. But all hell broke out in 1929. It was the Depression and people way up in Hollywood were jumping out of windows and killing themselves after losing their money. The whiskey business blossomed to a new height. They wanted more whiskey all the way up to Chicago, and all over the country they wanted good whiskey. Rass and Stell worked diligently. Day and night, the money came in and their pockets were full. The people of the South grew their own food and didn't feel the pressure of the depression as those in the North did. Stella and Rass worked extra hard day and night. With Stella going to work for Mr. Charlie, they had to give up the whiskey that was going to LaGrange. Whiskey, whiskey, and more whiskey, the country was demanding.

Two years later, in 1931, the running and hustling were getting to be too much for Estell. He could barely make it in at one o'clock in the morning. Then, gets up at five o'clock so he can get to Kroger's Grocery Store at 6:00 a.m. The migraine headaches and severe stomach pains sometimes sent him into shock. He didn't dare tell Rass his problems, nor would he confide in anyone else. He kept his illness to himself. For some time, when he suffered, he would ask God to help him continue to be able to provide for those who depended on him. It was a cold March night Estell came home early about nine. He lived in Cousin Callie's house with his three sisters, Cousin Callie, and her two children. He came in through the kitchen door. There were only three rooms, a kitchen, a bedroom, and the living room where all the children slept-Zora, Mary Joe, Queen, Emma, Forest, and himself. From the kitchen, you could see the full length of the house. He lit the lamp. "Estell, is that you?" called Cousin Callie from the side of the bed. "Yes 'am. It's me!" "Well, before you eat, you betta go out 'n get some stove wood, some now' n mo for in the morning! You heath me, boy? There is no eating'n sleeping till that wood is cut!'

The headache was unbearable. He tried to stay calm. If she only knew how he was feeling, she would cut the wood herself. Besides, she has her son, Forest, there with her all day. He is fickle-minded, all right, but he knows how to cut wood. Forest was a big strong and tall guy, about three years older than Estell. He's a mama's boy and very lazy. Forest raised his head from the pallet, which is in the middle of the living room floor. "You heath what she said, boy, now get your ass out dar' n cut that wood, and don't mess wit dat some tin' to teet' till you are done cutting." "Cousin Callie, I don't feel very good, I just wanna lay down and get some sleep, no need for eating," Estell explained. "You cut that wood, you heath!" "There be no sleeping or eating 'til you finish!"

Estell walked out of the back door, got into the truck, and drove away knowing deep in his heart he would never return to live in Cousin Callie's house as long as he lived. He headed toward the creek where he and Rass fished. The moon shined brightly over the creek, Estell reached into the bed of the truck and got an old quilt that belonged to Rass. He got back into the truck and wrapped himself warmly. It was about 4:00 a.m. when he was awakened by a bell, which hung around the neck of a cow. Estell straightened and folded the quilt and placed it back in the bed of the truck. He drove to Rass's house. The cow stood still as the truck passed. Stell explained last night's occurrences to Rass, even telling how sick he had been for some time. They were just finishing the breakfast Rass had prepared when Rass suggested, "Hell, you got a little money saved. Go in today and see that doctor in town. Mr. Burdock's got that house up yonder on the river road, just enough room for you. It's about time you be on your own. I think he wants $3.00 a month."

Estell had driven to work to more bad news. When he arrived at the job, all the working folks had gathered on the docks, and the boss was saying "Due to this here depression, we will be closing down a week from Friday, and you, Estell, your last delivery will be next Thursday, seven days from today. Estell had been in the house a month and the people nearby had given him bits and pieces of furniture. Rass had given him a bed and a kitchen table. He had been very sick for a week now, and he lay in bed looking out of the window. He saw four people coming up the road. He could imagine who they were, but he knew they were women. His head collapsed as he lay back on his pillow, maybe 3 or 4 minutes had passed when he raised his head to get a better look. It was Cousin Callie, Zora, Queen, Emma, and a young lady named Elsie who lived with her cousin, Lillie who was married to Cousin Callie's brother, Kupie.

Estell hadn't seen Cousin Callie or his sisters since the night he left. Rass had told them where he lived and that he no longer worked for Kroger. Maybe Rass had told them of his illness. Inside the house, Cousin Callie took off her shawl and said, "Estell, you are just as stubborn as Cousin Marshall, your pappy." She placed her shawl on the foot of the bed and continued talking. "I didn't mean any harm by telling you to cut wood. You know my boy Heno (Forest) is a lazy fool and don't have any sense at all. So, I want you to get well and come back home. You can give me that $3.00 you have given that peckerwood." "No," Estell replied softly so as not to anger her. She still had his sisters living with her, and they needed a woman to raise them. He knew she made them work harder than she did with her own daughter, but they need the upbringing. The harder the whip, the better they will be as women. "Now cousin Callie you see, I won't be no help to you. I went to the doctor and he said these headaches are called migraines headaches, he also said I have an ulcerated stomach. I gave that peckerwood a year's rent. I ain't working, and the doctor said I gotta take it easy for a while. Besides, your husband, Buddy, and son Forest, or Heno as wants to be called, want to be the men of their own home. Me, I might get married one day, and I'll need a place for me—" Estell was cut off by the outburst from Elsie. "Who will you be marrying? 'That woman, Mable?" The outburst shocked everyone in the room, including Cousin Callie. Estell turned his head from Cousin Callie to Elsie. He had known Elsie for a long time. She used to play with his sisters in their yard on the farm. Elsie lived on the farm next to theirs with her mother, brother (Heard), and other kin folks. She had always been that little girl next door. Then, when her mother died, she moved in with Cousin Lillie and her husband, Kupie, Cousin Callie's Brother. She was a little girl people pitied after her mother passed away. Her other kin folk headed North to Chicago and took Heard with them, leaving Elsie alone to fend for herself. Except for her cousin Lillie, she had no one. But now, for the first time, Estell looked her up and down. He wasn't looking at the little girl. What he saw was a full-grown young woman of 18 years old, with a shape that was out of this world and all the matching parts he thought. She stood about five feet six inches with a teasing tan complexion and big brown eyes. Her hair was cut short, making her look even younger.

"Estell, you may be somewhat older, but Elsie's been in love with you all her life." His sister Queen stated. "She told us so years ago, didn't you Elsie?" The question embarrassed Elsie. She batted her eyes and smiled over at Estel, "Ain't you going to fix that chicken soup for him, Cousin Callie?" She asked. "Yeah! You fast-ass gals get over there to that fireplace and get a fire going. Get that pot on the hook, and fill it with water," said Cousin Callie, removing a large bowl of soup from a shopping bag. She also had a cake of cornbread. Estell stared at Elsie as she stared back at him and Queen was just as fickle-minded as Heno, but she had told the truth as Elsie was thinking as she hurried to fix the soup.

The Depression was getting too hard to bear for Elsie. She had a job cooking in town. Her bring-home pay was one dollar and twenty-five cents a week. She made a promise to Cousin Callie and Estell that she would be there to help him every day after he leaves work at two o'clock. She was just coming up to the front of the house when she saw Mable going out of the back door leading into the woods. Elsie had been helping Estell around his house for about two months, doing all his cleaning and washing. She would bring him a pan of food from her job. She loved doing little things for him while nursing him back to health. But today her hand tightened around the pan she had in a bag. She could kill him, the thought! She busted through the door, pushing it wide open. Estell sat on the bed in his underwear, and his hair was uncut and unshaven. He looked up in shock as she came into the room. "I thought you were through with that hussy!" She screamed. Her eyes were big and brown as she stared at him angrily. She placed the pan on the small table. "Well, I done had it with you, Estell, I tried to show you how I feel about you, but you don't care how I feel! You can only think of Mable. Well, you can keep her. I won't be coming back!' Can I say something for a minute?" Estell asked, "You got a mouth. Speak what you want." Elsie said. "Do you know the difference between a woman and a girlfriend?" Without allowing her to answer, he went on talking." You see, Mable was my woman. She took care of my man's needs. You are my girlfriend, the one I hope to marry. This is what I told Mable today. This is why I have never tried to touch you because I respect you in all respects. So, I am asking you straight out, will you marry me"? Nothing seems more important to me in these two months than you. I don't have a job, I don't have anything, but I love you, not Mable, not Sally, no other woman I know, it's you." Before Elsie could think, she was on her knees in front of Estell kissing his forehead, jaws, eyes, and lips. "I love you too. Yes, yes, I will marry you. I will take care of you. I will love you for the rest of my life." Elsie promised.

The years passed, and in 1934, his first child, a son was born, and the child was me—Al Wynn! A big brown-eyed, sandy-haired boy weighing 6 1/2 lbs. In 1936 my sister, Sarah Frances, was born into the family. And that same year Estell went back to work with Rass working as hard as ever. They roamed the woods and roads at night making their liquor and stealing other people's goods. One night in 1937 Estell and Rass had followed one of Pluke Smith's workers, a cousin of Estell's, to his house. He pulled into his backyard and left six gallons of liquor in the back of his truck under some bags, Rass had stopped a half block from the truck parked in the yard. About an hour had passed when the lights in the house went out. There were no dogs around, so the picking was very quick and quiet. Estell and Rass laughed loudly as they pulled into the rear of Cousin Callie's house and sold four gallons to her.

The stealing had the sheriff's office upset! Everyone figured it was Rass but couldn't prove it. Pluck Smith stood in his honky-tonk store behind his house. Three of his whiskey makers sat at a table, staring at him as he spoke. "I know it's that nigger Rass, Thomas, and that yellow son of a bitch cousin of mine, Estell. I know that sick bastard is stealing my shit. If it wasn't for that damn peckerwood daddy of Rass, I would blow their damn heads off their mother-fucking shoulders. Luke was an average-sized man dressed very neatly in a plaid shirt and denim pants with suspenders. His hob-knobbed brogan shoes were shined to a tee. He prided himself on being neat every day because he felt this makes him feel equal in the white world, the human world, and somewhat of a god to the average nigger. His daddy Henry had plenty of land that he had gotten from his white pappy. And when his pappy died Henry gave his son the best of everything, the brick house his daddy lived in, the grocery store on the side of the house, and the honky-tonk out back that Henry Smith's daddy had sold whiskey in for over 40 years.

Life was good for Pluke. He was the overseer of the farmland, and on Saturday nights, all the blacks who worked on the farmland came to his honky-tonk. He would pick out all the pretty black girls in his place for the crackers who frequented his joint. They came for the whiskey from the woods, which was cheaper and better than that shit in town. His old white pappy had paid the police while he ran the place for over forty years, but Pluke was paying more to them to keep operating. Estell and Rass had to be stopped one way or another, Pluke thought. A snagged-toothed, bald-headed guy named Robert Fisher, one of Pluke's whiskey makers stepped closer to Pluke and said," I know that's your cousin, but you don't have to kill him. I know just what to do." Pluke said, "What is that?" Bob looked around at the rest of the guys. "Let's; play the same game that he is playing. Let me go down there and put four gallons of liquor back in the truck and notify the sheriff where the liquor is. And he won't be around here to bother anybody else." "Take care of it," Pluke said. "Then I won't have to kill that yellow bastard." Within the next three days, Estell was sentenced to one year on the chain gang. He only stayed for one week due to a retired white judge that Cousin Callie had worked for who spoke up for him.

In 1938 Estell and his family moved into the little house on the corner of Mountain Spring Highway, next door to his cousin Callie.

The houses were joined together like duplexes. His son, Al, was born on January 10, 1934, his daughter Sara Frances on January 4, 1936, now his son Robert was born on January 2, 1938. Cousin Callie was the midwife for Elsie. She stood by Elsie's bed with Robert in her arms. "This is a big baby, an eight-pound boy and he is a fat goat," she said, laughing aloud. Elsie, exhausted from the birth, gave a little smile, not really understanding Cousin Callie's meaning. "Yes, sir," Cousin Callie went on, "You have three goats. My book tells me goat stands for the word *"Capricorn"* and that means *they're good climbers in life.* They can climb Lookout Mountain in Chattanooga very well. You can never tell about goats," the book say, . She placed Robert beside Esie and went on talking as if to herself. "Did you know that my precious Lord Jesus was a Capricorn?" Come on, little Al Franes is asleep in her bed, so you will have to be going with me!" She took me by the hand and led me across the porch to her apartment.

On December 7, 1941, Pearl Harbor was bombed, and West Point, Georgia was coming to a boil. The revenue people were cracking down on the whiskey makers. Pluke and all the other whiskey makers were poisoning their whiskey, trying to catch the persons who were stealing their whiskey. One night while lying in the weeds underneath the weeping willow tree by the creek, Rass and Estell overheard Pluke's men as they jugged and jarred. The workers asked while tasting the whiskey, "What about the poisoned whiskey Pluke told you to jug?" One of the workers asked while tasting the whiskey. "Yes sir, I'm glad you asked because the poison is in the one you are about to drink from and all the other six brown jugs." "Yes, sir," the man went on talking, "We are going to kind of lay them old jugs around so them good old boys that like to steal other people's goods can get their square share of the poison. Twelve gallons will go behind the haystack, but four jugs will be hidden in front of the store, you get it?" The five men laughed as they filled the jugs on the truck and headed for the barn.

Rass and Estell from a distance could see the men unloading the whiskey. Sometimes later the men were gone. Rass and Estell approached the barn from the rear. Estell went to the corner of the barn to watch the farmhouse. Once he saw the truck parked in front, he gave Rass a nod, and Rass tore three boards from the back of the barn. Inside the barn, they quickly located the liquor and began to switch the bad whiskey to the back of the barn, making a total of eleven jugs. On their way home with the whiskey tucked away safely in the bed of their truck, Rass looked at Estell and said "hell, it is better for Pluke to sell that damn poison than us, wouldn't you say so, partner?" "Damn right," Estell replied, "And I hope he is his best customer." They both laughed as the moon gave light to the truck on Mountain Dew Road.

That night while lying in bed, he thought about his sister Zora who had married Elsie's cousin, John, and moved to Chicago. She was only a baby when she married, but that was what she wanted, and it would lighten the load on Cousin Callie. So, three years ago, she and John went north. That next year, Queen, his oldest sister married George Henry Hall, and they moved to Macom, Georgia. And now his baby sister Emma, fifteen years old had come to him yesterday asking for his approval to marry A.D. Billingsby, a cook, and the son of a preacher. A.D. was 32 years old, and maybe he would be good for her, someone to look after her, to love and care for her. Like a father! Estell had told her to let him think about it for a day or two. Maybe his thinking would be yes.

Everything was going smoothly for a week. Estell had married off his sister Emma. She and A.D. had settled down in his parents' home. Estell and Rass were just coming in from fishing when they heard that the State Police were all over Pluke's place and they were looking for Pluke. It appears someone had gotten hold of some bad whiskey at Pluke's place and had died. About eight people had been hospitalized. The police found the poisoned whiskey and now Pluke was nowhere to be found. They pulled into the backyard of Estell's house, Estell saw his son, Al, stick his head out of the door, and then vanish again. He turned to Rass and said, "Do you think that it was the whiskey that we…" He was cut short by Rass' voice. Rass could see the fear and guilt in Estell's face. "Look, Stell, don't give me that guilty look. We are hustlers. We don't go around poising people that was "Luke's doing. And besides, we don't know if that same whiskey is that whiskey or not. We didn't sell it to them. Remember, it's always best to be able to keep the cheat off you than to be the cheat. I feel sorry for the man that died and the people in the hospital, but damn, Pluke is getting what he deserves." Estell's spirit seemed to be lifted. "Yes, damn that bastard. He tried to kill us or send us away forever." "That's the way I feel," replied Rall. "Piss on his grave! His old daddy Henry Smith will save his black ass." They both laughed as Elsie and Al came to the back porch to greet them.

Two weeks later, the rumor was out that Pluke had sneaked back into Georgia dressed as a woman. He went and drew all of his money from the bank. The sheriff's office was right across from the bank. The laugh was Pluke got his money right under the sheriff's nose. Estell pulled the fish to the bank and placed it carefully into his basket. "As I was saying," Rass went on, "there is no better time to start packing and getting ready for our trip than the present. I'm getting ready to get the hell out of here and go to Florida. My auntie is waiting for one of us family kids to help her with that big house and those few cows she has left. My uncle did last year, and she is alone. She needs me, so I feel if we are lucky, we should be leaving here by the first of the year. Me, going to Florida, and you are going way up yonder to Chicago, Illinois."

The next month or two, Estell and Rass hardly slept. They had to be at least one or two steps in front of those whiskey makers. They had to know when each whiskey steel would be ready to be jugged, and after it was jugged, where would they hide it? Since Estell's brother, Willie had joined him and Rass, he would spend his nights in the woods watching each whiskey maker's every move. Every morning, Willie would give Estell every detail of the night's events. He informed Estell and Rass for some time now that Henry Smith was planning to run forty or fifty gallons of whiskey to Atlanta, Georgia. According to Mr. Smith's worker's girlfriend, they would start jugging tonight. Rass and Estell moved closer to the men as they jugged and boxed the liquor. "Where is that damned truck?" one of the six men asked as he rubbed his hands together. It's cold as hell tonight." "Give him time, he'll be here," another man answered.

Rass situated himself fifteen or twenty feet away from the steel, He saw Estell kneeling behind a bush with a rifle aimed toward the men who were sitting around drinking coffee, still packing whiskey. Rass looked over at Estell and pointed his finger toward the tree near the men, Estell nodded his head, and Rass moved to the tree. Once there, he placed the rifle belt around his shoulder and climbed to the center of the tree. He moved the gun from his shoulder and relaxed. It seemed as though half of an hour had passed when one of the men cried out, "I hear the truck! She is coming in now!" The truck parked. Willie and Leroy saw the truck come in from where they were sitting on the hill. They made their way over to Estell with their rifles in hand. The men were finishing loading the truck when the driver called out to one of them "Hey Howard, any more of that java left?" "Yes," a voice from the other side of the truck answered. "Come get a sip. You've got time." The driver jumped from the truck and went to the other side for the coffee. Rass was waiting for the driver to move, and he moved just where Rass wanted him to go, to the other side of the truck. All hell broke loose as Rass raised his rifle and shot. The bullet hit the top of the truck near the driver.

"Hawk, you black son of a bitch," the driver stopped dead in his tracks and hollered out, "Kill every one of those black bastards!" Simultaneously, Estell, Rass, Leroy, and Willie shot over the men's heads. "Don't kill us, boss!": One of the men cried out as they ran away from the truck and forty gallons of whiskey. After the men left, Rass and Estell inspected the cargo and the gas in the truck "Willie, you and Leroy get on to Lagrange, Georgia. Come back on the bus tomorrow evening. Estell will pick you up. Let's go home, partner." Rass said as he patted Estell on the shoulder. Estell and Rass left going to their truck which it was parked half a mile away down by the creek where two fishing poles lay awaiting them.

A week had passed, and Rass had left for Florida, Estell sat in the backyard with his 1941 Chrysler. It was fully packed. Cousin Callie was hugging Elsie and the kids. There were other relatives, cousins of Elsie and Estell, who crowded around the front porch to say their goodbyes. Today was the day they were leaving for north to Chicago. Cousin Callie held her hands, stretched out to Estell, and she walked towards him with tears in her eyes. "You take care of yourself, you hear," she said as she walked toward him, "and take care of that little wife and those kids of yours." Before long, the car had backed out of the yard and on its way to Route 41.

CHAPTER 4

Three hours later, the Chrysler pulled up in front of Mattie Hairston's house in Chattanooga, Tennessee. Mattie Hairston was a cousin of my father and Cousin Callie. Mattie Hairston was raising my uncle Prince, the baby brother of my father. We all went to the door, and Bubba, Mattie's husband, answered the door. He seemed surprised as he managed to smile at my father. He looked back toward the kitchen and said in a loud voice, "Look, honey Mattie. Look who's here at the door." Mattie was the opposite of the husband. She was very light-skinned and big-boned. "Estell!" She shouted with outstretched hands as she threw her arms around his neck. She looked over at my mother. "Hi, Elsie." My mother gave her hellos, and so did my aunt Queenie. "My, my, is this Al that's grown up so big?" she exclaimed while pinching me on my neck. "And Frances and Robert. My, how these kids are growing." She turned back to my father as we were moving into the house. "Why are you here? Estell? Are you upset because your brother has gotten his draft papers from the army?" "No, I didn't know anything about the papers." "He just got them yesterday" Mattie answered. "Where is he anyway? my father asked. "He just got him a little job at the grocery store, and he's still at work. He will be coming in about an hour. Now, why did you come if you didn't know about the papers?" she asked. "Well, you know, for some time now, I've been saying I was going to Chicago. It was getting kind of rough down in Georgia with the police. After doing that little bit on the chain gang, I promised myself I wouldn't do any more time."

"I suffered from extreme stomach pains, like an ulcer, and migraine headaches. It was a bitch being in jail, period. But it made it much worse being ill in jail. After doing one seven-day week, Rass went to that white pappy of his, Mr. Burnham, and begged him to speak to the judge on my behalf because I was ill. With one word being said to that honky to the judge, I was released, and only because of the good whiskey Aunt Callie had been selling to Mr. Burnham that he got me out. The judge even knew Aunt Callin. Mr. Burnham made the judge remember by saying, "You know the girl you used to et that good whiskey from, Callie? This boy is her cousin, and he is in jail very sick. That honky judge had given me one year and changed his mind after Mr. Burnham spoke about the good whiskey, he set me free."

After supper, everyone was sitting on the porch except my uncle Prince and my father. They stayed at the kitchen table talking. I guess they were talking man talk. I couldn't hear them. I stayed on the porch with my sister Frances still trying to kick me. I laid back on the floor of the porch, looking up at the stars. I looked over at the moon, a big shiny, bright moon, and I tried my best as I strained to see the face of the man in the moon. Were people just saying that or was he really in the moon? I tried hard this time to search him out. The next thing I knew, my father was pushing and shaking me. "Al, wake up, boy! Wake up! It's time to go." We all said our goodbyes again, and the big car headed for Route 41 north to Chicago.

That next morning when I woke up, father had parked in one of those gas stations. I heard my father say to my mother, "This is Indiana. It won't be long now before we reach Chicago. Go in there and get some breakfast." And he gave her some money. After eating, we were on our way again on Route 41 and headed for Chicago.

I admired the scenery. Every two miles you would see cows in the pastures. Then the scenery changed to horses. My father said those were soybeans. There were trees, all types of trees, in some fields you saw tractors sitting alone. Then, in some fields, you would see two tractors. The road seemed like forever, but we finally reached Chicago. On Thirty-First Street, my father had come to Lakeshore Drive (LSD) and made a right turn of Thirty-et. That took him to the sandy part of the beach. The trees and the hills had hidden the sandy parts of the beach. So, when he passed the hills and trees to the sandy parts of the beach, it is when he saw all of Lake Michigan, and it scared the shit out of all of us. The ladies started to holler, and the kids started screaming. "Oh, Daddy! Oh, daddy! Oh, daddy! We are going down!" We had never seen a lake before. The waves were high, and to a country person, it seemed like we would be engulfed by the whole lake. About two blacks from the lake, my father pulled to the curb and asked a passerby, "Where is 4714 South Prairie?" Sometime later, we were coming down to Forty-Fifth and Prairie, Forty-Sixth, and Prairie. I sat back looking at the huge buildings. I have never seen such a huge building in my life. I looked at all the black people on both sides of the street. Some were talking, some were hollering, and some were drinking out of bottles. We crossed the next block, which was Forty-Seventh Street. To the right, we saw big lights flashing on and off.

My mother thought that it was a church, but sometime later, we learned that it was the Terrace Theater. My father drove to the address and got out of the car. He went to seek out my aunt Zora. She was at home waiting for him. My father beckoned my mother and the rest of us to come into the house. We had all been seated there for half an hour. When my mother's brother, Heard, showed up, she started crying as she hugged his neck. "My brother, my brother, my big brother!" Then shortly after, my uncle John, Zora's husband, showed up. They had a beautiful, beautiful conversation until they tried to figure out where the children would stay. At that time, landlords had signs on the door stating, "NO CHILDREN, NO PETS." Aunt Zora said that my father would have a difficult time finding a place, and he had given her so little time to find a place that she had not found one. My aunt said that Mrs. Carrie, the lady who owned the building next door said that she would ask her cousin, who had a place on the west side. "Let me go and ring Mrs. Carrie's bell and see what she has to say."

About half an hour later, my aunt showed up with Mrs. Carrie. Mrs. Carrie came into the house, looking at my father in an admiring way. I could see that my mother didn't like that too much. "So, this is your brother, Estell, that you have been telling me about, Zora?" She grabbed my father's hand and held it, looking him straight in the eyes, saying, "I've heard so much about you." I could tell my mother wasn't going to like that lady at all. I looked at Mrs. Carrie really hard. She was a dark lady with a mole at the end of her nose. She looked to be about sixty or sixty-five with a heavy body and really skinny legs. She had long feet and wore cotton stockings. I didn't think I liked her too much myself. She was still holding my father's hand. She had on a flowery dress that looked like it had three aprons on top of it. "You know Estell," she said looking at him smiling, "if this little wife of yours can keep her children in order, I have one room that I can let you have for ninety days to give you a chance to get a job and get your children in school if you can pay your rent. Zora said she would let her sister Queen stay with her. That way, your family can stay in one room. It will be a squeeze, but that's the best I can do. You will be with me, my husband, and my son Jake."

I was enrolled in Farin Grammar School. It was located on Fifty First and Wabash. My father was lucky enough to get a job at Wilson Stockyard. My father worked the evening shift, from four to twelve in the morning. He had left my mother, Robert, and my sister all evening at the house. We had to fend for ourselves. I remember one Saturday when my father was off to work. He sent me to the grocery store on Forty-eighth and Indiana in the basement. I always walked the allies under the L-track. I like walking under the L-tracks and listening to them go by overhead. From nowhere, a boy came up to me. "Hey," he said, "are you going to the show?" I said, "I might, are you going?" He said, "Yeah, where are you going now?" I said, "I'm going to the store for my father." He said, "What are you going to buy?" I said, "Soybean Jr." He said, "I learned a good trick the other day. I can take a dollar and make five dollars." I said, "How can you do that?" He said, "Would you like me to show you? How much money do you have, boy?" "I have ten dollars. Can you make it twenty?" "If I do, you will split it with me?" I said yes and handed him the ten. He said, "I got the ten, and I will meet you at the store." He then took off running. With him knowing the shortcuts of the alleys and the streets, he lost me. I will never forget that day because it is the first day I got conned, and the first day my father shipped me with an ironing cord up here in Chicago.

CHAPTER 5

From the time of that notorious ass-whipping my father had given me, I learned from hard knocks and slick-talking niggers about the con and other street games that the street produces. We stayed on Prairie for one year in that tight and dimly lighted room. There were only 40-watt bulbs throughout the apartment. Every morning when Francis and I would leave for school, we would have to rub our eyes from the glare of the sun. Going to Farin Elementary School every day was routine. Every day we would stop about three times at different buildings up the street to wait for our classmates. Some of them were girls, and they would walk with Francis. The boys would walk with the boys. With all students doing the same thing every morning walking the six blocks to school, they looked like a herd of horses coming straight at you at the same time. Some of them were catching and throwing the ball. Some girls were jumping double-Dutch rope, some were singing, and others were talking as they walked to school. Every day going to school or coming back from school, there was a fight! The kids would gather around, making themselves a boxing ring cheering on the fight. I had about three fights during that year. One boy just didn't like me. Every day he would say, "Hello country boy." Then he would say "Country, country, country."

That one day I just wasn't up to his fun. So, I swung on him, coming from the hip with a haymaker that landed dead on his chin.

We were about three steps from the sidewalk in front of the entrance door. The way he was standing sideways looking up at me gave him no defense against the blows. He fell hard on the ongoing crowd. He fell, knocking three girls to their knees and hurting a boy's back. The principal and the Truant officer came out of the building, while one male teacher was holding me by the arm like I was his prisoner. The principal pointed to one of the teachers. "See about that boy that hurt his back and take him to the nurse. The teacher that the principal was talking to was looking at me as if she could kill me for my stupidity and ignorance. Her hazel eyes left me as she faced the principal. "Yes, Sir," she answered and took the boy into the building.

As they were going into the school, the boy caught my eyes, "I'm going to kill you for this," he whispered, and his eyes promised. The principal took me to the office and had me sit in the chair by his secretary. Then he came and got me, and he sat me in his office. "Does your mother have a telephone?" I said, "Yes," He said, "What is it?" I said, "Fairfax 5-7228." He had a big office with big statues of dogs in one corner, golf clubs, and a lot of pictures of birds all over the wall. I looked back at the principal. "Is this Mr. Elsie Wynn?" He asked on the phone. Thre was a pause for what seemed like two or three minutes, and he continued to talk. "Is this Mrs. Wynn? Mrs. Wynn, your son Al, has been in a fight again and this time I'm afraid I will have to suspend him. So, I would like to see you or his father in my office at nine in the morning."

The next day, my mother and I sat for three hours from nine o'clock until twelve o'clock, waiting for the principal to arrive. He made it there at twelve o'clock on the dot. We waited until one o'clock before he called us into his office. The day was long and rough and was getting rougher by the minute as he asked, "Do you know Aaron's mother wants the school to pay for the treatment of his back? These kids, I don't know what to do with them." The principal was saying, mostly talking to himself. "I do know what I am going to do for you," he said pointing a finger at me. "I am going to suspend you for 30 days, and if this doesn't work for you, I am going to send you to a school that can deal with your level."

"What do you mean suspend? What is suspend? What are you talking about?" My mother questioned. She only went to second grade in school in West Point, Georgia. The white man looked at my mother hard with no kindness or understanding of her lack of schooling. His eyes narrowed as he snapped at her. "Suspension means that he doesn't have to come back here until a month, and it means that he will be behind in lessons and all the other good things she should be learning instead of fighting, now I have other business." He stared at me until we were outside his secretary's door.

"Your daddy is off to work by now, but you are going to get it in the morning. You know better than to be fighting at school, and the landlady is not going to like you hanging around the house every day for a month. What am I going to do with you, Al? What am I going to do with you fighting all the time?" "Mom, I told you that boy was picking on me. Every day he would be just picking at me calling me names and all." I answered my mother with tears in my eyes. She grabbed my arm and slightly pulled me across the street. "Come on here, boy before the car gets here." The only thing I was thinking about while walking the six blocks to the house was the ironing cord and the hollering my father would do before he used the cord. That was enough thinking to make a person never want to go home or face my father again.

The next morning, I was just getting back from the store with my mother's coffee and fat-back meat. I had closed the entrance door of the apartment behind me as I heard my mother's voice telling my father about the suspension. "And the principal said he would be out of school for a whole month. I told Al that you would see him this morning." There was a hard knock at the door, "I'll get the door, Mom," I shouted. I took two steps back and opened the door. My mother was out of the room and in the hallway with me. "Stop all that loud talk Al, before you wake up everybody in the house." I looked over at the two big dining room doors closed in the middle. I doubted if that old lady could hear anything through those big oak doors with gold plate and gold knob. Simultaneously, my mother and I spoke to my uncle A.D. "Hello, Uncle A.D.!" "Hello," my mother said." Hey," he answered. "Where is Bubba?" he asked, talking about my father. As long as I can remember, he called my father Bubba. I never in my eight years knew why. "He is in the room drinking coffee." "Hey, Budda, where are you?" Not letting him answer, he went on talking. "I have good news for you today." "Alright," my father answered, "come on and tell me about it." "Well Bubba, you know that Hillman's Grocery Store downtown on Washington Street in the basement I told you that I put in for the butcher job?" "Yes," my father's head was bobbling up and down. "Yes, I remember," he replied. "Well Bubba, they called me in and I start tomorrow." "This is good news. I was talking to one of the colored ladies over at the vegetable department. We were just talking, and she asked me where I was from. I told her Georgia. She said, "How do you like Chicago thus far?" I said, "It's alright, just nowhere to live. I can't find a decent place to live. I am packed up with my cousin in his small apartment."

"You are looking for a place, huh?" She asked. And I said, "Yes." "Well," she went on talking. "There'll be an open house for kitchenettes at 2720 S. Prairie tomorrow at twelve o'clock." Then I asked her, "What is an open house and kitchenette?" "That means that the whole apartment has been cut up into two or three rooms." She went on to explain. "You don't have to share your room with anyone else. Just your apartment all by yourself." "You think they have an apartment for us too, A.D.?" my mother asked, all excited. "Cousin Elsie, that lady said they have two buildings, one stacked in front of the other one. Today is Saturday, Bubba, you get dressed and I'll run next door to see if John or Zora will take us to see the kitchenettes." I could have kissed my uncle for saving me that day. Finding a good house was like finding gold. My uncle saved me that day from the cord and from the thought of it.

The house on Twenty-seventh Street looked like a big, huge, gray castle. It looked like a haunted house that you would see in a movie. It was a big gray stone building with two round stone banisters. There was a huge black entrance door with a mail slot. The door opened into the hallway with shining hardwood floors. The first door to the left had a number on it. The second door had a number too, and so on. Apartment 13 was in the basement. The office for the building was on the second floor. Us kids, my mother, and my aunt. Stood on the front porch. After a while, my father and uncle came back with a big grin on their faces. They both had apartments. My father was 103 in the building. My uncle A.D. had number 1 in the rear of the building they call the coach house. The coach house was two flats with small windows and bars.

CHAPTER 6

That Saturday night, we moved into our apartment at 2720 South Prairie, apartment number 103. The apartment had a huge room with a closet-like kitchen and a closet about five feet by five that was located on the south side of the kitchen. There was a small door that led to the bathroom. There was another door that led to another apartment, apartment 104. Both apartments shared the same bathroom. The lights were very bright, which made a great difference from the dark rooms of our old place. My mother made pallets on the floor for us kids. She kissed us good night, and we said our prayers. I could hear my mother praying, saying, "Thank you God for this place, for my husband's job. Please take care of him. Father, for he is working." She cut off the light and went to bed.

The sun shone brightly the next day, being Sunday morning. I had gotten up really early while everyone in the house was still sleeping. I was walking down the hall, getting ready to go out the entrance door when the door to apartment number 1 opened. She stood there; the prettiest white woman I had ever seen. She had long folding hair with blue eyes that stared at me. I stared back, but the only thing I could see was the sheer nightgown and the patch of hair that lay beneath it. "Hi there," she said. I said, "Hi ma'am," shaking and keeping my eye on the patch of hair. "Would you like to make a quarter?" She asked. I said, "Huh," like an afterthought, still looking at the hair. "Yes, ma'am, I would like to make a quarter." "Would you like to empty my two wastebaskets? The trash can is in the basement. Your family is the ones who moved in last night?" "Yes ma'am," I said and stepped into the door to get her wastebaskets. I almost ran tripping over myself trying to get to the big garbage can to empty the baskets and get back to that nightgown.

When I got back to apartment 1, the door was slightly ajar. I knocked on the door, and the door came open. To my surprise, instead of seeing the nightgown, I saw a very neatly dressed man in a gray flannel suit. He was very dark and hard looking. He had holes in his face like someone had taken an ice pick and stuck him in his face everywhere. He looked at me and said, "Well, now, who do we have here?" I said my name is Al Wynn, and we moved in here last night. He said, Oh, yes. Give me the baskets. Betty is in the bathroom." Her apartment did not share a bathroom with any other apartment. Shortly she was at the door. This time, she was wearing a bathrobe. She said, "Thanks a lot, hon," and handed me a dollar bill. She said, "Check back with me and Tim again in a couple of days and I might want you to take out my garbage again or I might have something else for you to do." She closed the door. I stood there for a while; spellbound from what I had seen. I wondered if her husband knew I had seen that thing. I couldn't wait until the next time to knock on that door.

I went to the porch and sat on the banister looking up and down the street. The birds were chirping and singing. I saw three white ladies come out of the building next door on the south side of me with funny-looking hats sitting on their heads and long black dresses together with two white guys with their shirt collars backward. They walked north. I watched them until they were out of my sight. I watched the people leave the building as I heard a voice say "Hi there. You must be the son of the people who moved in last night?" I said, "Yes, I am." And as I turned around, I saw a girl that was about eight or nine years old. She had a light complexion with two long braids. She wore glasses and had on a skirt with Bobbie socks. "My name is Alice," she said, "and I live in the first house over there from the fence going south." I said, "I want to ask you a question. Who are those white people with those long black dresses and funny hats and the men with their shirt collars on backward?" She said, "Oh, you are talking about the nuns and priests. They belong to Mercy Hospital." "I never heard of a nun or priest. What is that?" Alice said, "Those are the white church people." We were so deep in conversation, me and Alice, we did not see a boy who was approaching us through the gate. "Hi, Alice," he said. She turned back to face him, and Alice said, "Hi Pap." He looked at me and said, "Hi" and gave me a wave of his hands. I waved back and said, "Hi." Alice said, "Oh Pap, this is Al Wynn. Al is the new boy who moved in last night." "What apartment?" Pap asked. "Huh," I said, staring at him. He was an odd-looking boy with a hole or dent under his left eye and a piece of meat in his left eye that looked like milk. He had a big round chest with a big know that set right on his back. "Huh?" I said again, "What apartment?" he repeated, knowing that I was staring at him. "One hundred three. I live in room 103," I said. "Where are you from?" Pap asked. "What do you mean? Where I just moved from?" "Naw.," Pap said, "Where were you born?" I responded, "West Point, Georgia." "So, you just got to Chicago?" Pap asked. "I have been here for a year," I said.

Then I asked him, "How old are you?" He said "Twelve." Another voice called out from the street. "Hey Alice, do you want to play touch football?" "Yeah, she shouted back. "Come on, Pap," she said as she started to run, then she looked back at me and said, "You too, Al." I met Roland Lane that day. We all had a great time playing touch football—me, Alice, Pap, and Roland. I did not know anything about touch football, but that day I really enjoyed it. During the next three months, I met all the girls and boys from Twenty-Sixth Street to Twenty-Ningh Street and Prairie. There was an older boy who lived in the 2900 block named Baker Martin. He was about nineteen years old, and he was a big brother type to the whole neighborhood of us kids. We used to have fun with him as we would make street scooters. He made them out of 2x4's, skates, and a milk crate. He would put bars on it like a motorcycle made out of 2x2's. Some of the boys would deck their scooters out by putting tin cans on the front like lights and bottle tops that shined. Some would put rubber horns like a car. Yeah, they would deck them slick. We would ride those scooters to school, to the store for our mothers, and everywhere we went. We would park them like a car.

Right in front of 2720 was a nursing home and behind the nursing home was a coach house where Pap lived. They had long wooden steps that led to the second floor. Next door south to them was a vacant lot where a house had been torn down before. It left a rocky hill that was about the length of a house and about eighteen feet tall. On the other side of the hill going south was a grey stone building where old folks lived. You did not see them until Sunday when they went to church. On the other side, south of that building was a huge vacant lot where at least eight houses had been torn down. In this lot was where the neighborhood kids would play baseball and football, and even try to ice skate in the winter. From the lot, if you went east, you would come up Calumet Alley, another vacant lot. To the right, you would see houses lined up. On the left side of the lot was an apartment building that seemed like it might have been a hotel before. Straight across from the vacant lot and the apartment building was Drake Elementary School. You could see the school from my porch on Prairie. Drake School is the school where my mother enrolled me and my sister Sara Frances. The teacher set me back a grade because even though I should have been in third grade, the teacher said I was doing second-grade work. I met with the kids in my building. Earneil, a girl who lived in apartment 105, and Henry Jones who lived in apartment 210 on the second floor. We all went to school together, fought together, and played together. All in all, we had lots of fun together. Mr. Tim and Mrs. Betty from apartment 1 would not let any other kids empty their garbage but me.

Now at twelve years old, I cornered Earneil in one of the dark corners in the basement. I was feeling all over her as she said, "Stop, boy, quit," in a soft voice as she raised her legs and twisted them around the lower part of my back. "Stop, boy, don't do it," as she kissed me. I raised her dress up slowly and pulled her panties to the side slowly she squatted just a little bit as I strained myself trying to penetrate her body. Five days later I came in from school and threw my books on the bed. No one else was home but me. I had to use the bathroom badly with a burning feeling. So, I ran out the back into the bathroom unzipped my pants and tried to pee but the sting and the pain hit me. I looked down and the water was dripping down. I tried to hold myself and look at it and then I saw the sore and as I pulled the skin back, I saw more and more sores. I waited nervously for my mother to come home. I just knew that my father, when he found out was going to kill me, ironing cord and all. I explained it all to my mother. She went to the drug store and when she came back to the store, she called me into the bathroom and told me to take my clothes off. The hardest part for me was her pulling the skin back and rubbing the salve on me. I felt so ashamed, but I asked her, "Are you going to tell Daddy?" She looked at me and said," We will keep this one to ourselves." She kissed me on the forehead. She was my mother again, by sparring me from the ironing cord.

CHAPTER 7

I'll never forget it. It was on a Saturday morning in November. The wind was cool, and the day promised rain. As I stepped off the steps of my porch, I heard Pap call me from across the street. "Hey Al, Al, ask your mother if you can work. Fat, the vegetable man needs two boys. He pays ten dollars for a day's work. If she says yes, come back to the alley to the barn. I'll be waiting." I was so excited cuz this would be my first job. I almost stumbled over the steps leading to the second floor running trying to get to my apartment.

For years Mr. Tim used to thrill everyone in the building with his music. He was really an expert piano player. You could hear the notes rising all over the building as he played. All of us kids, and even my mother, when my father wasn't around, would say that she thought my father bought the piano and was taking piano lessons because of Mr. Tim's beautiful playing. Today as I rushed into the room my father sat at his piano hitting the notes and saying the words. "doe Rae, me, fa, so, la, ti, doe, doe, ti la, so, fa, me, Rae, doe." I ran into the room and interrupted my father and also scared my mother as I busted out, "Mamma." My mother ran out of the kitchen with a plate in her hand that she was washing. My father stared at me as I shouted out in a loud voice, "Momma!" "What is wrong? What's the matter?" "Fat, the vegetable man over in the Calumet alley wants me and Pap to work for him. He is going to pay us ten dollars a day. Can I Momma? Can I?" "Ask your daddy.

He's sitting there." "What time will you be getting off, boy?" "I don't know, but I guess he will bring me home. His barn is right by Pap's house in the alley." My mom quipped, "Estell, he's the man who sold you the watermelon." My father stared at me for a minute and said "Yes, you can go."

I took off running, Pap was waiting for me at one of the wagons filled with all different vegetables, fruits, greens, rabbits, and squirrels. The wagon was loaded. "Come, boy," Fat said to me, "let me tell you about these here tin buckets." He gave me two tin buckets that were small with about five plums in one and about seven peaches in another one. "Now these plums sell for $1.00 a pail, and these peaches sell for $1.50 a pail. If these people want anything else, you guys come and see me at the wagon. You got that?" "Yes, Mr. Fat." I enjoyed the scenery. I had never been around so many horses, wagons, and fruits. Just meeting the people, wagon drivers and fruit sellers was enjoyable. "What did you say your name is, boy?" "Al," I said. "You and Pap get up on top of that wagon and we'll be going." One of the other fellas said, "Hey Fat when is quitting time?" Fat said, "Quitting time is ten o'clock. We'll all meet back here no later than eleven o'clock tonight.

Every Saturday, Pap and I would work with Fat. When the end of November came, Fat went from selling fruits and vegetables to coal. I worked with Fat for one week selling coal, but it was too cold. I was born in January, so I guess it was too cold in winter for me to be out there. I remember the last day I worked for him, and we all went shouting simultaneously, "Coal, man, coal!" Some guy hollered back to us, "Shut up all that damn noise! Everybody knows it's cold out there."

I always loved Christmas time on 2720 Prairie. In 1946, the snow was deep. The wind howled and had blown signs from the sides of buildings and businesses. There was a joyful noise at Christmas in the business section of Twenty-Sixth, Twenty-Ninth, and Twenty-First Streets. Everybody was waving, hollering "Merry Christmas!' and you could hear Nat King Cole as he sang "Chestnuts roasting on an open fire." On the radio, you could hear Bing Crosby as he sang "I'm dreaming of a white Christmas." You could hear some of the blues singers enjoying singing the Christmas songs. I enjoyed every minute going to the store with my little money trying to stretch it to get a gift for my mother and father on Christmas. I never in all my life of being a kid ever knew my father to buy us anything for Christmas, but we knew our mother would buy us something even if it was only a banana and two oranges. She never forgot. Regardless of what we got for Christmas, we were happy because we loved each other, and we were together.

It was a Wednesday, and it was teachers' meeting day at my school, so all the kids got out of school at twelve o'clock. There was a crowd of kids walking my way across a vacant lot toward Prairie. The children who lived on Indiana, Michigan, and Wabash would walk across the lot through the gangway between the nun's house and my house past the coach house across the Prairie alley to the Indiana lot, and back to Indiana Street. I was just approaching Prairie when I saw Mr. Leroy, the blind man who lived in the nursing home next to Pap's. He was walking very slowly and swinging his long stick from side to side. But six or seven feet from where he was walking was a hole about three feet deep that the sewerage people had left unfinished. I called out to him. "Mr. Leroy, stop! You are fixing' to fall in a hole!" He turned toward me as I was running up to him. "Who is this" he asked. "I'm the one who walked you to the drugstore last Saturday." "I'm trying to get to the shoeshine parlor on Twenty-Sixth Street. Do you have enough time to help me get there?" "Yes," I said and grabbed him by the arm and took the bag that he was carrying. Then I led him to the other side of the street.

We walked very slowly to Twenty-Sixth Street. We approached the shoeshine parlor. It had Expert Shoeshine on the window, and Thurman, the shoeshine man was an average size in height, thin, and dressed very neatly. He had on black house shoes with what seemed like a gold rim that went around the top of them, black slacks, and a white shirt. He was wearing a shoeshine apron tied neatly around his waist. He was very black with wavy black hair, and he was even nicer looking when he smiled. I watched his every move. "Hi, gentlemen," he said in a low voice as he smiled at us. We both said "hi." "How can I help you today, gentlemen?" he said with another smile. Mr. Leroy said "Give him the bag, boy. I have two pairs of shoes here and I want them shined and shoestrings replaced, and when can I get them back?" Thurman pulled out two pairs of old worn-out shoes, a black pair, and a brown pair. You could see where one string on the black shoes had been broken and he had one-half-inch heels on both pairs of shoes. "I remember you," Thurman said, "You are Mr. Leroy for the nursing home, aren't you?" "Yes, I think you've done my boots for me before." "Yes, I did, but you need two heels on these shoes before I shine them and put the string in them." "Oh, you think I need the heels?" "I know you do." "So," Leroy said. "How much would it cost for two heels and for you to taps on them?" "That would be $2.75 a piece with taps making a total of$8.10, including the shoestrings and shines." "That will be fine, sir. And when will I get the shoes?" "What's today? Today is Wednesday, isn't it? So, what about Friday?" We turned to the door when I noticed sitting on the floor, a sign that read "SHOESHINE BOY NEEDED." I TURNED BACK TO Thurman. "Say, pardon me, sir." And he turned back to me with that same grin. "Can I help you, sir?" I said, "Did you get a shoeshine boy, yet?" "No, I didn't. I'm looking for one now. Do you shine shoes?" "No, sir," I said, looking down. "We didn't shine shoes where I came from. In fact, most of us didn't have shoes. We walked barefoot." "Where are you from?" Thurman asked. "I'm from West Point, Georgia. I've been here a little more than a year now." Thurman looked at me with that same smile. Henry said, "I like this boy."

Mr. Leroy said, "I do too." Thurman looked over at Mr. Leroy and Mr. Leroy said, "One thing you can say is that he didn't lie to you." Thurman asked me "Would you like to learn and what did you say your name is? "Al, Al Wynn, and yes, I would love to try to learn how to shine shoes." "You go to school, boy?" Thurman asked. "Yes, sir, I do." "Well, it starts being busy on Friday, and I close up at 8:00 p.m. You come on in on Friday. What time do you get out of school, at three o'clock?" "Well, you come in at 4:00-8:00 p.m. on Friday, and 9:00 a.m.-9:00 p.m. on Saturday, "If your mother doesn't take you to church on Sunday, you will be working with Mr. Buddy, he works weekends." Mr. Buddy is an older man, and you will like him. You report to Mr. Buddy on Friday at four o'clock p.m." I thanked him and we left. I couldn't wait until my mother was home from work. I told my mother and father about the job that was offered to me by Thurman. They both agreed to let me work.

CHAPTER 8

Friday seemed like it was forever in coming. Finally, it was here. Inside the shoeshine parlor, Mr. Buddy was my first customer, showing me how to brush the shoes. "You hold the sole of the shoe with your left hand if you are right-handed, and the sole of the she with your right hand if you are left-handed." "You come straight to the shoe with the brush, but as soon as the brush touches the shoe, you tilt your brush in an upward stroke. Do you understand that, Al?" "Yes sir," I said and tried again. But every time I tried; I would hit that corn again on his foot. "Damn boy, I said turn the damn brush up, not into my toe." It took me about three weeks to get the brush thing together, and about the same amount of time to give a decent shine.

But I wanted so badly to be like Mr. Buddy. He would take the shoeshine cloth with both hands and go down the shoe real fast and then he would snatch the cloth from the shoe and make it pop two or three times before he let go of one end of the cloth. Make it pop, then he would throw the cloth behind the back end of the shoe and snatch and let one end go and the cloth.

Several times two or three guys would come in and would not want anybody but Mr. Buddy to shine their shoes, and that's when the fun and the show would begin. He would pop that cloth from one chair to the other, and it would sound like a person was playing hambone on their leg and thigh, the rhythm had a beat to it. Every

Sunday after we would get off from work, Mr. Buddy would take me down to Harrison and State to the show. He would pay my show fare and buy me all the candy and popcorn I could eat. This particular Sunday night, as I entered my hallway I could hear my sister crying, "Daddy, don't hit her anymore." My heart started to race as I ran as fast as I could to the door. My daddy's shirt was torn from the shoulder to the elbow and my mother lay on the floor, cursing at him and my baby brother was curled up in a knot under the table crying softly. I went over to my mother, crying, saying "What's the matter mama? After my mother had straightened herself up a little and wiped away her tears, my father turned to me and told me. "Boy, I want you to go to the store for me to get me some soybean junior." I was holding onto my mother's arm while she was trying to do the dishes, and she was mumbling something under her breath to my daddy. Me and my sister Francis said, "Don't say nothing, Mama, be quiet." My father screamed to me, "Boy, did you hear what the hell I said?" My mother kind of gave me a shove and said "Go to the store, Al. I'll be all right." I halfway ran and walked fast to the store and prayed to God, "Please don't let them fight no more. Please don't let them fight no more." There were other experiences that I experienced coming up as a young boy. We ate beans most of the time while my father ate steak and lamb chops broiled due to the illness in his stomach. Those beans would make me walk two or three blocks trying to belch [it was the gas coming up], but I became more nervous with the arguments and fights between my mother and father.

I was fourteen now and I had almost had a fight with most of the boys in the neighborhood that was my age from Indiana to Calumet, Twenty-Sixth, Twenty-Ninth, and Thirty-First Street there were fights some boys wanted to pick on Al. With all the fights, I was getting pretty good at boxing. A man named Bill who lived in the attic, an athletic type of person asked my father to let him teach me how to box. Joe Louis was famous during those years, and I remember every fight. The whole neighborhood would come out of their house praising Joe Louis's victory. Bill had once been a boxer. I really don't remember what made him stop or quit, but it was something he saw in me that he thought would one day make me great or make me successful in the boxing game. The boxing started off well. First of all, he made me start doing the duck walk when you squat with your hands on your hips and then sling your legs as you walk. This position makes your whole body tired, which I hated. Then there was rope jumping and shadow boxing and the running that lasted well for a year.

I was fifteen years old, coming home from school when I saw about six police cars in front of my door. Crowds of people were circling around. My heart seemed to come through my chest. The only thing I could think of was my mother and father fighting again. I ran as fast as I could to the crowd. When I squeezed through the circling crowd, that's when I saw Mr. Tim handcuffed with his nose bleeding and his face in the dirs. While the big Irish Police pushed his feet into his back. He turned his head toward me and I could see through the big, bruised eye that someone had hit him. He seemed to be staring right at me with his good eye. 'Go and get Betty, Al." I took off running and knocked on Mr. Betty's door. She slept most of the time. Deep down in my heart, I thought I would see that red patch of hair. I knocked for what seemed like ten minutes. "Who is it?" she asked from inside. "Al, Mrs. Betty, Mr. Tim wants you to come right away. The police have him out in front." She cracked the door and looked at me and then she opened the door and said, what did you say, the police have Mr. Tim outside?" I said, "He wants you to come right away." She had on blue pajamas with a matching robe and hose shoes. She ran out the door and down the steps to Mr.

Tim. They lifted him from the ground. One man was holding his are. They had him handcuffed in the back. You could see the whole face now, the big eye, the dirt that was in his nose, his nose bleeding down on his lips He had on a beautiful pinstriped suit, where the blood had tainted the collar. He looked at her with a good eye. She ran to him, throwing her arms around his neck as she cried out, "Tim, Tim, what have they done to you? What's the matter, baby? What have these damn bastards done to you?" One white policeman came up and pulled her away from Mr. Tim and said, "Who in the hell are you?" "I'm his God damn wife, that's who I am, and his name is Tim Rogers, and my name is Betty Rogers and I want to know what the hell has he done to deserve this shit."

"We are taking him to Twenty-Seventh and Wabash. If you want to know anything more, come over there and ask our captain. Otherwise, step aside." They led him to the car and put him in the back of the squad car. I walked close to the car with Mr. Betty holding my hand. "Stay with her, Al, and take care of her. I'll see you when I get home." Mrs. Betty rushed back into the house and took me in with her. "Paul's still doing delivery, ain't he?" I said "Yes." "Will you go and find him and ask him to take me to Twenty-Seventh and Wabash? And when your mother and father get home, remember what Tim asked you to stay with me." Paul was there in his car and they drove away leaving me on the porch. Paul was Earneil's uncle who lived in apartment 106. He was a carefree person. He had a 1945 Buick. He did a delivery service. He always wore a motorcycle cap and a jacket, everything like motorcycle junkies. He had a Harley Davidson that he rode. Everybody had it out through the neighborhood that every girl that rode on that bike was going to give it up. With that thought, I wished I owned a Harley Davidson.

Mrs. Betty and Paul returned half an hour before my mother came in from work. Paul spoke to me saying, "Hi, little Estell." I said, "Hi." I asked Mrs. Betty, "Is Mr. Tim coming home:" She said, "No, he has to go to court on Wednesday, and did you ask your mother and father about staying with me?" "No," I said, "but they will be home in about half an hour and I will come and get you." After my mother and father had eaten their dinner and had asked everybody about what had happened that day, I told them about the version I had seen. I told them that Mr. Betty wanted to speak to them. It was sometime after I knocked that she opened the door. "Hi Al," she said, seemingly sleepy. "Come on in, Mrs. Betty, my father and mother are waiting." "Okay, hon, take it easy. Come on in and close the door. You don't want your mother and father to see me like this, do you? I must brush my hair." When you entered Mrs. Betty's apartment, there was a short hall. On the east side was the bathroom door, two or three feet up into her room was another hallway going east, then another short hallway right at the corner of that hallway was a stove, and on the other side at the stove was the refrigerator. Right in front of the refrigerator was an archway that led out into the big room.

As I stood there glancing around the room, right in front of the entrance door in the hallway leading to the room was the kitchen table, and on the table was a pint of Gordon's gin bottle with only about a short left in it. Beside that bottle were Prince Al's can and Prince Al's tobacco papers lying in the middle of the table. A long red pack of Pall Mall that seemed to have one missing cigarette lay at the end of the table. "Excuse me, Hon," Mrs. Betty stepped out of the bathroom, passed me, and went to the table. "How do I look now?" she asked and turned around slowly in front of me. I saw that she had brushed her hair in a nice row. She seemed a little more stable now I said, "You look nice, Mr. Betty. You look just fine."

"Thank you, hon," she said and pinched me on my jaw. She took a Pall Mall out of the pack reached got her lighter and lit it. She took a puff of the cigarette, and we were on our way to my apartment. As we walked down the hallway towards 103, the notes from my father could be heard throughout the hallway as he played the song "Laurel." "Your daddy is getting good, Al. He is getting really good, but he'll never beat my guy, Al." We both laughed as I opened my door to the apartment. My mother was standing in the middle of the floor as we walked into the room. Mr. Betty acknowledged my father and said, "Your music is very smooth." We both continued to mother while my father continued to play his Laurel. "Mrs. Wynn," Mrs. Betty started, "of course, you heard about the incident with Tim today. He had been having trouble with the police before. They are jealous of him, his car, and the way he carries himself. I will have him home soon. Of course, we send Al to the store for us, we trust him with our money, with everything. Tim and I would both feel more comfortable if he knew I had someone to look after me by being alone in the apartment and all." "Well, you know Al is only 15 years old. Mr. Betty, can't you find some lady to say with you?" My mother asked.

"Well, you know me, and Tim have only been here for a year. We just moved here from Detroit. I don't really know you that well, Mrs. Wynn. I don't know any people in the building, but we trust Al." "Well, Mr. Betty, it's not up to me, you have to talk to his father." She turned to my father and said, "Well, Mr. Wynn, I know you heard the conversation. Of course, you know I will be paying him for staying. That will help him with his school things. I will pay him whatever you think is fair." My father stopped playing the piano and said, "You're telling me that Tim, your husband asked him to say, and you heard it with your own ears. If you heard it with your own ears, then he can stay." For some time now, when my mother and father would argue and fight, I wanted to slap him with a baseball bat, but tonight I wanted to hug and kiss him for saying yes. Mr. Betty and I took off to her apartment.

CHAPTER 9

We had been in the apartment for about an hour as Mr. Betty was toying with playing cards. She asked me "Did you know I could tell fortunes with cards?" "No, I didn't know that. How do you do that?" She pulled one card off the deck, and it was a king of diamonds. "This card tells me that you want to ask me something, but you are afraid." She pulled another card off the deck. It was a ten of clubs. "This card tells me, she said "that a person doesn't get anything out of life unless you ask for it. You must ask for what you want in order for another person to understand what you're trying to say." Her whole conversation was interrupted by an alarm clock that sat on the end of the cocktail table in the other room. "Oh man, I set the clock to go off this morning and it's going off tonight." "Al, go and turn the clock off. What time is it anyway?" She said while checking her own watch. "Oh, it's eight o'clock already." She grabbed her gin bottle and tilted it up. "Hon, you've got to go to the store for me." She reached for the phone and dialed a number. "Hello," she said, is this Sam's lounge?" "Let me speak to Bill. If Bill is not in, let me speak to Henry. Oh yes, hello Henry, yes, this is Betty Rogers.!" Yeah, I'm fine. How are you doing?" Yeah, I'm going to send a young man up there, Al, just bag what I want and give it to him. He will have a check. I need a pint of gin and a pack of Pall Mall. He'll be there in about 15 minutes. "Did you get the price?"

"How much do I owe you?" "Okay, fine." "He'll be there shortly." I was out of the door and on my way to the liquor store.

Nightlife people always excites me. I entered the door of Sam's Lounge and went over to the carry-out section. The bartender was a big heavy guy who hollered out to me. "Say, boy, you don't belong here. "Get the hell out of here!" Another guy there was smiling at me pleasantly and asked me "Is your name Al?" I said "Yes." "He asked me, did you come for Mr. Rogers?" I said "Yes." He hollered to the other guy, "He's alright. Leave him alone!" I handed the guy the check. He gave me the bag and I rushed out of the door and back to Mrs. Berry hoping that she would continue telling the truth about that fortune telling. She let me into the house and sat back at her table. She had a glass already for the bottle. She had placed a glass with ice in front of her. She opened the gin, poured a half glass straight over the ice replaced the top, and gulped that gin down. Then she reached for that Prince Al can and the cigarette papers and started to roll her Prince Al tobacco. "That's the first time I have ever seen that done, Mr. Berry." "Seen what?" She asked. "I mean my uncle smoked Prince Al tobacco too, but he doesn't smoke any other cigarette but Prince Albert tobacco. You smoke both."

"Well, you see Prince Albert tobacco is much stronger than Pall Mall and less strong than a cigar. So, I smoke the Prince Albert other than the cigarette, but most of the time, I smoke the Pall Mall." Then she threw those big round green eyes at me after she had finished smoking her Prince Albert. "Well, hon, I think that I'll take a shower and get ready for bed. Remember what I said. You don't get anything out of life unless you ask for it." She went into the bathroom to take her shower. I sat there at the table with a little knot in my pants about to tear the zipper loose. After a while, she was back at the table. She had on just a thin housecoat with only two buttons fastened in the middle. She had a towel tied around her head. She sat in the chair across from me at the table with her knees locked together, but the gown slipped from each side to her hips. She took another drink from the bottle as she reached over for the cigarette papers and the Prince Al can again. Her legs parted and as she sat back in the chair her legs were wide open now facing me. I couldn't tell you to the day whether it was the fire from the stove or the temperature of my body that seemed to make me sweat all over.

I sat there as she puffed on that Prince Albert cigarette. I almost trembled from fear of being ashamed to look at that red patch that was looking back at me. I peeped at it nervously one or two times. I glanced quickly and then stared at her; she was staring back at me. I knew that she knew then that I wanted to look. The words seemed to ball up in my mouth as I tried to speak. "Mrs. Betty," I said shockingly. "What is it, hon? Speak up, what is it?" "I know that my father is going to kill me, but I want to do it to you." "You want to do it to me? What do you mean? Sya it hon, what do you want to do?" "I want to fuck you, Mr. Betty." I looked at her as though I had gotten braver by the minute. "I want to fuck you very badly!" "You have made yourself very clear." And she led me to the bed by the window.,

CHAPTER 10

The house coat was wide open now as she lay on the couch panting and looking up at me as I crawled between her legs. I penetrated her opening and I started to buck as if I was bucking a horse. Up and down and as hard as I could. Her hands came around to touch the sides of my butt as she squeezed me on it very gently. "Slow down, Al," she whispered, "slow down, hon," she whispered even lower. "We have all night." I don't know how long we lay there in what seemed like slow motion to me before the heatwave hit my body. It appears it was starting from my toes and gradually moved up between my legs. My motion became much faster now as I was trying to capture this feeling. Before I knew it, my body had exploded into a million pieces as I slipped into ecstasy. "Oh hon," Mrs. Betty was whispering. "My sweet baby." She said as I rolled off her in amazement and exhaustion. I had set the clock for four o'clock. I knew my mother set her clock for five o'clock and would come to check on me. I had to be sure that Mr. Betty wasn't drunk and was aware of everything that was going on before my mother came knocking. I had placed the divider in front of her bed by the window. She had dressed in her pajamas and had her robe placed on the end of the bed as she went back to sleep. I sat on the couch in the room across from the table in the hallway with one end of the couch in the corner three or four feet from the window where Mrs. Betty slept. I sat there thinking of that excitement I had last night and wondered if her pussy was the only pussy that had dynamite in it. I dozed off for what seemed like a minute or two before the knock came.

I passed the rest with flying colors and my mother was pleased with the ten dollars Mrs. Betty gave me. “Give me $2.00 Mommy and keep the rest for your carfare and lunch money.” “Thanks,” she said and kissed me on the top of my head. He held hands as we walked back to our apartment. That day at school I told all my friends about the explosion, and everything seemed to leave out nothing. All the boys wanted to spend the night with me. I said “No, I can’t do it. My mommy won’t let me.” But I did let my best friend Kenneth in. We had a lot of fun that night. The word had gotten around that I was staying with a white lady. All the men were trying to bribe me to let them into the apartment. They didn’t know, but Mr. Tim had picked a good watchdog when he picked me to guard that dynamite pussy. Every night I thought about that explosion I would say, “NO, NO, NO. My mommy will whip me and tell your wife.” All the men in the building hated my guts. I didn’t give a damn. That was my pussy until Mr. Tim got back. And as the weeks passed, I wished he didn’t make it.

My mother wasn’t checking on me every day anymore. She would let me go and come as I pleased when I was working for Mr. Betty. Mrs. Betty was getting drunker and drunker every day. She would send me to the store at least twice a night. She would write a check each time that she sent me. I would hide the change from her, sometimes $15.00, and other times as much as $50.00. The next morning, she would tell me when it was time for me to leave. “Get the change off the table, Al, and lock the door when you leave.” She would sleep all day and about six o’clock that evening she would want me to go get her something to eat and drink from Sam’s. They had a fish and rib joint in the rear of Sam’s bar. They all knew the pretty white lady, Mr. Betty, I overheard one man say to another

"You never have to worry about her checks, man, it's as good as gold. I tell you that woman is rich. That's why she could buy that man of hers a car lot on Twenty-Fourth and Michigan Avenue." "But isn't he in Jail?" Another man asked another question before his question could be answered. "And what did he go to jail for?" I walked over to the Coke box as if I didn't hear the conversation. I lifted the top of the box. The man went on talking. 'h was bringing cars from Detroit to his lot." "So," the other said, "So they were stolen,' the man said. "He should be getting out in about three weeks. The paper said he only got six months." "Six months?" 'He got off easy. Who in the hell does that nigger know That goes to show you," the bartender said, 'money talks and bullshit walks."

Damn, he will be home sooner than I thought. The shoeshine job was nice on the weekends. I made nice tips, and I kept my mother with carfare and lunch money. And with the money I got from Mr. Betty, I was doing very well. But this would all stop when Mr. Tim comes home. I was boxing every now and then, and anyone who came into my yard. My mother had taken some of the money I had given her and bought me a pair of sixteen-inch gloves. One day while boxing, I saw one boy standing with four or five other boys. He was staring at me through the fence. I had never met him, but I knew that he was Leroy Greene, and he was a very good fighter. Everyone around his age feared him. He had three of four guys with him all the time. Sometimes were older, and taller, and some were his size, but he could beat them all. He and his friends were standing on the sidewalk looking into the yard through the fence. "Do you want to box me, man? "He asked me. I said "Yeah, I don't mind if you want to box. I'll box." I turned around, watching him come through the gate. When out of the other corner of my eye, I saw my father, mother, Mr. Betty, and two other ladies on the porch watching me. *Damn, I thought, I'm gonna get my ass whipped right in front of my whole family.* He was in in the yard now and Pap was taking off the gloves, giving them to him to put on. The crowd of kids that were playing touch football in the street knew Leroy and his reputation. "Come on, y'all. Let's go watch. It's going to be a real fight now." They all gathered around the fence. My heart started beating fast, and my tongue seemed to thicken in my mouth. It appeared that my throat went numb, and I couldn't swallow. This is only my nerves I thought to myself. The only thing you must do now is act as though I'm Joe Louis in a real ring, fighting the worst person in the world. I got to remember everything that Bill taught me about Baker Martin. Bill had said, "Al, Joe Louis fights in a circle, and he only throws six-inch punches. You get nothing by swinging wildly. When you stick that left out there, you must twist it with a snap. You must put your shoulder behind it so that the blow will have weight." Baker said, "Watch the person's eyes that you are boxing. His eyes will always give him away when he's fixing to throw a punch." We tagged gloves and started the match I moved in a circle very slowly. Leroy danced on his toes. He shot a left at my head, a light blow which was blocked in the air. I kept coming closer and closer to him as he threw a couple of jabs to the left and the right. I blocked them all and continued my aggressiveness. I started to bob and weave as Bill had taught me. He kept throwing a left jab at me which was blocked each time. I had practiced that pivot move when the right hand is thrown at you. Instead of trying to weave under it, roll with the punch. I was almost begging him to throw that right punch so I could try that out. I kept bobbing and weaving, moving closer and closer to him. Then I dropped my left hand down a little so he could see my jaws. Just as I thought, he drew back, and I could see his eyes flinch as he threw that right haymaker at me.

I knew that I could connect if I did it properly. The haymaker was coming after my jaw, and I did it very smoothly. I rolled with the punch. The haymaker went by my ear, then I rolled back with a weave and my right hand went into his midsection very hard. I heard him grunt" Ummph!" The right hand seemed to slide off into his stomach as I gave him an overhand right hook in the jaw. He was falling backward now, and I was almost running to keep up with him as I tagged him one more time with that right. He hit the ground hard, very hard. You heard the kids on the fence saying everything. "Man, did you see that?" Man, I know that hurt." It was a little while before Leroy could get himself together and he asked his biggest friend, Moody to untie his gloves. After his gloves were off, he came and pushed me and said, "Let's see what you can do with those gloves off." I said, "I don't want to fight. We were just boxing." "No nigger," and he pushed me again. Then a voice came out of the crowd. "Don't be a jerk, Leroy. Maybe you will have another match, and the next time you'll get him. But you were only boxing." Baker Martin said. Leroy looked at Baker and then at me and smiled. "I'll see you again. I'll see you again," he said as he left the yard. The four of them crossed the lot going to Calumet where they lived.

It was Saturday night and I had put up my gloves from boxing Leroy and left my apartment and come back to the front porch. Mr. Betty and two ladies were still on the front porch as I came out of the hallway door. Here's the champ. Here comes the champ." "You're getting very good hon. You hit that guy from heaven, didn't you?" "Yes," the other lady said in a flirting kind of way. The other lady continued, "I just told your mother that she should send you downtown to Eddie Nicholas gym. My nephew goes down there and he's getting ready for the golden gloves." The other lady said "Pardon me, Louise, for interrupting, but I would like to ask you a question. Al, do you still work for the vegetable man?" I said "No, I don't. I'm shining shoes but I still go over there. Why?" "Oh, because I would like to have some good mustard and turnips from over there and I know MS Hudson from the basement said she wished she had some okra and corn." "Would you like for me to write that down for you, hon?" I said, "Sure, Mrs. Betty." She left for not too long, came back with the paper, and handed it to me. "I must go to work at the shoeshine parlor at 10:00 a.m. I will see if I can get that for you." "Just tell me how much that costs and we will have your money."

CHAPTER 11

I had set the clock for 4:30 a.m. Mrs. Betty was on the bed asleep butt naked with one leg on the floor. She turned towards me, and that red patch had put me to sleep at about 1: 00 that night. The clock went off at 4:30 a.m. I was dressed and ready to go at 5:00. Mr. Betty had rolled on the side with her back to me. I went over and pulled the covers up on her. She would not awaken until about 12:00 o'clock. I took her keys and eased the door closed quietly behind me. I was climbing the hill across from my house. The moon was still bright and as I reached the top of the hill, I could see the vegetable wagons lined up in front of each other. I passed to search for old man Jimmy who was the caretaker of the barn.

The wagons set between two garages and as I stepped into the alley to the right of me about ten feet away on the east side of the alley was the barn. I saw Mr. Jimmy sitting in a chair near the door. He was snoring. The dog that lay beside his feet recognized me and yarned and went back to sleep. Another dog was nudging me on my leg. It was a raggedly looking German Shepherd with Kuka bugs all over his tail. I knew the dog's name. Its name was Queenie. "Go on, Quennie," I said while making a gesture with my hand. It ran about two or three steps and turned and looked at me again. "Go on," I said, and still making a motion with my body, it started at a slow pace running up the alley where two or three other dogs were waiting for it. After a while, the dogs all disappeared through a vacant lot.

I walked softly over to Jimmy and shook him very softly. "Jimmy," I said, "Jimmy." "Huh." He rose a little in the chair, never opened his eyes, and took the back of his hand and wiped his mouth. His arm fell by his side as the snoring became louder. I said "Jimmy, the ladies in my building want some greens and corn>" I noticed the pint of gin borde and a wine bottle that lay on the other side of his chair. I heard the horses kicking in the stalls as they seemed to be talking to each other in horsetalk. Then it dawned on me that Jimmy was out of it like Mrs. Betty. I tiptoed away from him and headed for the wagons. I hit the first two wagons in the back.

The only thing I could see was some crumbled-up bananas. The next two wagons had what I needed. There was a half basket of peaches, turnips, and mustard greens, and hanging on the side of one of the wagons were about ten rabbits. It took me about 45 minutes to carry two baskets of greens, mustard, and turnips, one of each three rabbits and those peaches to Mr. Betty's house. I looked over at the clock and it was 6:30 a.m. Man, I said to myself, I forgot the bass. I was over the hill and to the wagons. In the first wagon, there were paper bags, 10oz paper bags. I was back at Mr. Betty's in a flash. I filled bags up with the turnip greens, and then I bagged up the mustard greens. I had ten bags of mustard and turnips, five gabs of mustard, and five bags of turnips. I bagged up the peaches and placed six peaches in each bag. I had eight bags of peaches and three rabbits. At 8:00 o'clock, I went to the basement apartment first. Ms. Hudson's. You could smell the aroma of bacon and eggs coming from under the door. The smell made me hungry as I knocked on the door. Ms. Hudson answered the door. She was a short fat lady in her bathrobe with a towel around her head. "Hi, Al," she said. I said "Good morning, Ms. Hudson, I was told that you wanted some corn and okra. I'm sorry, but we didn't have that today. We do have some nice mustard and turnip and peaches and good ole peaches and rabbits." She asked, "How much are your greens going for?" I replied, "A dollar and a quarter a bag." "And how much are your rabbits?" she asked. I responded, "The rabbits are $1.75 each." She said, "Let me see, Al, a bag of turnips and mustard would be $1.25 a piece, that's $2.50 and the rabbit is $1.75, that would be $4.25." "Man, Al; I have only $5.00, I guess you could bring me those items of greens and rabbit." "I don't have your $.75 change, Ms. Hudson. But I can go to the store and get it for you. Those are some delicious peaches. I let them go for a dollar, but I'll let you have them for seventy-five cents if you want them."

"Boy, you're a born salesman, aren't you? You have just stood up here and taken all my money." She handed me the $5.00. I was up those steps and back with all her bags and rabbit. The next hour and a half, I had sold all I had, and they were still begging for more, but it was too light outside for me to go back. So, I said, "We're sold out, we're sold out!" For the next two years that was my hustle every Sunday. All the ladies in my building in the back building thought I was the real vegetable man. With Ms. Betty giving me money every day, my hustle on Sunday, and the shining of shoes, I began taking Mr. Buddy to the show. "Boy," he said, "you sure have a lot of money there." "Where did you get all of that money from?" We would laugh and eat popcorn and candy, laughing as loud as we could at Bud Abhor and Lou Costello. I enjoyed those Sunday visits to the show with Mr. Buddy. He was fun to be with.

That Monday, I felt good running home from school with the rest of the kids. I would first stop and see Mrs. Betty. I would then go into my apartment and do the chores that my mother had left for me. Sometimes I washed dishes or cleaned up the house, or whatever chores she had told me to do. When I stepped into the gate and into the yard, my sister Frances met me. "Daddy's in the I said "What's the matter? He doesn't get home until five. It's just three-thirty." "He had one of those headaches again, so he came home early. He said as soon as I see you tell you don't stoop anywhere. Come and see him. He said, "Don't stop at Mrs. Betty's house, but come and see him now." My sister said it like she was my daddy. I went into the house. My father sat at the piano playing his favorite song, "Laura." I said, "Did you want to see me, Daddy?" He said "Yes, Tim's back home. This is what he left for you." He reached up on top of the piano and there were three crisp one hundred-dollar bills. "He thanked us for letting you stay with Betty. I'm going to give your mother your money to put up. That will be between you and her. I'm telling you now, I let you stay there because he asked you to. Now, I'm telling you. I don't want to catch you in her house anymore. Do you hear me?" "Yes, sir" I answered. My father went back to playing "Laura." My heart was pounding, and I damn nearly wanted to cry because Mr. Tim was back. What was I going to do now? That was the only pussy I knew and the only one I could get when I wanted it; and that money, that money was going to stop. I thought. Why did he have to come back now?

I was through washing the dishes. My father was playing on an arrangement of George Sheraton. As he was playing "Bamboo Buggy." I asked "Can I go out to play baseball? I'm through with the dishes." "Yeah," he said, continuing to play as I walked out the door. I was just fixing to go out of the hallway door as Mr. Tim was entering the door. He was dressed very sharply. I always admired how he dressed. He had on a pinstriped gray suit with black and white shoes. His silk black hat was turned down around his forehead. You could smell the cologne from his body. "Hi, Al, did you see your father yet?" I said "Oh yeah. Thank you, Mr. Tim." "You are very welcome, Al. I appreciate everything you did for her and me. She told me how well you took care of her." I wondered if she had told him everything, including her smoking two different kinds of cigarettes and drinking. I wondered very seriously if she told him everything, I was looking sideways at him and said, "That's okay, Mr. Tim, I did the best I could." "I would invite you to see Mr. Betty, but she's sleeping now." "I would like to tell you something. I don't want to tell her, but Mrs. Betty has been drinking very heavily and taking aspirin. Bayer aspirins. She sends me to the store for these items." "Yes, I'm going to get her treated for her drinking, and thank you for the information," as he stepped into his apartment and closed the door.

My spirit was low for the next three weeks. I wanted so badly to see Mrs. Betty. I would see Mr. Tim now and then coming and going. I never saw her. Sometimes I would knock on her door early in the morning before going to school, hoping that the red patch would answer the door, but it was always Mr. Tim. "Do you want me to empty your garbage or go to the store" "No, not today, Al, but get back t me." He would give me a dollar. A couple of weeks had passed since Mr. Tim had been home. I was getting desperate and more desperate to see Mr. Betty despite what my father had said. I should have gotten some keys made when I had them so that when Mr. Tim went to the store or something I could have just run in and said hi to Mr. Betty. Yes, run in, get killed, I thought. I wasn't that big of a fool to have gotten keys made. My luck seemed to have changed as I walked from the rear of the house to the front of the house, Paul and Mr. Tim stood in conversation on the front porch. "Oh, Al," Mr. Tim said "I was looking for you. Would like to go to the store for Betty?" "Yes, I would." "She wants you to take this note to Henry at Sam's. Wait let me give you the money." Mr. Tim went into his pocket and Paul just went on talking. "So, you got to go to court on Wednesday, huh, Tim?" "Yes, 26 and California at ten." "Hopefully they will throw it out," Paul said. "I hope so." Mr. Tim said. "I hope so." Mr. Tim said.

Today was Saturday. I could hardly wait for Mr. Tim to go to court. Just four more days and I would be with that red patch. Mr. Tim handed me a twenty-dollar bill and I was on my way to the store. That Wednesday I walked my sister and brother to school; they both went to Drake School. I went through the front door, said goodbye to my sister and brother, and made a swift dash. When I was no longer in their sight, I went through the side door and went back home. It was a quarter to nine that Wednesday morning. There wasn't anyone on the porch. The day promised rain as the sun moved behind the clouds. I walked swiftly through my hallway and went to my apartment. I wasn't in the apartment ten minutes before there was a tap on the door. It was Earniel, "Hi 'al. I haven't seen you in a long time. You don't like me anymore?" I said, "You're all right." "' So, what are you doing at home? Why aren't you in school?" "My mother is going to buy me some brand-new shoes Friday and I had pink eye bi I'm well now." "Do you want some company?" I wanted to say, "HELL NAW, BITCH!" As many sores as you put on my dick. I should never speak to you ever again and I should call the police and doctor when I see you coming. But instead, I smiled at her very politely and said "I have the runs and that's the reason I'm home from school, I just shit all over myself all the time, and I have to stay close to the bathroom. I know you don't want me to be bothered with a shitty nigger." I kept running out checking on Mr. Tim's car. At nine fifteen he was gone. I could hardly wait until ten o'clock came because I knew he was well on his way. The hallway was empty. I also checked the porch. No one was there. I dashed back to her door and knocked three or four times very hard. Finally, she answered. "Yes, who is it?" She said in a weak voice "Who is it?" "It's Al," I said anxiously, "Open the door." She said, "Hon, I can't let you in because I don't have the key." Then I said, "Can you open the window?" She said, "Come to the window on the side." I stood at the window on the side of the house as she tried desperately to open the window. Every time she tried to open the lock she would fall to the side or lose her balance due to her drinking. Finally, she unlocked it and I struggled and climbed through the window. "Oh, hon. I missed you." She spoke. Her dress was wide open.

I missed you too, Mr. Betty," I said, staring at that red patch. She tried to reach out and hug me but stumbled and started falling. I caught her and pulled her closer to me. The little knot in my pants had stiffened. I walked her slowly backward to the bed in front of the window. "Fuck me hon, fuck me," she said looking up at me. I was just about to unzip my pants when I heard the key turn in the door. I said, "Pull the covers up over you, Mrs. Betty because here comes Mr. Tim." She said "Hon, hon, I want you to fuck me, hon." I seemed to be looking at Mrs. Betty for the first time now. She now seemed older with her hair all tangled and her face unmade. I looked at her and it looked as though she had lost a week's rest. Lord, I said, I should have listened to my father. I'm about to get killed for an old drunk woman. The footsteps were coming much faster, not down the hallway. "Come on hon, come on, hon," she said, "fuck me." "No, Mrs. Betty. I can't go to the store for you to get no liquor and aspirins." I didn't know whether I should drop down on my knees and pray or just run and jump out of the window. I said in a louder voice, "Come on, Mrs. Betty, get back in bed and let me cover you up. I can't go to the sore for you." Mr. Tim was behind me now, "What's wrong, Al?" Oh, Mr. Tim, she wants me to go to the store and get those aspirins I told you about." At the same time, Mr. Betty is still pulling at my pants saying "Come on hon, fuck me. I want you to fuck me." Mr. Tim reached into his back pocket and pulled out his wallet and gave me a five-dollar bill. "Good boy, Al. I'll take care of her from her." He walked me to the door and took the key from his pocket and opened the door from the inside. That was the first time I had seen that lock. And as I walked to the porch sweating, I thought about the window that was still up. I knew then that Mr. Tim knew that I had climbed in the window and that Mr. Betty had never asked me to go to the store. Mr. Tim was a nice guy. And if he didn't tell my father about me being in his house today. I swore to God I would leave Mrs. Betty and her red patch alone forever. So, in my mind, I said "Goodbye, Mrs. Betty. I thought you were sweet."

CHAPTER 12

For the next couple of weeks, my Uncle Willie came to live with us. It was a big day for my daddy as he went shopping for a daybed for my uncle. We, kids, have always slept on a pallet on the floor. It was like a family reunion that day. For some time now, my Uncle John and Aunt Zora had moved into the building at 2801 S. Prairie on the second floor. My aunt Queenie and their cousin Joe, who had moved from Georgia, moved on the first floor. They all were in apartment 103 that night reminiscing about the good old days. My father was telling them what Rass used to tell him, “You got to give the people what they need.” He always told the story of how they ran the people off and took the truck from Pluke in the woods. They would always have a big laugh about Pluke coming back to the bank dressed like a woman getting his money.

It was the twenty-third of December 1947, and I sat in the classroom. The teacher was teaching math on the blackboard and her back was to the class. I turned to Deloris, a classmate who was sitting in the back of me and dropped a note on her desk. “Let me see it one more time before we go to recess,” the note said. Deloris leaned forward in her seat, and only my ears could hear them whispering, “One more time. Come on, hurry up!” There was no one on the right side of Deloris. That seat was empty. So, I dropped my pencil to the right and bent down in my seat to get the pencil. I turned my head to the back of Delors’ desk. Her dress was up to her waist. She had scooted really low in her chair and had pulled her bloomers to the side. I saw her pussy with a little fuzz just starting to grow around it. She quickly closed her legs and sat upright in her chair. PI picked up the pencil and as the teacher was turning to face us, the recess bell rang. After recess, we were doing lessons about math. Deloris' feet tapped my seat very gently. She said, "Reach your hand back here. I've got a note for you." I reached my hand back and got the note. The note said, "Would you like to walk me home?" My mother's at work." I turned back and whispered to her, "Yes, I'll wait for you over by the hotel building." After I met with Deloris, we walked a half block to Twenty-Eighth and Calumet. She lived in a basement apartment. "You will have to wait in front of the house until I close the dining room sliding door because my grandmother lives in the rear, and I can't let you in until I close that door."

After a while, she was back and let me into the apartment. It was a dinky little apartment, one closer when you first walk in with curtains used as a door. They were pulled to the side, and you could see all the junk clothes stacked on each other inside. There was a big clothes hamper that sat on the side of the closet. Then you walk into a big, huge bedroom with mixed-match furniture. Big heavy drapes hung at the two-floor windows which were pulled together giving the room a dim light. Deloris put her finger to her lips telling me to be quiet and pointed to a chair in the corner by the bed. "I'm coming Grandma," she said in a loud voice. Deloris was through the door and into the kitchen. Deloris reached into the refrigerator and took out the sandwich that her mother had carefully wrapped for the grandmother. She put the sandwich on a plate and placed it on the table, then she poured a glass of milk and placed the mild jug back into the refrigerator. She went into the room by the rear door. She got her grandmother who had gotten out of bed and into a wheelchair. The grandmother's room was so stuffy, and it seemed as if you stepped into a rear closet. The only light was a 25-watt light bulb, and it gave a very dim light. Deloris pushed her grandmother to the table. "You go on and eat, grandma. I must go and start cleaning up before momma gets here."

Deloris was out of the kitchen and back into the room sliding the door behind her. I sat in anticipation of my next move. Deloris was in the room now. She reached up and took of her panties really quickly and said, "We have to hurry up before my grandma gets through eating." She jumped up on the bed. I dropped my pants and was on top of her, fumbling trying to insert her opening when that grandma hollered out "Deloris! You know I can't eat without taking my medicine. Where's my medicine and the water and what are you doing up yonder anyway?" Once again, Deloris was in the kitchen getting the water and saying "Grandma, you know I have to clean up before momma gets home. She gets home at four-thirty. You all right now, grandma?" Deloris was saying as she was leaving the kitchen. I kept fumbling trying to insert her. She moved one way; I moved another way. I couldn't really get it right. It seemed like we had been wrestling there for about half an hour. She finally whispered to me "You know I haven't been broken in yet?" I said, "WHAT!" She threw her hand up to her lips and said "Boy," raising up shocked when we heard her mother's voice in the kitchen.

"You just now eating momma? You aren't finished eating yet, momma?" "That girl has just been running in here and running there giving me a sandwich. I'm just now eating." Deloris pushed me off of her, almost on the floor. I, in turn, was trying to pull up my pants and almost fixing to run into Deloris. She then pointed to the door. I went to the door. First reaching for the lock, Deloris tapped me on the shoulder when I could hear her mother calling out. "Deloris, what are you doing up there?" Deloris pulled quilts and covers off the hamper and told me to get in. As I squatted into the hamper, those big heavy covers came down on me. "I'm coming, momma." Deloris was saying. In the kitchen, Deloris told her mother that she was cleaning up the closet and the house like she had told her to do. She had a headache and lay across the bed. "Well, her mother said, "I have to go out and get something for dinner. I want you to mop the kitchen floor and wash those dishes on the side there. They better be done before I get back. And open that damn middle door so Grandma can talk to you. Deloris was back and let me out from under that quilt. I was about to smother under there. My whole body was wet from sweat. When she opened the door and peeped out, she almost pushed me out the door. Not saying a word. I heard the lock behind me. The air was cold and refreshing from being under those quilts. I was late getting home and once again I showed up in the middle of one of those fights between my mother and father. I never did get used to those fights. It only added to a nerve condition.

The next day was Saturday, and I went to my shoeshine job. As I entered the door Mr. Buddy was popping that rag on four customers' shoes. It got good to him as he jumped back and did a little tap dance and went right back popping that rag on those shoes. I smiled at him as I took my apron off the door and tried it neatly around my waist. I got one of the shoeshine rags off the hook and gave Mr. Buddy a nudge with my hands telling him to move down to the next two customers and gave it two pops. Mr. Buddy went back into his tap dancing again. We both started to make those rags pop on the customers' shoes. "Watch it, Mr. Buddy," one of the customers said, "Al is getting just as good as you are." I was still popping the rag as Mr. Buddy went back into his tapping. Then he put the cloth around his last customer's shoe and pulled it really fast making it pop. He said "I told Al I don't want him to be like me. I want him to be better than I am." That Sunday morning, I had gotten up at five as usual. But for the first time in two years, there wasn't a grape left. There wasn't anything for me to sell. So, I went back and sat on my porch thinking of Deloris and her mother! First, Ronald came out and waved at me as he was coming to the yard. Then Kenneth Boyd, a boy who lived on Twenty-Fifth and Prairie, was a close friend of mine. Before long, we had a crowd and we played touch football in the side yard. As I went back for a pass and caught the ball, I looked over to the left of me and saw Mr. Betty standing in the window giving me a big round ao applause. I waved at her and felt saddened. The thought that I had neglected her from the day that Mr. Tim had caught me in that room, I never did come back to go to the store or empty the garbage or anything for her. I looked back at her and smiled and waved and she waved back. My side of the team went into a huddle. When we came out of the huddle, I looked back at the window, but she was gone.

The next couple of days I stayed on Deloris's back about letting me come to her house. She whispered in my ear in school while the teacher's back was on us, "My mother is on vacation, but she goes to the beauty shop tomorrow. I can come over to your house for an hour." "Okay with me." That next morning, I met Pap and Otha in the lot on the way to school. They were waiting in the vacant lot for me. Otha was a slim boy, with a fair complexion with a long head. He was a newcomer to the neighborhood and had moved into Pap's building on the first floor. We called him the seven-ring man because of his head. "Hi, Al!" They both said as I approached them. Pap said "Today, that teacher is going to give us a test. And I know I don't know that test. I'm going to wait and take the nest on Monday. Come on and go with us," Otha said to me. "Go where?" I asked. "To the beach, Thirty-First Street beach." I looked at Pap for a moment and said, "Why not?" And we were on our way to the beach. Before long we had walked all the way from 31 Street beach to the Field Museum at Soldiers Field. We had fun playing in the grass on the swings throwing rocks in the water. Before long it was two o'clock and he had to hustle back from the museum to 27the Street. I had told Pap about the date I had with Deloris with the quilts and blankets on me. I told him I damn nearly fainted in that basket. We separated at the lot and they went home and I went back to Drake School to wait for Deloris. I was sitting on the steps of the building that looks south across the field and elsewhere. Before long I saw Deloris coming with the next crowd of people walking, mainly with a fat dark-skinned girl who wore her hair very short. They were passing me as I ran up behind Deloris and grabbed her from behind the neck and said, "I got you now."

Her girlfriend said, "Turn her loose." She said "I'm going to tell her momma, and the bitch took off running. Deloris told me "I wanted to tell you, but you didn't come to school that. I can't go to your house because my momma did not go to the beauty shop." I said, "Ten minutes in the hallway." Deloris replied, "I'm not going to be there more than ten minutes." We walked through the gangway between the fences and the building on the north side. We got to the side entrance door into the building. It was a long hallway. I said, "Let's go under the stairs over there in that corner." She said, 'Let's go into this bathroom over there." The bathroom door said "Toilet." And the door was ajar. There was only a sink and a toilet in the bathroom. She said," Where do you want me to go?" I said, "Lay on the floor." She pulled off her panties and lay on the floor. I dropped my pants and pulled down my underwear and was on my knees between her legs. When I heard her momma say "Deloris, where are you?" She damn nearly kicked me in my face again and she jumped up and pulled on her panties. I jumped up and zipped my pants. I said, "What should I do?" She said "Shhh, boy be quiet. I saw the window and it was easily raised. I said, "I don't want your momma to catch me with you so I'm going to jump out of this window." She said "Go ahead. Go ahead." I said, "Close it behind me and tell your momma you had to go to the bathroom."

I jumped. It was a short distance to the sidewalk, and I landed on my feet and ran to the rear of the building across the alley through the vacant lot. All the neighborhood kids were playing baseball. A big curly-haired boy named Curly Joplin had hit a home run. As I ran, the neighborhood cheered him around the bases. I stood in the crowd watching the game. There was no need to rush home because it was my sister's turn to do the chores. Maybe half an hour had passed when I saw Kenneth running towards me. "Man, come here, Al." Let me tell you something. You know that girl Deloris you were telling me about; you were with the other day? I was in the playground and there were about 50 police around there. Her momma said that some man had tried to rape Deloris." I said, "What man?" "Yeah, and he left his cap." That was the first time it dawned on me that I didn't have my cap on. My heart started beating fast as my tongue seemed to get numb. I said, "What the shit you mean a man, Kenneth?" He said, "What the matter, "l?" I said, "That man is me." He said, "You mean to tell me that you were the one?" "That's what the shit I'm saying, yeah. They can see that she ain't raped. The bitch is still a virgin. I was going to rape her." "What are you going to do?" I said, "I don't know!" "What do you think I should do?" He said, "I don't know, man. She knows you. She said it was a man, so she must not want to tell on you." I felt better until Kenneth opened his mouth with the next words. "But they have got your cap, man. They will know it was you, they have got your fingerprints." I could hardly sleep that night. My stomach was nervous, and it seemed as though I had gas. I tried to belch but I couldn't. So, I did what I usually do, walked from Twenty-Ninth to Twenty-Sixth Street two or three times trying to belch. I wanted to tell my mother about the episode, but I was afraid to. I went to sleep. The next morning on my way to school, I didn't know what I was going to do. I walked to school by myself. I kind of lagged behind the rest of the crowd. As I was crossing the lot in front of Drake School, I could see the patrol officer and by the red building, I saw Mrs. Scott, Deloris's mother looking up and down the street like she was a detective. I came closer to Mrs. Scott. "Good morning Mrs. Scott," I said. She looked back to me and said "Hello, son," and went back to looking up and down the street. I said, "Mrs. Scott," and she said, "What is it?" I told her, "I am the one that was with Deloris."

She said, "WHAT?" And grabbed me by my collar and said, "Help police! Police!" The police ran over and grabbed me by my arm and before I knew it, I was in the principal's office. With all the people staring at me like I was something rare. The truant officer looked at the police and said, "A car is coming." About half an hour later, I was at the Twenty Seventh Street police station. They had me sitting in a little room off the side of the desk. Ever so often, a police officer would come past and say, "That's him right there. Is he the one who raped the girl at school?" After a while one big fat Irishman came in and said, "Al, this is for you.' He gave me a piece of paper that had the date and time for me and my mother to be back, which was a Friday at 10:00 that morning. We were to ask for Detective Riley and Grasberry. "Okay, boy, the officer is going to take you home, and you be back here tomorrow with your mother at ten o'clock. Do what the note tells you to do." So, I was on my way home to 2720 S. Prairie. It was hard telling my mother what had happened to me that day. My father looked as if he wanted to kill me but momma, she was telling me to tell whatever I did. I said with tears in my eyes. She said, "Boy, tomorrow is my payday and I have to be at that police station at ten o'clock. Boy, you better not be done taken nothing from that girl. I assured my mother and my father that I did not do the things that she said. I wasn't the man. That next morning, when we arrived at the police station, we were sitting outside on the bench of the little room that I was in that day before. One black officer came out of the room and said, "Is this the Wynn family?" I said, "Yes," "And you are Al," I said, "Yes." "Well, we're just about through with Deloris. They've been here since nine 'o'clock. You should be in the room in the next ten minutes and out of here no later than eleven 'o'clock if you tell the truth, and your truth pans out to be the truth, you should be out of here before twelve." About half an hour had passed before they called me and my mother into the room. Deloris's mother sat in the chair by the window. She was a tall, stocky lady, really stocky. It looked like she could have knocked out Joe Louis with one punch. She was looking at me now like she could kill me. She had Deloris dressed really pretty in a short dress like the ones that Catholic kids wear.

You could see her big legs and thighs. It seems like I had a flashback from lying in that bathroom on the floor. This wasn't the time to be thinking about that now. They were trying to send me to jail. She gave me a half-smile. I looked over at the officer who was seated on the other side of the table by Deloris. He was a white officer who looked like he had never played a game of cards in his life or anything else. He seemed like he never played anything but the police. Stand up in front of me. This is no play game, Al. Do you understand that? These are some serious charges that have been placed against you. Do you understand that?" I said, "Yes, Sir." "Deloris said that you twisted her arm. Forced her into the building, took her into a bathroom or toilet in the building, and attempted to rape her. Are these things true. "Some of them," I said, looking up at him. "What part is true, and what part is false?" "I did twist her arm, but I was playing with her." "What do you mean playing?" The white police spoke up. All of the kids played like that. We don't hurt the girl when we twist her arm, it's al play. The false part is I did not force her into the building. I did not force her into the bathroom, and she took off her panties willingly."

"Is this true, Deloris?" The officer asked as she stared at her. "He is lying," Deloris started crying. "He took off my panties before he jumped out of the window." "

"So, if he took down your panties and jumped out the window when did he have a chance to rape you? He just took down your panties and jumped out the window, when did he have a chance to rape you? He just took down your panties and jumped out the window." Deloris was crying hysterically, not answering the police. She said, "He did rape me, momma. He did rape me. I don't have to sit up and lie. He did rape me." "Why don't you tell us, Al, in your own words what took place between you and this young lady, starting from the beginning," I told it all from the beginning. That shocked her momma when she found out I was under the quilts that day. I said, "Deloris told her momma that it was a man. That's the only reason that I told her mother that it was me. All the things I did, she had said yes to. All the things I did, she wanted to do as badly as I did. In fact, he was the one who asked me." At this time, Deloris had her head down between her legs sobbing and sniffling as you would say. "Okay young lady," the black officer said. "Do you still want to stick to your story, or do you want to be truthful to your mother? Did Al try to rape you?"

"No, sir," she said, half crying "Did you give him your permission to go into that bathroom and lay on that floor?" "Yes sir," she said, still sniffling. "You hussy, you had me to come down here getting ready to send this boy to jail and you were the one who did the initiating. You wait until I get you home!" The black policeman said, "You all can go as soon as Office Kelly gets through writing the report.: He looked over at me again and said, "Al, you be careful and leave these little girls alone. You will get yourself in a world of trouble." He looked over at my mother, "See you again, Mrs. Wynn." She flashed those big brown eyes at him and said, "Thank you Officer" and left the room. My mother had to be at Drake School that Monday. All the kids were looking at me saying, "That's him." In the principal's office, it didn't take him long to explain that he couldn't have a student acting the way that I was acting. So, he was transferring me to Foster School, at Union and Halsted in Jew town as they called it. My mother had to teach me how to ride the bus. Foster School was less tough than Mosley's school, and Montessori. They were a boys' trade school and at other schools when a new student got there, he had to show his ability to be a boy, a crybaby, a homosexual, or a Joe Louis. I proved myself with the best. I had all the boys within a month saying, "Al, I'm on your side." Everything I did, they wanted to be on my side. One boy told me after I had hemmed up one of the boys in the basement and played tic tac toe with his head. He said, "Man, Man, Man, a, you can chump." I said, "Yes," after I took my hand because my knuckles were bleeding from the print of his teeth. I was expelled from school for three weeks.

CHAPTER 13

It was a hot day in June as we boys were just finishing playing touch football in the side yard of 2720 Prairie Avenue. "It's getting hotter," I said to Pap and Roland Lane. "Yes," Pap said, "it's getting really hot." We were just approaching the gate to go out to the sidewalk when we saw a sailor man standing there dressed in a full uniform and jacket. The other boys were just catching up to us at the gate. The sailor asked, "Do you boys know Davis S Smith?" "Yes, I do," I said. "Can you tell me where I can find him?" ha asked. "Yes." I answered. "He is right over there sleeping in that car." We boys were separating up and down the street as I heard the man ask, "Are you Davis Smith?" Davis had sat up in the seat when the knock on the car window awakened him. He strained his eyes trying to see the guy that was asking "Are you Davis Smith?" Davis lowered the window in the car and said "Yes, I am Davis."

The man stepped closer to the car as he took the .45 caliber automatic pistol from under his jacket and shot Davis three times in the head and chest. The noise from the pistol was a shock to us as we started running and shouting, "He is killing Mr. Davis." Mr. Davis was Paul's brother and ten years older. He didn't ride a motorcycle or chase girls like Paul did. He kept a low profile, wore suits every day like Mr. Tim and my father did. Some people said he was a businessman that was into everything that was not legal. I ran to Paul's room and kicked and banged my fist against the door. "Yes, who is it?" Paul asked, sleepily. "Paul! "Paul! A man just shot Mr. Davis!" I yelled. The door came wide open. Paul was dressed just in pants, no shirt, or no shoes. "What did you say, Al?" I was crying now and didn't know why. Maybe it was the shock or just plain scared as hell, but through the tears I said, "A man just shot Mr. Davis in your car." Paul took off ruing to his car. I was right behind him. When we reached the car Mr. David had fallen back, leaning in the seat. It seemed as if the bullets had torn half of his head off. Blood was everywhere.

Paul hollered loud, "OH GOD! Davis! Davis! My brother," He cried hard and loud as he fell to his knees in the street. From a distance you could hear the sirens of the police and fire trucks coming from Mercy Hospital on Twenty-sixth Street heading our way. The word had gotten out and people lined their porches, yards, and street looking and talking among themselves. It was a memorable day and I know in my heart that I would never forget that I was the one who told the sailor man where Mr. Davis was, and no way would I forget the scenery. It seemed that all the people in the building were on the porch when one of the adults asked Roland Lane what happened. "How did the man know that Davis was asleep in that car?" My heart started beating fast as Roland answered. "You see, we were all coming out of the gate when the man asked us where Mr. Davis was. And we all told him he was in the car. He was a sailor. We didn't know!"

"Of course, you didn't," of the ladies said that was standing next to the boy. She reached over and brought him closer to her. "Don't cry. It wasn't anyone's fault." The next day the newspaper, The Chicago Sun Times read, "Davis Coleman, a black south side landlord was killed yesterday by a sailor whose mother, wife, and kids were killed by a fire that was in a run-down house on the west side owned by Davis Smith." This fire occurred two weeks ago while the sailor was stationed in Florida. There was some talk that the fire was deliberately set. There haven't been any charges brought against the sailor yet. My life took on a different outlook after Davis Smith's death. It seemed to me life was much shorter than we believed it to be. Anything can happen to shorten it or at the age of seventeen, maybe I was just growing up.

Two more characters came into the neighborhood. One was Jimmy Smith, Davis Smith's son. He was twenty-one years old, slim, and very nice looking. He had two gold teeth, and when he brushed the wavy bangs from his forehead, they reached the back of his head. Every time he muttered a word, he laughter. I guess that's why he had the gold teeth because it made him have a nice smile. He was a jittery sort of person with what seemed like too much energy. He had only been around for two weeks, and his uncle Paul had bought him a Harley Davidson motorcycle the same as his. He wore the Harley Davidson jacket, a cap, and I guess the gloves; he never took them off. Paul's Livery Cab Co was running really good now, so he bought Jimmy a car which made him have 2 Livery cabs.

I had two or three, or maybe four fights with Earneil throughout the years. She never could whip me or my sister Frances, but now she was boating every day so that no one better not mess with her. She seemed as though she was mad because I didn't want any more of her infected pussy. She would look at me sideways and say, "Nobody better mess with me now because my big cousin will kick their ass." I would ignore her remarks and continue doing what I was doing at the time.

It was on a Saturday morning at about seven when my aunt Queenie came knocking, banging on our door. My mother let her in. My father was shaving by our mantlepiece. "Estell, you are going to have to say something to A.S. He's just out there beating Emma and stomping all in her stomach." My father stopped shaving and looked at her and said, "What are you doing out to their house so early?" "I was washing, and I wanted to know if he needed anything washed for her>" "I don't know why you are out there in their business, sister," my father said. "Well, I'm going back there to help her and if he kills her, it will be your fault. Don't say I didn't tell you." And my aunt went to the door. "Wait a minute sister, I'm going with you." He grabbed his shirt off the chair and put it on half buttoned, got his hat off the mantlepiece and reached and got the straight razor that he kept on the shelf. My mother had sat back on the bed after she opened the door dressed in her slip. She grabbed my father by the arm, "Don't go, Estell, send Queenie back home. She had no business going out there dipping in their business anyway." My father snatched away from my mother, and they left for the rear building. My uncle Willie sat up on his daybed in his underwear. "Oh, she's telling you the right thing, Estell; I wouldn't go out there. It will only get you in trouble." My father went on out there and knocked on the door. The door came open. My uncle spoke to my father. "Hello, Bubba." But before my uncle knew it, my father had grabbed him in the collar and snatched him up to him and cut him from his head through his face to his chin. My aunt Queenie had got in the back of him and hit him as hard as she could with one of those pots from the stove. I stood there crying, "Don't do it, daddy! Don't do it daddy! Don't do it daddy!" It was too late to stop as blood started running down his face tohis shirt. When my auntie hit him in the back of the head with that pot, he lunged forward, knocking my father against the hallway wall. There was a front door and a rear door. My uncle ran through the hallway to the rear door, going to Twenty-Sixth street. It wasn't long before my father was caught by the police for the assault against my uncle.

They went to court and the judge gave my father six months in the Bridewell Correctional center. He sentenced my father to six months after he heard the testimony of my father's baby sister, Emma. The prosecuting attorney had asked Aunt Emma, "Did you have a good husband?" She said "Yes, he was a very good and was a good provider for me and my child." "Did you send your brother to help you?" The prosecutor asked. "No, I didn't send for him. My sister came to meddle in me and my husband's affairs and went and got my brother. He had no reason at all to do him like that," my auntie said, putting a tissue up to her nose and sniffling. "He had no reason to cut him." Do you still love your husband? "Yes, sir." "Are you back together?" "Yes, sir." "Are you staying in same apartment?" "No, sir. My husband moved, and I'm going to move in with him."

The next character that moved into the neighborhood moved into my Aunt Emma and Uncle A.D.'s apartment on the first floor. His name was Bobby Lewis. He was slim. He was twenty-three years old and looked as though he was eighteen. He was light-complexioned with a small number of freckles, and he also showed an open face gold crown when he smiled. He was a very neat dresser. I was on my way to empty the garbage in the alley when I saw him at the rear door looking up and down the alley. I put the garbage in the can, and he said 'Hi." I threw up my hand and spoke back, "Hey, how are you doing?" He said, "Man, we moved in last night. My mother and I moved here on the first floor." I said, "Yeah, that was my uncle and Auntie's house that you moved into." He said," Yeah." And I said, "Yes." He said, "Well, do you know the old man up stairs called Buddy Peterson?" I said, "Yes. I know Mr. Buddy." He said, "He is my grandfather. He is the reason we got the apartment." He said, "Man, I really need a cigarette. Where is the store around here?"

I said, "You can go down," and pointed to Twenty-Sixth Street. "Or you can go down to Twenty-Ninth Street to the corner store or the drug store is on Indiana." "Would you like to show me, or would you like to go with me to the store so I will know the next time?"

I'd been standing there for an hour. It was Saturday, I thought to myself, there was no one else out, and there were no chores for me to do. He seemed pleasant to talk to, so I said, "sure, I'll show you, come on. We'll take this short cut right across this alley." So, we walked across the vacant lot to Indiana Street. As we walked to the drug store on Twenty-Ninth Street, all the girls that I knew would say, "Hi, Al, "but they would be staring and smiling at him. "By he way," he said, "my name s "Oh, I go in every Saturday at one and work until eight. You know we close at nine." I said my good-byes and told Bobby, "We can go over to the drug store and get those cigarettes. "Don't tell they sell cigarettes at the liquor store?" I said "Yes." He said, "I want me a beer, so I'll get them here." I said, "Okay, I'll go into Bobby Lewis and yours?" "My name is Al Wynn." "I see all the girls seem to know you," he said. "We all go to school together," I replied. "What school did you go to?" I asked. "Oh, I… uh, came out of college about three years ago. I stopped three years ago. I didn't finish. You could say I'm a dropout, man." "How old are you? I thought you were about eighteen." Then he told me his age, "Twenty-three."

Twenty Ninth Street was crowded on a Saturday morning. Jitney picking up people and other jitneys were letting them out. We passed TJ's Food and Grocery, and we were coming up to Smitty's Shoeshine Parlor. Smitty could beat Mr. Buddy shining shoes. Smitty was a short black handsome West Indian with wavy black hair. He popped this rag in Mexico, West Indies, New York, and now he pops the rag in Chicago, ain't that right, Al and I would always praise him for his good shoe shining. I met Smitty at the show downtown with Mr. Buddy. We were just coming into the show when Mr. Buddy saw Smitty standing at the candy counter. They hugged each other. "Smitty, this boy is going to be better than you and me. Wait until I get finished with him. Al, this is Smitty, an old friend of mine all the way from New York. We popped them rags." Smitty had come down to Twenty-Sixth Street four or five times to see us. We had fun when Smitty visited us, and we would laugh and drink colas. Smitty had come from New York ten years ago, bought an old junk us, had it towed over to Twenty Eighth and Indiana. It was a good spot for the bus. It sat between TJ's Food and Grocery and Henry's restaurant. The liquor store and bar had sat on the corner. It was a good place for a business. The automotive company that was on the next black stretched each way north and south and east and west. A lot of people worked there on a Friday, Saturday, or Sunday. Business was good for everyone.

Across the street from the automotive factory going west was Dollar's Grocery store next door from Dollar's, sitting on the corner was one apartment building. The drug store sat on the north corner of Twenty ninth Street, right in front of the liquor store across the street. I soke to Smitty and quickly introduced him to Bobby. "Why aren't you at work, Al? Smitty asked. "Oh, I go in every Saturday at one and work until eight. You know we close at nine." I said my good-byes and told Bobby, "We can go over to the drug store and get those cigarettes. "Don't they sell cigarettes at the liquor store?" I said, "Yes." He said, "I want me a beer, so I'll get them here." I said, "Okay, I'll go into Henry's restaurant and get me a pop." He said, "Okay," and left me in front of the restaurant door. I went into the restaurant. "May I help you?" A lady asked as I sat on the stool by the door. "Yes, get me a grape pop," I said. "You want a glass?" she asked. I said, "Yes, ma'am," I took a sip of pop and looked around the room. There were four men sitting in the back. All of them were dressed sharply. I recognized all of them from going to the store for Mrs. Berry. The darker guy in the crowd who sat on the inside booth in the back was Wadell, and they called him Boack Chocolate. He was a ladies' man, and a gambler. The ladies called him Chocolate because they said he was sweet, and he was black with an open-faced gold crown that sparkled when he smiled. He was nice looking, average height, weighed about 137 lbs. Across from him sitting in the booth with his back t me was Tommy, another Ladies man, and a gambler. He was tall, slim teasingly tan with wavy hair. His mustache was cut thin and neat. He had ladies' fingernails, and they were long, shaped, and shiny. Leroy, a gambler, sat at the end next to Tommy. He owned a gambling house on 30th and Indiana.

Drug store Bob stood on the side of Wadell as he looked over at me, "Hey Little Pimp," he said. "What is a pimp?" I spoke. "I ain't no Pimp." "Ain't he the one that lived with that white woman named Betty Rogers?" Wadell asked. "Yes, he's the one," Drug store Bob answered like he had been knowing me for a while. He stayed with that broad for a year. The men of the building that lived there said that little nigger's pocket was packed everyday with money. "Is that true?" Tommy said, turning around in the booth looking at me. "Did you get money from that bitch?" I said, "Who are you? Are you Mr. Tim's friend or something?" He said, "Who in the hell is Mr. Tim?" I said, "He's her husband, that who he is." "You mean to tell me you were getting money from her every day," Bob asked. "And you didn't know you were pimping?" "I ask you again," I looked at Bob, "What is Pimping?" "Pimping is when you get money from a lady, and you are not doing any hard labor for her and she's giving you her money freely. You were getting money from her for a year, and you weren't her husband. Who do you think you were?' Currently. Bobby was at the door looking for me and we left.

In the next two or three months, I mostly hung out with Bobby. He was an exciting kind of fellah, and I thought that I could learn a lot of things from him. I was tired of playing baseball and rooting the peg and hide and go seek. I thought I had grown up above that now. We mostly hung out in his apartment. He would tell me wild stories about the girls in college and this one girl called Mary Ann that he wanted to marry. He also asked me everyday to ride in the jitney with him to 24th Street with him, we walked into the tavern part of the building. This day I had gone to 24th Street with him, we walked into the tavern part of the building. There was one lady by the telephone booths dressed neatly. She had a scarf around her head with a knot in the back. She was looking at me and Bobby up and down as we approached her. "Hi, Karen," Bobby said." Hi Bobby," she said, looking at me with dreamy eyes. "This is Al. He lives in the building that I live in. Look out for him, will you, while I go up to the 3rd floor?" There was a long radiator sitting over by the window. I went over and felt it. It was cold and I had a seat on the radiator. I pulled a Batman Comic book out of my back pocket and started to read it. Every now and then, I would look over at Karen, who was seated on the barstool near the rear of the lounge. Every time I would look over at her, she would be staring at me. I sat there reading that book for what seemed to be an hour. I got restless and walked over to Karen. "Do you know the apartment that Bobby went to?" She said, "Yes, it's 303. But why don't you wait for him" You don't want to go there."

"Well, I can't wait here all day. I'm going to see what happened to him." I started up the steps to the third floor. As I was walking up the steps, I heard voices. When I reached the second floor, there were two men arguing. One was tall with long hair that was curled. The other one was a kind of short fat guy. I walked past them, headed for the third floor. When I got to that landing, I stopped to observe the argument. "Bitch," that little, short guy was saying to the tall guy with the curls, "didn't I ell you to stay out of that hoe's house?" "I just got my hair curled, daddy. Don't you see it, don't it look pretty?" That startled me because I had never seen anything like that before, two men arguing like husband and wife. "Yeah, fuck your hair. If I see you in that hoe's house again, I will put my foot up your ass." The tall guy that was talking like a lady switched voices on me. The tall guy in the gross voice said, "Don't get too god damn happy mother fucker. I will put this purse down and kick your ass." The little guy pointing his finger at him said, "You might have a chance to do that if I catch you in this bitch's place again." He was shaking his fingers while going down the steps. I continued to the third floor. The building had six floors. I reached the door. Bobby came out of it walking fast. "That god damn elevator," he said, "I've been waiting on this elevator for half an hour. Come on, Al, Let's go." He started running down the stairs. I followed him. We were in a cab and back to his apartment in no time. I had never seen him like this before. He was very jittery and sweating.

Inside his apartment, he told me to have a seat at the kitchen table. He went int the room and came back with a skinny rubber hose in his hand. He placed the rubber hose across his lap and tore at the button on his shirt. After he rolled up his shirt sleeve, he told me to tie his arm with that rubber hose. "Pull it tighter," he told me. He got up from the chair and walked back into the room. When he sat himself back in the chair, he placed a shiny object with a needle on the table. He balled his fist up one or two times like a person does when they are taking a blood test. As he balled his hand up two or three times, he took his finger and hit the vein in his arm two or three times. Then he took the needle and inserted the needle into his arm. Then whatever the substance that was in the needle went into his arm, and when he pulled the needle handle back out, there was blood in the needle, then he shot that blood back into this arm. He untied the rubber hose. He sat there for a while as though he had gone to sleep. He rubbed his finger across his nose as he stood up, he said, "Man, man, man, that's good, really good!" He had placed the needle on the table and the rubber as he had tried to pull up his pants. As he stood there, going into a long nod. He hit the floor with a bang. I was out that door. I pulled the door back and ran around to the front of the building. I ran dead into Jimmy, almost knocking him down in the front yard. "Hold up, Al, where are you going?" I said, "Oh, hey Jimmy. How are you doing?" He said, "I was just looking for you, man. I need twenty dollars bad. Al, Percy ain't here, and I got a date and I need it bad. I'll give it back to you on Thursday." I said, "I'm going to be needing it on Thursday now, Jimmy, I must buy me a jacket with that money.

He said, "You'll get it back on Thursday. Don't worry about it." The next week, I avoided Bobby. And that Thursday, I didn't see Jimmy. I hung out with Pap and Roland Lane. I had gotten good for the sixth month down at Nickolas's Gym on Congress. A golden glove bout had picked out a white boy to spar with me in the ring for three rounds. To show all the people down there How good I was, I thought. When I saw the white boy, I didn't care anything about how wide his chest was. It seemed like he had football pads in his shoulders. I only noticed his legs. They were ostrich legs, long legs with little knows I them. I was short and stocky; my legs were big, and I thought that made a difference. I didn't know at the time that when I first joined the gym, that he was here. I didn't know that he had been there for three years and had all that experience, that he showed me in the first round, he damn nearly killed me. I knew then after that good ass-whipping he had given me, that I was through with boxing. I got home, defeated, and disgusted. I was just coming up on the porch when Jimmy came through the hallway door. "Hey Jimmy, I've been looking for you, man." He gave me a slight grin and pulled one of his gloves tighter on his hand. He looked at me with that smirk on his face. "If you are talking about the twenty dollars, I don't have it. I don't know when I'm going to have it and stop asking me for it." I had just gotten my ass whipped an hour before now and I'm fixing to get my ass whipped again, I thought. But I knew in my heart that I couldn't let him get away with that loud-mouthed bullshit he just told me about my money. I was too close to Mr. Betty's door and my own door. I wasn't about to let my father and mother see me get my ass whipped on that front porch. I figured that Jimmy had the advantage because of his age, so I invited him to the basement. "Say, Jimmy, you can't just say it like that, let's go into the basement and discuss this."

"You want to what, go in the basement?" he asked, tugging, and pulling at his glove. "Sure, I'll go to the basement with you. Let's go." Before I reached the basement, I had a change of heart two or three times. I wanted to say go ahead and keep the money, but something in the back of my mind said, "That's bullshit. I'm not going to let this skinny mother fucker take my money. Just because he is twenty-one or twenty-two years old." He said he would pay me back and that's what he's going to do, or I'm just going to have to take this ass whipping. We were in the basement. Jimmy was standing wide-legged at the bottom of the steps. I was in front of him, kind of looking at him. "So, what are you saying, you're not going to pay me back my money, Jimmy?" "I'm saying just that, and I don't know why you brought me in this goddamn basement to get your as whipped." He tugged at his glove just one time when my right hand went into his midsection as hard as I could. He grunted and farted at the same time as that right hook caught him on the side of his jaw. Now once again, I was Joe Louis, and stepped into him before he could fall sideways and hooked him with that left hook, and that straightened his ass up. Blood rushed from his nose as he threw up his hand in defense, but that right hand cracked his ribs. He screamed, "Don't hit me no more. Don't hit me no more! I'll give you your money." He begged so pitifully that I felt sorry for him. So, I said, "just keep the money, man." I turned to walk away when I noticed Ms. Hudson standing at her door observing the scene. Mrs. Coleman and her husband, Mac, who lived in the first apartment in the basement had come out into the hall. "Do you need a towel, Jimmy?" Mrs. Hudson asked. "No, thank you, I can make it," he said, staggering and falling up the steps. I looked around at Mac, Coleman, and Ms. Hudson, but I could tell by the look on their faces they didn't approve of that fight, but they didn't know the essence of it.

CHAPTER 14

The next couple of weeks after the incident with Jimmy in the basement, I was hanging. out with Bobby again. We were sitting around talking and Bobby was telling me about his girlfriend in Cleveland, Ohio, the city he grew up in. I had stopped boxing, so I had started smoking cigarettes with the approval of my mother and father. The cigarettes that Bobby was smoking looked like one of Mrs. Betty's Prince Albert's tobacco cigarettes. I said, "Oh, you don't smoke Pall Mall anymore, huh?" You got to smoke Prince Albert tobacco." "No, this cigarette got a different taste from Prince Albert tobacco. Here, you take a puff." I took a puff off it, and it almost strangled me. He said, "No, you took too much. Do it like this." He took the cigarette and pulled off it just a little bit. And he made his lips and jaws into a balloon-like shape. He held his lips real tight and then let the smoke out. I said, "Why do you have to do all that?"

He said, "Come on, Al, just try it one more time, and then I'll tell you. Make your mouth into a balloon, like I did. Inhale it, then hold your lips tight and blow as hard as you can, but keep your lips tight, then blow the smoke out." Each time it seemed as though it was getting easier and easier for me to do. Then a strange feeling started creeping up on me. I said, "What is this, Bobby?" He said, "Its's China Red, the worst reefer I know." He seemed to be ten blocks away, hollering back at me. Then something scary happened to me. Bobby's head had gotten big as a stove. I jumped, I said,

"Damn man, what's wrong with you?" Bobby was laughing almost into tears. He said, "You're just high." I said, "No, man. Your head is as big as that stove." I said, "Man, I've got to go home." And it seemed as though my voice was ten blocks away. He said, "No, Al, sit down and calm yourself. You can't go home like that. Calm yourself. I'm going to turn the radio on, just listen to the music." The music was very soothing. After an hour or so, I had calmed down and was on my way home when I heard a voice calling after me at the rear door. "Hi, how are you doing?" The rear door was propped open, and you could see the truck in the alley. I said, "I'm doing fine." She said, "Would you like to make some money?" I said." "Doing what?" She said, "Helping me to take these chairs, tables, and clothes up to my apartment."

She lived right across from the old man Mr. buddy, Bobby's grandfather. She was dark brown skinned with real bush black hair. She was average looking and very hairy. She had hair all up to her legs and arms, thick eyebrows, a thin mustache. She had one little baby in a crib. She had paid the driver of the truck, and he left, she closed the door behind him and said, "Come you have a s eat, and I'll pay you in a minute as soon as I fix the baby a bottle." I had a seat in the chair on the side of the bed. She sat on the bed in front of me. Her dress was half up to her thighs. I could see the inside of her thighs, and there were no panties. The little knot between my legs began to rise as she reached over to the dresser and pulled out a half-ping bottle. "Would you like to celebrate with me?" I said, "What are you celebrating?" "This house," she said, "I'm celebrating my new house." She took a sip out of the bottle and passed it to me. I didn't drink, so I faked a drink. She went on drinking and talking and before long, she had told me the whole history of her life. Now she was tipsy, and she went from telling me the history of her life to telling me how pretty my eyes were, and how tan my face was, and she rubbed my jaws. I looked over at the clock of the dresser. It said five-thirty. There was a string that hung from the pull chain on the light in the ceiling that was tied to the head of the bed. She reached up and pulled the string as she reached over and pulled me on top of her. She was twenty-four years old and gave me the ride of my life. At seven-thirty, I was walking bow-legged home. When I reached the door to my apartment, I straightened up as good as I could. "Where have you been, Al?" My mother asked.

"I was with Mr. Fat, the vegetable man. He wanted me to help him work today and tomorrow, and he's going to give me $15 tomorrow." That lie had come very quickly. I know I had promised Lilly that I would be back in her apartment the next day as six. I didn't know where in the hell I was going to get that $15 that I had promised my mother. That night I slept very hard, and I dreamed that I had really fucked Deloris.

The next day, I came from school in a hurry and did my chores around the house. Half an hour before my father and mother came home from work, I told my sister I was going to meet Fat for work. I closed the door behind me and made a big dash past Paul's apartment to the basement and out the back door of the basement to the rear building. I was just getting ready to knock on Lilly's door when I heard Bobby's voice call after me. I turned around to the steps. A tall lady about 24-26 years old smiled at me. She had a little boy in her arms and another one holding on to her black slacks. She was very tan and had curls around her ears beneath a skull cap. I said, "Hi," then I saw Bobby when he stepped from behind her. "Hey man," he said. "Where are you going in such a hurry?" "I'm going to visit a friend of mine that I met yesterday." "Oh, you know that young lady already. "My, you're fast," he said, smiling. "no, man, nothing like that," I said. Smiling back and catching Mary's bedroom eyes staring back at me. "This is my cousin, Mary," Bobby said. "Ms. Mary is Grandfather Buddy's wife." I said, "Oh, I know Ms. Mary." She said, "Oh, you do?" I said, "Yes."

When the door behind me opened, Lilly stood there with what seemed like a white nightgown on. She opened the door a little wider so she could get a view of all the people in the hallway. "I heard voices, were you coming to see me, Al?" she said while looking directly into my eyes. I said, "Yes, this is Bobby Lewis. This is his cousin, Mary." They all nodded at each other. "Bobby lives downstairs and his grandfather and grandmother. Mary's mother lives right here next door to you." She said, "It's nice meeting both of you." Then she grabbed me by the arm and pulled me inside the door. I said, "Bobby." He said, "Yes," just before he got ready to turn into his grandfather's door, he turned to face me. I said, "Man, I got something very important to talk to you about when you get time." He said, "In about ah hour." I said, "Yeah, that will be good." And I closed the door. I turned to face Lilly standing behind me. She walked up close to me and looped her arms around my neck. She said, "Did you miss me today, Al?" I said, "Yes," and got mad at myself because that little know between my legs had started to bother me again. "I know, I missed you." She said as she started kissing me on my face and neck. I walked her to bed, and she was still kissing me on my neck. We fell on the bed as I kissed her hard. We rolled from side-to-side kissing and hugging and whispering into each other's ear until the baby started crying loudly. "Don't you want to see about the baby?" I asked as she steadily kissed me.

Only one of two things could be wrong with her. Either she's hungry, and I just fed her, or she's wet. Well, let's see which one it is." She stopped." The baby was wet, and the baby wanted a bottle. It was a funny thing about a baby when they get dried and get a bottle. They toy to talk. I was just listening to the baby when Bobby knocked at the door! Lilly answered the door. "Is Al still here?" he asked. She turned to me, "It's your friend Bobby." I stopped into the hall with Bobby and pulled the door up, but the door swung back open and left a crack. "Say, Bobby, you have to come through for me tonight., man," I whispered. "What do you mean?" He spoke. "Man, I'm going to be out here 'til about ten or eleven o'clock tonight. I told my mother I was working with Fat's, and I would have 15.00. You must lend me that until I go to the shop on Saturday." "Man, I don't have any money. Mary and I want a reefer and a beer, and we don't have money for that. That's the reason I came and knocked on the door because I thought maybe you had some money." I walked back into the house and closed the door behind me.

"How bad do you need hat $15?" Lilly asked. "Well, I told my mother a lie last night. I told her I was working. She is going to expect me to have that $15, and I don't know where I'm going to get it from." "Sure, you do." She said, putting that loop around my neck again. "First, you must answer my question. Did you miss me?" "I missed you really bad," I said, kissing her softly on her neck. "I could hardly wait to get here," I said as I kissed her hard and fell back on the bed with her. She sat up quickly and said I wanted something to drink. Would your friend go to the store with you and buy what I need?" She gave me a $50.00 bill. "Get me a pack of Pall Mall Red, a Canadian Ace beer, and a pint of gin. You can keep the rest." I knocked on Mr. Buddy's door. I spoke to Mr. Buddy and Ms. Mary, and I smiled at her daughter. "Bobby, do you want to go to the store with me? He said, "I'll go. What are you going to get?" I said, "Some drinks for the lady next door." Mary said, "I want to go with you. I need some cigarettes." She said, "Is it all right?" I said, "Oh yeah."

We were standing in front of the restaurant. I knew who I was looking for, and I saw Drug Store Bob seated on the stool talking to a lady and another man seated in the booth. I hollered through the door, "Hey Bob, can I speak to you for a moment, please?" He turned to face me. Hey, how are you doing, Litle Pimp? What do you want? He was on the sidewalk with me now as I pulled him aside from Bobby and Mary. "I got two friends here but. I don't know anyone else to come to but you." "You seem like a nice guy." He said, "What is it?" I said, "I need some reefer." He looked hard at me, "How much reefer do you need, Little Pimp?" I said, "Three or four joints." He turned around and looked over at Smitty's bus that had a group of men standing in front of it. "Hey Rabbit," he hollered out. "Yeah, "Rabbit answered. Rabbit was a light complication guy, slim and dressed very sharp in a suit. Later, I found out that he was a gambler and a doe dealer. "Come over here for a minute, Rabbit," Bob said. "Yeah," Rabbit said as he walked up to us. "This is Al" Bob said. "The Little Pimp I told you about that conned all that money out of that white bitch." "He needs some reefer about four or five joints." "Can you look for him?"

"No problem," Rabbit said, but "I have to go over to my car." Pointing to a convertible Cadillac. I said, "I have to go over to the liquor store and by the time you get back, I'll be out." I told Bobby what I needed and gave him the money. He went into the liquor store. I told him to get the beer and whatever he wanted for himself. Before long, Rabbit was back with my package and handed it to me. I handed him his money $4.00 as we passed Smitty's shoeshine parlor going back to 2727 Prairie. I looked over at the group of men and recognized Wadell as one of the guys in the crowd. He gave me a smile and a nod at the same time. He said, "I'll see you again, Little Pimp." I laughed back and told him, "I'm going to tell you again, I ain't no pimp. I don't even know what it means." We were past the bus now and were walking in front of TJ'S grocery store. The store was closed now, but there was still a little light in the window. I stopped and said, "Bobby, what about Mary's cigarettes?" He said,

"She gave me the money in the house. Here are her cigarettes in my pocket." I said, "Bobby, you got your beer, right?" And I said, "This is for you, Mary." I handed her the four reefers. She said, "Oh, how did you know I wanted this?" Bobby butted in and said, "I told him."

Bobby said, "Wait a minute, Al. You just asked me for a loan of $15, but you gave me a $50 dollar bill to go into the store with. Whose money is this?" "Who gave it to you? I know who gave it to you, that woman gave it to you." "It's none of your damn business who gave it to me." I said with a smile. "Well, I just want to know one thing," Mary asked, "Why do they call you a pimp? Do you take money from all your women?" "I only take it from the ones who like to give." We laughed as we walked home. The next three or four days, I had fun with Lilly during the couple of days I ditched school. I had gotten suspended from Foster Vocational School again for fighting. We went over to Montefiore Boy's school and tore up the lunchroom. About a dozen boys got expelled. I had started smoking reefer, and for two weeks, I hadn't gone up to Lilly's house in the evening. So, I told my mother I had a night job so I could get out of the house at night.

When I first met Lilly, I asked her if she was married. She said "No," and she didn't have a boyfriend." She put her arms around me and said, the only person she had was me. This night I told my mother I was starting my job from six to twelve. It was on a Saturday night. I had just entered the hallway of the rear building when Bobby ran down the steps and met me coming in the door. "Hey man, where you been?" he asked, with that weird look in his eyes. I knew what he had been doing. He said, "Man, I'm higher than a mother fucker. Man, guess who's upstairs and wants to see you?" I said, "who, Lilly?" He said "no, I'm talking about my cousin, Mary." I said "What?" He said "Yeah, man, my cousin, she wants to put pussy all around your neck!" Instead of going to Lilly's house, Bobby and I went to Mr. Buddy's and Mary's apartment on the second floor. Mary was sitting in the chair by the window. "Have a seat," she said." Bobby, did you bring my cigarettes?" "Yes," he said and gave her the pack from his shirt pocket. Mr. Buddy was just going over to close the door that Bobby had left ajar. I was smiling at Mary as I turned back to face the door when I saw a tall black fella that was dressed in police clothes. He had a big bag in his arms as he knocked on Lilly's door loudly. Bobby turned to the door and caught a glimpse of the man standing in front of Lilly's door as Mr. Buddy pushed the door closed. "Damn!" Bobby said, "who the hell was that, Al? "I don't know, man," I answered. I was kind of glad that I wasn't at Lilly's house when that guy came knocking. Whoever he was, he was big with African features.

We had fun that night, laughing, talking, and playing cards. As old as Mr. Buddy and Ms. Mary were, they were the champions in playing bid whisk. We were playing "rise ad fly." Sometimes Bobby would play with Mary when we lost, but most of the time I would play with her. Mr. Buddy would laugh at Bobby and say you are my favorite grandson, you know that, but you just can't play whisk as he banged the cards of the table. Ms. Mary said, "we done won again." At about 11:00 p.m., Mary was putting the coats and caps on the sleepy little boys of hers. We walked mammary to 29th and Indiana where she caught her cab, a jitney to 46 and Indiana where she lived. After she was gone, Bobby and I went into Henry's Restaurant. It was more crowded than the tavern next door. Some people were eating food, drinking coffee, pop; some people were drinking beer and every now and then you could see someone pull a half pint from out of his coat pocket or pants pocket and take a sip. We squeezed our way to the rear and there they were. Wadell, Leroy, Bob, and

Tommy. They all sat in the back boots except for Bob. Bob had the floor, and everyone was laughing.

He was telling his joke about the signifying monkey. We walked in on the part where Bob was saying the monkey said, "oh, Mr. Lion, I apologize." The lion said, "I ain't going to whip your ass because the elephant whipped mine. I'm going to whip your ass about the motherfucking signifying." The monkey said, "wait a minute motherfucker, you ain't raising no hell, the whole jungle has seen me when I fell." You let my balls up out of the sand and I'll fight you toe to toe like a natural man." The lion jumped back on one knee, and the monkey jumped to the top of the mother fucking coconut tree. He turned his ass to the northeast wind. He said, you stupid hair faced motherfucker I done tricked you again. He said this is the future motherfucker, not the past. If you think I'm going to slip out of this tree again, that's your motherfucking ass. Everybody gave an applause. One guy said "Drug Store Bob, you just take the cake. Where did you learn all of them goddamn jokes from?" "From your mammy," Bob said, and everybody busted out laughing again, even the guy that Bob was talking to. Bob looked over at Bobby and then at me and acknowledge me saying, "what are you doing up so late, Little Pimp?"

"If he's a good pimp, he'd be trying to catch him a good hoe." Wadell said in a loud voice. What's your name anyway?" Wadell asked me. I said, "Al." "Al, what?" Tony said, fucking with me. I said, "Al Wynn, and this is Bobby Lewis." Drugstore Bob went in his pocket and brought out a pint of gin and uncapped the bottle and took a sip from it. "Do you drink, Little Pimp?" He said offering me the bottle. "No, I don't, but he does." Bobby took the bottle and took a swallow out of it. "What did you say your name was? Bob asked." Bobby Lewis," Bobby answered. "Damn, you've got a snout for a throat, haven't you? You've been swallowing a long time, haven't you? How old are you?" "Twenty-three and soon will be twenty-four," Bobby said. Someone in the crowd hollered out, come on Bob, tell us another joke." The crowd had kind of thinned out around Wadell and Bob. There were three counter stools empty across from them. Bobb and I seated ourselves, getting comfortable for the next joke. I looked up at the clock behind the counter on the wall and it said ten minutes till twelve. I had told my mother that my job was from seven to eleven and that I would be home about twelve. Bobby and I were leaving as Bob said, "That white lady asked, 'Shine, Shine, Shine, save poor me. I'll give you more pussy than you ever could eat. He said, 'I love pussy and I ain't no rat, but I don't love pussy like that." The night was cool as we walked two blocks home.

CHAPTER 15

I was feeling pretty good this first day of July. I had just come in from school when my sister met me on the porch. Two nice-looking little boys sat on the steps eating a piece of white bread my sister had given them. "Guess what, Al?" I said, "what?" "You know the young lady that Mr. Smith used to go with?" I said, "Yeah, what about her?" "She was here right after I got out of school with these two little boys. And she told Paul's mother and Mr. Smith's mother, Gloria, that these were Mr. Smith's sons. She doesn't want them anymore because she can't take care of them and wants to give them to Ms. Gloria. You should have heard all the names Ms. Gloria called her. Slur, bitch, and that these were not Mr. Smith's sons. Even Earmiel screamed and hollered at her saying that wasn't her uncle's kids." "What did Paul and Jimmy say?" "They weren't here," my sister answered, "but if you look at them real hard, they do favor Mr. Smith to me." I went over to them and asked the oldest boy, "What's your name?" "COD, they all me COD." "And what's your little brother's name?" "His name is Davis." I reached my hand in my pocket and pulled out $3 and gave it to my sister. "Do we have any more white bread in the house?" and she said "Yes." I gave her the money. "Run down to the street to the basement store and get a large can of Pork and Beans and bologna." We were all full when my mother and father got home. I explained the situation to my mother. She, in return, explained it to my father. I begged them to let me take care of the boys with the money I make. I said, "They wouldn't be any trouble, would you please let me keep them?"

They said "Yes." My uncle Willie kept them while we kids were in school. I enjoyed coming home everyday for the next three days. Playing with them, tickling their fat stomachs and running around the yard with them. People would come on the porch, even their grandmother, Jimmy, and Paul observing the fun, but they never did say anything. Then on the fourth day, my heart was broken. When I left the shoeshine job, coming home with a quart of milk and a whole cake for the boys, I could hardly wait to get home to see them. They were so lovable, but to my surprise, Ms. Gloria and Jimmy had come to my father and mother and admired the fact that the girl could have been right. Those could be her grandkids. She hugged and kissed them and took them home. It was a sad night for me that night and I messed them dearly. Yet, deep down inside of me, I was very thankful to God for Mr. Gloria. The boys needed a mother, and most of all, a friend.

My mother could see the hurt in my eyes as she told me their grandmother has them now. They will be fine. "You did what you could, you gave them a home, you fed them, and even thought I gave you he money, you with the grace of God clothed them. You did everything that God talked about in the Bible." She placed her arms around me and whispered in my ear, "God loves you, Al. Rember, the more you do for people, the more God will do for you, never forget that Al." She kissed me on my forehead. I couldn't have been rewarded more because I worshipped and loved my mother way beyond words.

CHAPTER 16

My family was getting ready for another celebration that night because my father's baby brother [Uncle Prince] was coming home from the army. My father had bought a second-day bed for my uncle. Although all the working people went to work, they told me to stay out of school to watch for him. Pap stayed out of school with me. He and I were pitching horseshoes in the dirt by the sidewalk. It was about a quarter to one when the yellow cab stopped in front of 2720 S. Prairie. I don't remember my uncle, when he left for the army, but I knew the soldier that stepped out of the cab with a real thin mustache and light complexion was my uncle Prince. His features were a younger version of my father's. I shouted from the sidewalk, "Uncle Prince." "You must be Al," he said, setting his suitcase on the sidewalk. He hugged me and ran his hand across my hair. "My, you've grown," he said. "Did you know the last time I saw you; you couldn't even reach my knew, and do you know who you are named after?" He said looking at me.

I said, "yes, you, your name is Prince Al, ad my name is Al." He said, "That's right." We smiled as Pap looked on. I reached for his bag. He said, "No, I'll carry that. It's a little to heavy for you, Al." We were just getting ready to go up the steps when Mr. Tim and Mrs. Betty came out of the hallway door and down the steps. Mr. Tim was very sharp as he always was, dressed in a brown flannel suit, tan shoes, and all other matching accessories. Mrs. Betty was sharp, too. But she was dressed in gray. "Hello, Mr. Tim and Mrs. Betty," I said. "Hi, hon," Mrs. Betty said. I looked into those beautiful greenish eyes of hers. It seemed just for a moment that they had lit up just a little more for me. I quickly diverted my eyes back to Mr. Tim. "Mr. Tim, this my uncle Prince out of the army. Uncle Prince, this Mr. Tim, and his wife." Uncle prince had lowered his bag again to the concrete and extended his hand to Mr. Tim. "Nice meeting you both," he said. My uncle looked over and gave a nod to Mrs. Betty. She, in return, gave a wave and said "Hi," in a soft voice. They continued their walk to their car. Me and Uncle Prince and Pap went to the apartment. It was not too long before we were inside the apartment, then he suggested he should take a nap because it was a long hard trip. I told him if there was anything he needed for me to do, I would be on the front porch or in the front yard.

It was like a family reunion again that night. My aunts and mother had begged my father when he got out of the Bridewell House of Correction, to make up with my uncle A.D. So, with the family being a family again, they were all there. Greeting and enjoying my uncle Prince. They talked about the old days, Ras Thomas, Pluke Smith, cousin Kallie, and my mother told the story again of how her aunt Lillie lived out in the woods away from everybody raising ten kids. Just imagine how my mother would ay "But there in the wood as dark as it was and wasn't scared." She told me about that last night when Aunt Lilie had made p her mind to really move from the country, uptown, near her people. She had owed the white man $40 for a bad crop. After she had loaded all the rocking chairs, beds, and everything else into the wagon that she was moving, with the smaller kids riding on top of the wagon and the bigger kids walking, they went to the big house where the boss lived. "Well, Mr. Dansler," looking up at him. He was standing in his front yard. A big bellied tall, white man that was bald straight down the center of his head. Two of his sons between the ages of 24 and 30 sat on the steps of his house listening to the conversation. "I done found me a place up yonder in town where my cousin stays. I'll be coming back to see you when I get some washing to do." "Oh," he said, looking down at her. She was a short lady, about 5 feet, 1 inch tall with mangy gray hair and Indian features. They said that she was mixed with Black Feet Indian. "Oh, you mean to tell me that you don't have that $40 with you?" he asked.

"No, I don't have the $40." She spoke. "I didn't have it last month when you told me to move, and I don't have it now because I didn't have any washing to do. Nobody comes way out here for washing no more. Ain't nobody getting no dresses, or anything made, so I don't have any work. But I'm sure there in town I'll have work and I'll have your $40 in no time." "Well, I don't know what we are going to do about this, Lillie," he said. "This here is a mighty fine-looking horse," he said, grabbing the reigns and rubbing the horse's head. "Boys come down here and unhook this horse. Looks like these darkies are going to be walking into town." She said, "Oh, boss, Mr. Dansler, please don't do this to me. Don't take my last horse! How am I going to get my kids and my stuff uptown? Please don't do this!" she said. "Do you think I give a damn about these little black bastards or you? What I do give a damn about is my god-damn $40. Get them off the wagon before I have to do it for you." My mother continued with tears in her eyes. That night, it was cold as we walked the five miles into town. This is why, at the age of five, I hung on to my cousin, Lilly, because she was the only mother I ever knew. As I grew up under her, I respected her independence."

The talk went on with each person giving their likes and dislikes of the south. It wasn't long before my father had gotten Uncle Prince and Under Willie a job with him at Wilson's stockyard. My mother would constantly argue and cry out for a bigger apartment or house because the one we were living in was too small for three adults and three children. Each Saturday, my father would dress in his finest suits, ties, etc. and go to his five- or six-hour piano lessons. And every time my mother would argue that piano lessons don't last for any five or six hours. One Saturday morning as my father was dressing, he put on a blue surge suit that he had just tailored for himself. He stood looking at himself in a full mirror. I stood by sizing him up, too. "This looks pretty good, don't you think so, Al?" He asked. "You look really good, "I said, smiling at him. My Uncle Price and Uncle Willie sat at the table in a far corner. "Well, Al, when you grow up and get a job, you can dress just like your d addy," my Uncle Prince said. "Yes, sir," I answered. "I'm going to buy myself a lot of pretty clothes." That next Friday night was my payday from the night job I didn't have.

I had hung out with Bobby, Mary, and Lilly that week, but that night was pay night, and I didn't know where I was going to get the money from. Lilly had gone to visit her mother on the newest side. Mary didn't show up for her weekend visit to her mother's house due to a cold and Bobby had disappeared on me. It was about eight-thirty at night when I reached Smitty's Shoeshine Parlor. I had $6 in my pocket. Smitty's door was locked. I knocked on the door two or three times softly. Some man came and took the cloth away from the window in the door. He peeped out at me. "We're closed!" He spoke. I said, "I'd like to see Smitty because I knew they were gambling in there and Smitty was the only one who could get me in." He said, "What's your name?" "Al." "Al, who?" he said, "Al Wynn." Before long the door opened and Smitty looked up and down the street and then he said, "Come on in Al," he said, "What do you need? "I said "I need to shoot the dice. That's what I need." The place was crowded. "Let him on up here, Smitty. We take pimps' money, hoe's money, all money. Let that little nigger up here. "Come on over here. You can stand by me, Al." Wadell called out from the table next to bob, I squeezed through and got to the table. "It's your shot. What are you shooting, Little Pimp?" Bob asked me. "How is he going to butt me?"

"Who in the hell says it's his shot" Some guy said at the end of the table. He was tall with about three teeth out in the front. "I said it," Bob said, "and I'm the houseman tonight.: Okay, Bob, if you say so. What is the little nigger shooting?" "I'll shoot five dollars," I said. "Ten dollars he wins" Wadell said. "I got some of that," Tommy said, "Thirty dollars he wins, it's a bet." "Fuck that little nigger," the snaggle-tooth guy said He threw he five dollars over to Bob and put he thirty dollars in front of him on the table. "Open your hand, Al," Bob said. I held my hand out open in front of me. Some guy said, "He never shot dice before. What the hell is he doing? You think Bob is just going to put them in his hand?" Wadell said, "Al, put your hand on the table and make a fist, then open your hand into a cup. Bob will throw you the dice. You catch them and shoot." I did what Wadell told me to do with my fist. Bob threw the dice at me. I caught the dice. Shook them real fast in my hands, then I threw them as far as I could on the table. One dice stopped on one and the other dice spun and stopped on a six. "Seven, the winner," Bob called out. Odell said, "I knew he had talent. That's my boy, AL." Throw that goddamn thirty dollars over her nigger."

Bob said, "What are you shooting now, Al?" I said, "Ten dollars." He said "Oh, he is shooting it all." The same tall guy with no teeth said, "I got him, I got him. I'm not going toilet him get away this time." Wadell said "Do we still have a bet nigger for thirty dollars?" "Yeah, we still have a bet," going into his pocket for more money. The dice were in my hand one more time. I shook them real hard. I didn't know if it was right to pray to God, but I needed the money. So, I asked God to please let me get that money. I threw the dice again straight across that table. "It's eleven!" Bob shouted! I had twenty dollars. I wanted to just quit because that was enough money to give my mother, but something inside of said to keep going. I pulled ten dollars from the twenty dollars and put it in my pocket. "What are you shooting?" Bob asked. I said, "Ten dollars.," I was looking for Wadell to say something again. He said, "You're on your own this time, Little Pimp. We are not going to ride this stagecoach with you again." Some fat guy standing next to the tall guy was betting me, saying, "And ten dollars you don't hit. Coe on out of your pocket with the ten" Before I knew it, that ten dollars were out of my pocket and bet. I said, "Once more," I said. "Please, God, let me hit just one more time." I threw the dice across the table. The dice was out of my hand again, rolling across that table. The dice stopped at ten. Bob hollered out. "Ten is the point! Come on Little Pimp, come on, make that ten!" I must have thrown those dice five times still praying before the dice rolled and one dice stopped on four. The second dice spun for what seemed like seconds and stopped at six. "Ten points!" Bob shouted. "Okay, Al, what do you want to shoot?" I said, "Nothing, really." The snaggle-tooth guy said, "You can't quit and done won my money and it's your shot." Some elderly guy dressed real neat stood about three persons from Bob said "Hey, houseman, can I buy the dice?" He said, "Yes, you can if you pay the man that shooting." He gave me five dollars. And I said "Thanks," and I thanked Smitty and Wadell. "See you around, Wadell." Tommy said "That nigger knows when to quit when he done won. He has that much sense." And I hit that door. Leroy let me out. It had begun raining after I went into the place, and it was raining hard when I came out. I ran up to the restaurant and there were only two customers there eating their dinner. They had lima beans on the menu. I love beans. They were only $.35 a bowl. I ordered a bowl and corn muffins and a pop. When I finished eating, it was ten-thirty by the clock of the wall. Two and half hours had passed. The rain had slacked up and I came out of the restaurant. I jogged back to Bobby's house. Bobby still wasn't home, neither was Lilly. I sat there for an hour and a half on the steps leading to the second floor.

That Saturday morning, I gave my mother twenty dollars of my salary. I messed around with Roland and Pap until noon. I went by the rear building. Bobby was still in bed and Lilly hadn't made it in yet. I went to work at the shoeshine parlor. I had a nice time with Mr. Buddy. I told him I threw those dice, and I hit them every time. Mr. Buddy would say, "Hot damn, boy, you're something!" I got in about eight-thirty and Bobby was sitting on the porch. "Damn, man, I've been sitting here all night waiting on you. I started to come down to that little shoe parlor." I said "What's the atter, man? Mary is over three and she wants to see me." "No, man, that dope dealing Karen, hat bitch acts like she's going out of her mind. Every time I come down there, she says, where's your friend?' she sent you this note, man." He passed the note to me. The note read, "I would like to see you as soon as possible. Karen." "Man, what's with those bitches," Bobby asked. "I mean a pretty motherfucker like me, and they send for you. Man, I wish I had that bitch Kaen, she keeps a know." "Man, I didn't say nothing to that woman. I don't know what she's talking about. Wants to see me for what? What the fuck she wants to see me for?"

Mary said that she would be sown tomorrow after church," Bobby said, and he left for home. The next night, that Sunday, I rode back with Mary to her house. Her husband worked for U.S. Steel from three to eleven. That night was the first time that she and I had good sex. Although I enjoyed myself, there with Mary, my mother's words would steadily eat tat me. "don't get caught in any man's house, Al. He would have all the grounds to kill you or do anything else. The law would be on his side." She would constantly tell me, "Don't smoke any cigarettes after anyone. You don't know where their mouth has been and stay away from them sissies because they carry a knife, and they will cut you." As I thought about the words of my mother, the more frightened I became in that bedroom with Mary. I was glad when it was over, and I was back in the jitney on my way to Twenty-Ninth Street.

CHAPTER 17

I had made enough money from the shoeshine parlor. And he little money I made from shooting dice with the fellas on the sidewalk was enough money to give my mother that Friday night from the job, the job I didn't have. I had given Drug Store Bob enough money to buy me a pint of Seagram's gin, a Canadian Ace beer, and a pack of Pall Mall Red. I had taken the bag from Bob and started my walk to Lilly's house. I was in a good mood after I walked past TJ's store. I started thinking to myself. I wanted to surprise Lilly and to have my first drink with her. Lilly was a nice girl. I thought, single, and didn't have anyone, she said, but me. What the hell, everybody makes a mistake. Who knows, maybe that baby that she wasn't a mistake to her. Why in the hell was I thinking this way? I thought. Shit, I wasn't ready to get married. I was too young for that goddamn love shit, what the hell was I thinking about? I noticed that I was relieved when she told me that the African looking guy was her cousin, Bob, bringing her and her baby some food. "That's the only person in my family that keeps up with me and looks out for me and my baby," she said.

"Why did you ask about him, Al? Were you jealous?" Before I could answer, she rubbed in between my legs and kissed me on my neck. I forgot about the conversation and grabbed her and pulled her close to me. I was thinking as I knocked on Lilly's door. She let me in. "What's in the bag., Al? Is this for me?" "It's for you and me."

"Oh, you're going to drink some too," she said. "Good," She got the bag and was going to get us some glasses. We sipped the gin and the beer for two or here hours. We laughed, kissed, hugged, and drank some more. It was after 12:00 A.M. when we both were naked and I was lying on her in the dark, in her bed. She began to moan under the pressure of my body. I could hear her whisper two or three times, "Oh, Al, I love you, I love you," she whispered. The next thing I remembered, here was banging on her door. Then someone seemed to be kicking on the door. I woke up out of my drunkenness. Lilly had turned on the light and was sitting straight up in the bed naked. I looked over at the clock on the dresser, it said a quarter to four. She threw her finger up to her mouth in a hush position. I whispered to her. "Who is it?" she threw her finger up again, shaking it to her lops. Then leaned over ad whispered to me, "It's Bob." I whispered back to her, "So what. He's your cousin, open the door." She said, "You don't understand. He's my boyfriend, and he pays the rent and buys all my groceries." I said, "What, a damn policeman is your boy-friend?" She threw her finger up again shaking it for me to be quiet. I was wide awake now and my mind was working very fast now.

The words of my momma started coming to me in flashes. They can do anything to you, Al, kill you, and nothing will be done about it. I looked at their windows. One window was on the side, a two by three window. Two windows were together at the foot of the bed. They were three by three windows. Just in case, I could get through the side windows. I would have to be contented with the spiked wrought iron fence that reached from the rear of the house to the front. The deep concrete basement steps with an iron rail around it were beneath the two windows across from the foot of the bed. I looked at her again. "What do you want me to do, hide?" She nod-ded her head in a yes manner. The bang came at the door again. A voice from the outside of the door said, "Open this goddamn door,

Lilly before I kick the hinges off it." I was on the floor, grabbing my draws, shoes, socks, and everything, putting them in my arms. I went to go under the bed, and she waved to me, no. Lilly hollered out "I'm coming to open the door, Bob, I'm coming." I tiptoed across the floor to the closet like a kitchen that was straight ahead. In front of the doorway to the kitchen was the sink, the stove sat to the right. On the left side of the door was a refrigerator with its back to the wall. I stepped around with my back to the outside wall and faced towards the refrigerator. There was a small space just enough for me to stoop in. I held my clothes and everything in my lap as I stooped.

Lilly opened the door for Bob. "What took so you so goddamn long to open this goddamn door?" Bob questioned in a roaring voice. "Who in the fuck you got in here?" he asked as Lilly closed the door. "Nobody, Bob. I don't know what you're talking about." "You're telling me a goddamn lie. There's someone in here and I'm going to find his mother fucking ass." I closed my eyes and started praying. "Oh momma," I said to myself, "I'm so sorry I didn't listen to you." At that moment, it seemed as though my whole life was flashing before me. "What are you looking under the bed for, Bob? I told you there's nobody here." "Shut up, bitch, he said as I could hear his footsteps coming toward the kitchen. My heart pounded in my chest as my eyes tightened. He was in the kitchen now. I could hear him breathing. He took two steps, and I opened my eyes and saw his big shoes standing in front of me. "What the fuck are you doing in her?"" He said to me. "Get your mother fucking ass out of that corner and get your ass in this room." He asked me again, "What the fuck is you doing in here?" Not wanting to act like I was afraid in front of Lilly, I answered in a stupid manner "I'm looking for my quarter I dropped." "Get your mother fucking ass out of here and put on your clothes. How old are you?" I said "Eighteen." He said, "Put on your clothes and get the fuck out of here."

He sat on the bed with his head in his hands. That silly bitch sat in the middle of the bed holding her mouth to keep from laughing like it was a joke. I almost pissed on myself as I scrambled to get into my pants, putting my draws in my pants pocket and my socks in my back pocket. I had put on my shoes and pants and shirt. I didn't know whether to break out of the door, walk out of it, or what. So, I confronted Bob. "Since you told me I didn't have to hide in that closet, can I have one of your Camel cigarettes?" He said "The only cigarette you will get is a .38 through one of those brass teeth that you got in your mother fucking mouth." This is the first time your eyes met and through the tears in his eyes, I could see the hurt. He shook his head from side to side as he said, "You better get the fuck out that door." I was out that door and going down the hall as I looked back and saw Mr. Buddy's door closing slowly behind me.

Everyone's door on the first floor was open except Bobby's door. As I approached their apartment, they would close their door. Only one door stayed open and that was Carolyn Frazier's, which was the door by the rear entrance door. Carolyn had tried to give me a play two or three times. Her eyes had promised me anything that I wanted, and I could have if I just visited her instead of going up those steps. Her big eyes were staring at me as I approached her door. She was standing in her doorway with her arms folded across her breast when we both heard the screams form upstairs. "Oh, Bob," Lilly was shouting, "I didn't do anything. I wasn't doing anything!" "You're a damn lie, bitch. Do you think I'm supposed to be crazy or something?" "h, Bob," she screamed out again, "don't hit me no more." I spoke. "I'll kill that motherfucker. You got a knife, Carolyn?" She said "What are you going to do with a knife? Go upstairs and get killed. He's already whipping that bitch's ass. You going to let him kill you with a little knife and he's got a gun." I said "No, I'm not going to let him kill me. That lying bitch is on her own." I said, "I'll see you tomorrow, I kissed her softly on her jaw and I walked out the rear door into the alley.

I was shaking so bad that I didn't want to go home yet. So, I walked slowly back to Henry's restaurant. The words of Bob kept coming through my mind. The only thing that you will get is a .38 between them two brass teeth of yours, and I remembered the words of Mr. Buddy on Sunday. We would have a Bible reading from 1:00pm to 2:00pm, and then we would get ready to go downtown to the show. "I've been reading the Bible, Al," he would say, "from one end of the book to the other. It might take me a year to get through it, but I will start all over again next year. This particular book or chapter I like more than any other chapter in the book is in Proverbs where it says, honor thy mother and thy father, and your days will be longer. Always remember that when you honor your mother and father, their wisdom will see you through. It also says in Proverbs, chapter one, verse two, get wisdom, but above all things, get understanding. Bob's words and Mr. Buddy's words haunted me all the way to the restaurant.

It wasn't long after jimmy had come to live with Percy that my father had to go to the dentist. I don't know to this day whether Jimmy's smile with his two gold teeth had inspired my father to get a bridge with the identical two gold teeth. He would boast to my uncles about all the gold that was in the back of the bridge. He would say "I have enough gold in the back of my mouth to buy me another Cadillac." 'The third year that my father was here in Chicago, he had traded his old New Yorker Chrysler for the Cadillac. That same year, Paul bought him a new Cadillac. Everyone called him for delivery because they wanted to rede in a Cadillac. It wasn't too long after that that I, at the age of seventeen, played copycat either after my father or Jimmy. I bought myself two gold teeth at seven dollars apiece. I was sitting on the stool now in Henry's Restaurant. The waitress asking me now, "What do you need?" I asked, "Yes, do you have any beans?" She said "Yes, red beans and rice." I said, "Give me a bowl and a cup of tea and a slice of apple pie."

I settled down to enjoy my meal as someone had put a dime in the jukebox. The man's voice was saying, hit that five jack, put it in your pocket and lock it back, going downtown to see y man and I don't have time to shake your hand, standing on the corner full of jive, you know you're my man brother give me five. The record went on and on. It was three days later as I had been watching Lilly's house for Bob and getting enough nerve to go here. I finally went and knocked on her door. "I came after my cap, Lilly, I said. "There it is on the dresser. You can get it." I stepped into the house, and she shut the door. "Can I speak to you just for a minute, please, Al?" "For what, what do you want to say? You've got a mouth, say it." I know you are mad at me, and I don't blame you, but Al," she said, "I saw him, and I knew," almost crying. "You are the only person I love. The day that you saw him bringing the groceries, I told him that I didn't love him anymore. I knew then that you were the only one that I loved. This is why I told him that I never wanted to see him again." She fell into my chest, crying and threw that loop around my neck. "Oh, Al, Al, Al, please forgive me, baby." I damn near was crying as this point as I whispered, "I forgive you, Lilly. I forgive you."

This was Wednesday when I was with Lilly. That next Saturday, three days later, I could hardly wait to get to Lilly's house. She had her web on me, and I knew it. She was pulling me closer and closer to becoming a bigger damn fool than I had been, but I was enjoying it all. That night we drank, hugged, kissed, and whispered in each other's ear. Before long, we were naked once again and she was moaning under the pressure of my body. I don't know how long we were embraced before I slipped out into ecstasy. The next thing I knew, it was morning and I sat straight up in the bed as I felt for Lilly and noticed that she wasn't in the bed. I looked over to the right of me and got the shock of my life 'cuz I looked dead in the eyes of Bob seated in a chair with his legs crossed staring at me. My heart seemed to switch positions in my chest. "How are doing, man, and where's Lilly?" I said, not giving him a chance to answer my first question. "She had to go get something from the grocery store and she told me to tell you she'd be right back." "Man, what time is it?" I said, ignoring the clock that sat on the dresser. Bob turned to the dresser and looked at the clock. "It's eight-thirty." I said, "Damn, she knew I had to go to work." I jumped up naked and went to the foot of the bed. Once on the floor, I started putting on my clothes as fast as I could, avoiding Bob's stare. "Man, I might get fired this time," I said out loud. Once my clothes were on, I hit that door as fast as I could. I old him, "Tell Lilly I'll see her later," I could hear his voice dragging as he said, "Yeah."

I was really hurt by the lies and deceit that I had encountered with Lilly. I had to get away from her. Deep in my heart, I knew that she was trouble for me. And even though I cared for Mary with all the good smelling perfumes she wore, she was bad for me and my soul. I knew that s she was married. Mr. Budy would tell me after reading hat book. "Reading the Bible, Al, is cleansing for your soul." I figured it was time for me to change environments. I was getting too deep, too caught up in a web I knew nothing about. It was time to go see Karen.

CHAPTER 18

I had stayed to myself for the next week, going around Smitty's Shoeshine Parlor, shooting dice in the alley, and on the sidewalk. I was just coming across the lot from playing baseball when a black Buick pulled up in front of me and stopped. A pretty girl sat in the back and the driver seemed to be about for0five years old and was looking at Velma, the girl with the big grin on her face. She said, "Hello, Al." I said "Hello, Velma." She was about three years my senior. Her father was John Levi. He owned a two-flat building on Twenty-Sixth and Prairie. He was whiter than a white guy, but he had one percent black blood in him. He was a flashy kind of guy., her father. He wore the best of clothes and bought himself a brand-new Cadillac every year. The black people in the neighborhood had it out that he was some din to Louis Warner, who owned a Cadillac Company. He wore fancy rings. Some people said that he was pimp, and others said that he was a big-time gambler.

She was smiling at me. I smiled back. "Didn't you get Karen's note, Al?" She asked. I said, "Yes, Bobby gave to me last week." "Why haven't you called her? Why haven't you come down to see her?" I said, "I've bn busy.," She said, "Boy, that woman likes you. It's a whole lot of men that wish they were in your shoes." She spoke. "Come on, get in. I'll take you down to see her. She wants to see you now. She gave me this to come and get you.; And she showed me a hundred-dollar bill. I said, "I can't go right now, Velma, but ell her hat I'll be here Saturday night. Today is Thursday, Saturday night I'll be her for sure at about eight." Every day until Saturday, I talked to Bobby. Every night, I would start the conversation off with Bobby with, "Damn man, what he fuck she wants to see me for? What have I got to offer?" "Don't you know little punk ass nigger?" Bobby asked. I said, "No, I don't." Bobby said, "Karen is about forty years old and you are eighteen, soon will be nineteen. She wants that tender beef you've got motherfucker. She wants to gobble that thing up like it was apple pie or some sweet cakes like that. Do you understand that? Shit all of them old men around her. She wants something fresh. Something young, something that makes her feel like living the next day What's so killing about it," Bobby said as he sat on his mother's bed and kind of bounced on it lightly two or three times and pointed me to the chair that was sitting between the kitchen and bedroom. I sat down, facing him as Bobby continued to talk, "she's willing to pay for it?"

I said, "How do you know that, man?" "Didn't you tell me that Velma had a $100 bill for you nigger?" "No, I thought it was hers. I thought she gave it to her to come and get me." "Look, man," Bobby said. "This girl sells more dope than the grocery store sells baking powder. She is the number one dope dealer and keeps all kinds of money. She couldn't be sending for a punk like you if she wasn't interested." "Say, man, you can cut out all of that name calling," I said, looking at him real hard and rolling my eyes at him at the same time. "Man, you shouldn't get mad when a person's trying to tell you the truth. I told you the other night I wish I had the bitch. I would know what to do with her and you better learn what to do before she starts looking for somebody else." "What would you do if you were me, Bobby?" "Well, I would clean myself up best I could, and I would go and see her and party with her and talk all kind of shit to her. What I'm saying mam. I would do anything she wanted me to do to get that knot."

I thought about all the words that Bobby was saying before I closed my eyes to go to sleep on my pallet with my sister and brother. I thought about what Bobby had said, and I thought about the way he said to dress up in my best when I go to see her. Everybody seemed to be telling me to get the money, to get the money, and that went on and on in my mind. But I had a mind of my own, and if I was going to try to learn how to play this game that everybody else was playing, I was going to have to play it my way. I was going to have to think for myself. So that night, I reasoned with myself. On Friday evening, I really didn't have any dress pants or shoes. The only clothes I had were school clothes and kid's clothes. I was going to find out eh next day if Karen really liked me or was, she just toying with me. The next day, while everyone was at work and my sister and brother were at school, I went into the house and found a pair of dress pants of my Uncle Prince. He was taller than anyone in that house. My father had about ten or fifteen pairs of dress shoes. I stole a pair of the least ones that he would wear. The shoes were about a size to big for me. The shirt wrapped around me like an overcoat. I drew the belt tight on the pants that evening. This made them look straight in the back but bunched up in the front. I had eased all my clothes over to Bobby's house because I had told him I would dress there. After putting the shirt and pants and the shoes on, the pants were so long I had to give them three rolls, leaving the cuff showing where the tread was. Bobby was in the kitchen while I was getting dressed, raiding the icebox. I told him while I dressed, "Make me one of those bologna sandwiches, too."

"Okay, Al, here's your sandwich," he said as he entered the room. "Damn man, where did you get them clothes? You look like Little Abner! Man, I told you to dress up, not look like a fool. You don't go down there and embarrass yourself in front of that lady. Those damn blue jeans you had on look better than that shit you got on. What the fuck you want her to do? Do you want her to feel sorry for you, or do you want her to love you?" I said, "I want her to feel sorry for me, man. That's the reason I'm wearing this shit. You said she had a known. Let's see if she's going to spend some of it." Me and Bobby caught a jitney cab to Twenty-Fourth Street. The place was crowded as we came into the big building tavern. Karen was seated in the far corner at a table with three guys and two ladies. They all had their drinks and seemed to be having big fun. There was one empty table about two tables from them. We walked over to the table. Bobby seated himself with his back to the wall. I was still standing as I looked around the room. Two or three people seemed to be staring at me. Some would turn their heads around laughingly and whisper in their partner's ears, and I knew they were talking about me. The way I was dressed was getting the results that I wanted. Karen hadn't noticed me. Then I looked to the left. I could see Velma leaning over whispering in some guy's ear.

She was facing me as she looked up and saw me. She gave a wave and pointed over to where Kaen was. I pointed back to the chair that I was going to sit in with Bobby at the table. She nodded her head in a yes manner. I looked at Boby as I was seating myself at the table. He was laughing so hard that he had tears in his eyes. I said, "Cut it out, an, you're going to spoil my evening." He said, "I can't help it, man, I told you that you look like Little Abner!" Velma went over and touched Karen on her aback and pointed over to me. She turned and looked at me and smiled and put up one finger. We were sitting there enjoying the music from the box. Velma and Karen had disappeared. Before long, Velma was back with a pint of Cutty Sark. "Karen will be with you in a minute, Al. She's taking care of a little business. This is for you and Bobby." I said, "No problem."

She said "I'm going back to my gentleman friend. If here's anything you want, call me." Before long, Karen was back in the door and head my way; then the song "Glory of Love" started playing on the box, and the record was saying, "you've got to give a little, take a little, and let your poor heart break a little, that's the story of the glory of love." Karen was coming towards me now with her arms stretched out. Her eyes were almost closed tight as though she was high. "Do you want to dance with me, sweet baby?" she asked, holding out her arms. The record kept going on "That's the gory of, that's the glory of love," the record was saying. She snuggled uptight against me. And as the record would slow down just a little, she would roll her stomach on mine. As we danced the music continued, she whispered in my ear, "You are toing home with me." And I whispered to her, "Yes, if you want me to." She said, "We'll be leaving about one 'o'clock. It's eight o'clock now, can you stay around that long?" I said, "Yes," Karen didn't ever sit at the table with me and Bobby, but the whiskey continued to come. Bobby was giving the shit away to everybody he knew. "Hey, have a drink, man," he would say I went to the bathroom two or three times. I could see Karen through the crowd of people talking to someone at the entrance door. Our eyes would meet as I would turn and go into the men's room.

It was about twelve-thirty when a little short guy about 5'4" came over to our table. He was dressed very sharply. "Kaen told me to speak with you for a while. Can you come and go with me?" He spoke to Bobby. Bobby said, "Hey legs," and I was off that stool with the nod of Bobby's head to go with him. Before I knew it, we were behind the counter into what I thought was the kitchen "What's your name, Al?" I said, "Yes." "They call me Bowleg," he said. "What size coat do you wear?" I looked at him, stunned. "You don't know?" I said, "No, I don't know." He looked in his inside pocket and came out with a tailor ruler wrapped in a piece of cardboard. He said, "Karen told me to get some measurements of you. Do you mind?" I said "No." "Stretch out your arm." After the measurements, I was back at the table with Bobby. The crowd had started thinning out. I was high, and I didn't see Karen or Velma around.

Bobby was high now and standing by the table with some guy talking about going upstairs. I knew what that upstairs meant. I wanted to tell him, "Man, you're high enough. He said, "I'll be right with you, my man," I want to tell Al something." He asked, "Ok, my man, I'll be right over here. He asked me, "AL, do you know who you were talking to just a little while ago when you were in that kitchen?" "Yes," he said, "his name was Bowleg." "Yes, man, his name is Bowleg, but he's the worst motherfucker to ever hit this town.," I asked, "Who is he, man?" He said, "That mother fucker there is the world's greatest pickpocket, they have barred him from the ball games, Soldiers field when they have football games, and maybe Bowleg can't go to Las Vegas, man." "I don't know." "What did he want when he took you into the kitchen?" "He said Kate told him to take some measurements of me." "That hitch might be trying to build a coffin," I said, jokingly. "No, Al, you don't get the point. This goddamn Bowleg is awesome. He has five fo the prettiest boosters here in Chicago." "What is a booster?" I asked Bobby seriously. "Goddamn, man, what do know?" "Not too much." I said, cutting him a grin. "Let's put it like this. They steal pretty, pretty, pretty clothes, expensive clothes. It looks like you're going to get out of your uncle's shit," he said, patting me on my shoulder as he went upstairs. At two-thirty, Karen and I were in a jitney on our way to Washington Pak Court on Forty-Ninth Street. Karen had a neat looking kitchenette in an English basement.

Once we were there, Karen put on the music and fixed me a drink. The record was playing the song "Crying in the Chapel."

"You saw me crying in the chapel, the tears I shed were tears of joy. I know the meaning of contentment., I am happy with the Lord, just a plain and simple chapel, where all good people go to pray. I praise the Lord. I grow stronger as I live from day to day. I searched and I searched, but I'll never find no place on earth to find peace of mind, now I'm contented in the Chapel just to stop and praise the Lord." The music continued as we danced to it, slow as I pulled Karen tighter and tighter up to me. We kissed, danced, and drank the Seagram's gin that Karen loved. The music was cut down softly now as Karen pulled me on top of her in her bed. The little knot between my legs seemed to throb from stiffness. I was n top of her now, and I started humping as I did when I met Mrs. Betty. But Mrs. Betty's words came back to me through Karen. "Slow down, Al," she whispered. "We have all night." She placed both of her hands on the cheeks of my ass and guided me into ecstasy, and I could hear her whisper low, "Al, very slow. Yes baby, that's it."

CHAPTER 19

I was almost late getting to the shoeshine job Sunday morning, on account of Karen. She had asked me to call her when I get off from work at two o'clock. Mr. Buddy was disappointed when I told him that I wouldn't be going downtown to the show with him today. I had a date. I had my favorite jeans on, slightly starched like my mother fixed them, shoes shined, and a nice-looking shirt to match. I always wore hats or caps, and that particular day I had on a cap. I could hardly wait for Mr. Buddy to get through with reding the good book so I could get down to Twenty-Ninth Street. Mr. Buddy locked the door to the shoeshine parlor, and I walked him down to the bus stop as I did every Sunday. We waited on the bus at the bus stop. The bus was approaching the stop. He turned to face me. "You must be growing up, Al. So, you've got a date, have fun," he said as he stepped on to the bus. I stared at his back until the bus pulled away. He seemed to be getting older to me and maybe I had become too dependent on my being with him on Sunday. Maybe I was his comfort on a Sunday; maybe I was his friend on a Sunday; maybe I was his date every Sunday. Whatever it was, he could feel that it had come to an end.

I walked across the street and waited on a jitney that would take me to 29th Street. I walked into Sams bar, looking over at the bartender Bill who had always given me a break to come into the bar on account of Mrs. Betty. He never scolded me on account of my age. He would just look at me real hard when I stayed there a little too long and I would disappear out the door. I spoke to him, "Hi, Bill" I said. Not giving him a chance to answer or speak back, I said, "Have you seen Wadell or Tommy?" "Yes, I think they're next door in the restaurant," he said. When I entered the restaurant, they were seated in their favorite place, the rear booths. I walked straight up the booths. I said, "is this private, or can I sit down?" Leroy and Wadell sat with their backs to the wall and Tommy sat facing them. I sat beside Tony. "Where's Bob?" I asked, "where's Drug Store Bob?" "That mother fucker won one thousand dollars. Yeah, he'll lose a thousand dollars, too. So, it's not a big thing for Bob," Tommy said. "Well, man, I wanted Bob to be here when I say this but maybe one of you could relay the message." "What's the matter, Little Pimp? you aint fixing to die, or nothing are you?" and they were looking at me real serious."

I hope not, I said with a big grin. "I just want you to know, the four of you to know that you all have fucked me up big-time." "What do you mean?" They questioned me, looking serious. "I mean, with this Little Pimp shit that you all put on me, telling me to get a good hoe. I've been telling you all along that I ain't no pimp. And don't even know the meaning of the word. So, what has happened, according to Bobby---" "Who are you talking about? That little mother fucker that drank all of Bob's gin the night?" Leroy asked. "Go ahead," Wadell said," and don't cut him off anymore, Leroy." "Yeah, he one that drank Bob's gin, but anyway, according to Bobby, I have caught the biggest hoe that I could catch in this neighborhood." "No shit," Leroy said. "Who in the fuck is that, that me and Wadell or tommy ain't fucked, and don't leave Bob out because he has fucked most of them himself." I said, "Tell me something, how many of you mother fuckers have fucked Karen?"

Tommy sort of leaned to the wall in the booth with a toothpick twisting in his mouth. He sat straight up in the booth, and so did Wadell. They both stared at me. Tommy took the toothpick from his mouth. "Hold on Little Pimp. Are you sitting here telling us that you have FUCKED Karen?" "You damn right and fixing to fuck her again tonight!" Wadell leaned over a little, looking at me very seriously. "You're stepping into high cotton now, Al," "And some dangerous mother fucking cotton, too," Tommy said, butting in. "well, what the fuck is y'all talking about?" I spoke. "I mean in the first place, Al," Wadell went on, "I haven't ever heard of her being a whore, but I do know that she's a dope dealer and he has a killer for a husband who is doing sixteen months now for shooting a nigger in the big building. But the nigger didn't die. The word is out that he done killed at least five people." "His name is," Tommy butted in, "Ben Lucas. Everybody calls him Big Ben. He has gone to jail for murder and dope dealing." "In fact," Wadell said, "he should be getting out this month or next month, and Paul Will is Ben's best friend and a very dangerous character. That's who Karen is, dealing dope for now, and Will is looking out for Ben, taking care of his wife until he gets out. So that money Al, I'd advise you to let go, leave it alone. I haven't heard of any guy fucking Karen if they have. They haven't told anybody about it, and if I were you, I wouldn't tell anybody about it," Tommy said, looking casually at me." "

Shit, all that money that bitch carries ad handles," Leroy said. "Shit, I would have to live true to the game. The game says, 'pimp or die.' Shit, if that bitch really loves you, she ain't going to tell nobody you were taking her damn money." "Shut up, Leroy," Odell said, "where have you ever pimped?" "I'm just saying, didn't you say that a pimp takes pimps money, hoes money all money If he's a pimp, take the mother fucking money You better take fast before that bad-as husband of hers gets out of jail." "My thing Wadell," said taking his eyes off Leroy and looking back at me, “is to take anything that she gives you, but meet her in some place that you’re not known or she ‘s not known. Don’t let all your friends see her. After you have gotten all that you can, try to ease out of the relationship gracefully.”

I called Katen at the big building and agreed to meet at her house at nine-thirty. It was a cool night when I reached her house. I rang the bell, and right away, the door opened. She stood there smiling at me in a white House coat and matching house shoes. “Come on in, baby,” she said. “Would you like to have a drink?” I said “Yes.” She fixed me and herself a drink, a gin, ice, and Seven Up. I was sitting in a chair. She placed her drink on the table by me and went over to the closet. She reached up and brought out two garment bags and walked over to the bed and placed them on it.” “Come over here baby, let me show you what I got you.” She pulled one suit from the bag. It was a vest T-suit with the vest cut short to the waist. It was tan in color and looked very shiny. She told me it was silk. She pulled out another suit. It was a two-piece suit, white coat, and pants. She said “I’m going to love this on you, baby. This is raw silk. Are you going to spend the night with me?” she asked. I said, “Sure, I am. If you want me to

“You ae going to have to spend the night with me if you want to the other items that go with the suits.” We drank and ate Chinese food she brought from the refrigerator. The next day she took me to a hat shop and bought me a brown beaver hat, to match the tan suit. She also bought me a white beaver hat with a big black bow, “You can wear this white hat with any color,” she said. “Gus,” she said, talking to the hat man.” “Yes, ma’am, Mr. Karen.” We went off to the shirt and shoe shop. Karen had told me to pick up the hats and to be dressed by seven and meet her at the big building because Wadlee’s word told me not to be caught around anyone that knew her. She told me it was important for me to be down there on time at eight-thirty. Regretfully, I promised her that I would be there. She had given me two hundred-dollar bills. "Here, baby," she said, "put this in your pocket for tonight." I had gotten home at about five-thirty. To my luck, there was no one home except my sister and brother. I took out the white suit and black shirt and black Florsheim shoes. After I had taken a bath and dressed, my sister said, "Oh my God, Al, where did you get these clothes?"

"Here Frances," I gave my sister $3 and my brother $2. "Tell mom, that I got a waiter's job, and they are having a party and I had to rush right back to work. Give mom this $30." I couldn't wait to get to Twenty-Ninth Street to see Wadell, Bob, and Tommy. I was going to stop at Bobby's house just for a minute to show off my new shoes. To show him what he could have had if he had copped the bitch as he said. I knocked on the door, His mother's voice answered. "Who is it?" I said, "Al, Ms. Dickison." She said, "Come in." I stepped into the house and was face to face with Mary standing at the refrigerator getting ice. "My, My," she said, "what whirlwind blew you this way?" "I just wanted to say hi to Bobby, and how are you doing Ms. Dickinson and Mr. Buddy." "Bobby is in jail," Ms. Dickinson said. "They found a reefer on him, and he got six months today." I was saddened by the news and I told Ms. Dickinson that I was sorry to hear that and told her that everything would be all right. I noticed Mary had gotten bigger to me, but I just didn't want to stare at her. "Well, I just stopped by to say hello to Bobby. I really must be going, and I'll see you al later." I said and turned to the door.

Mary said, "Al, I'll walk you to the alley if you're going that way." We went down the hall to the rear door. Before opening the doors, I glanced to the right, and Carolyn's door was wide open. She sat at the door by her kitchen table curling her hair. She peeped up at me, I said "How are you doing, Ms. Carlolyn?" "I'm alright, Al," she said in a low voice. Mary said "hi" to her as she stepped behind me into the alley. "What have you been doing Al, since your girlfriend upstairs moved?" "Why you call her my girlfriend?" "Well, it wasn't your wife, or do you run around fucking strangers?" she asked me, and she was looking at me very seriously. I asked her, "who said that I was fucking her?" "You ain't got to lie to me, Al," she said. "It's not everyday that a man gets chased out of f woman's room naked, and by the way, you look very nice today. And I have one other thing for you before you leave. I'm pregnant and it's not my husband's and I don't mess around with anyone else. So, I'm not telling you this because I want you to take care of any baby," she said. "I just want you to know because you're the daddy. You won't be worried about me anymore because I won't be coming down here anymore unless my mother needs me in an emergency. If you ever want to see me again after tonight, you know where my mother lives." She turned and walked back through to the rear door, leaving me in the middle of the alley feeling like a damn fool, leaving me with the impression that I had done something very wrong to her because she was pregnant. Hell, I was the one that had been done wrong. She done fucked my brains out, made me slip into her husband's bedroom. She knew that was wrong. Hell, I was too young to feel guilty about fucking. I like her and all, but shit, I wasn't going to die because she didn't come back.

I walked out of the alley and headed for Sam's bar. I reached Smitty's Shoeshine Parlor. Smitty had just finished a customer's shoes when I stepped into the parlor. He said, Step right up here by this gentleman, I can get both of you at the same time," not even really looking at me. Smitty grabbed the top of my shoe and started rubbing them. "This here is some fine leather," he said. "And if I don't see my face in them, you're not going to get a tip." Smitty looked up at me and said, "Well, I'll be goddamn." He said, "Boy, what bank have you robbed? Goddamn, you're clean." I said, "I haven't robbed any band. I'm just trying to live and let live." He said, "Well, you're doing a damn good job of it."

After the shoeshine, I peeped into the restaurant window. A new record had come out, and it was being played on the jukebox in the restaurant. The record was by Johnny Mathis, "Chances Are." Chances are cause I wear a silly grin, the moment you come into view. They sat in their favorite booths and Bob was drinking his favorite gin. As I walked towards them, Wadell and Tommy and Leroy and some other customers were playing dominoes in the back booth. Bod stood, watching them. He turned and headed towards me, "Goddamn! Wadell, look at this motherfucker. This motherfucker here is cleaner than clean. Wadell and Tommy turned around to face me. Leroy said, "That motherfucker is pimping." Wadell said, "You're looking very good, Al. Very good." Tommy said, "Goddamn, Al, if I was a bitch, you could fuck me all night." The time that I was with them bullshitting and talking, I didn't tell Wadell about I was going to meet Karen at the big building.

I don't know why, but I seemed closer to Wadell than the other guys. He seemed more like a big brother to me. I don't know what it was about him. Maybe it was his flashy dressing, his smile, his gold crown, or maybe because the women called him Black Chocolate. Maybe it was his popularity. Whatever it was, I felt more confident and closer to him. Tommy had more Indian in him than he did black. I could tell that, but unlike Wadell's gratefulness, Tommy was cold-hearted, real cold0hearted when it came to women. He had all the attributes of a true pimp. I looked over at the clock on the wall, and it said twenty-minutes to eight. I eased out from Wadell and Tommy and went into Sam's lounge to the telephone booth. Most of the people that were standing around and sitting near the door seemed to admire how I was dressed. Bill didn't notice me as I went to the telephone booth. I called Karen "Where are you?" She asked. I said, "I'm at Twenty-Ninth Street. Look, Karen," I said to her, "wouldn't it be better if you meet me at Thirty-fifth street at Redman's Corner?" I said, "I heard that you are married, and I'm only concerned about you." She said, "I want you here because I'm celebrating my birthday tonight and I want you to look nice to me, baby, but Velma is here sitting right across from me at the table. So, baby, I'm going to tell her to put a seat there beside her, just for you."

CHAPTER 20

They had put tables together in the middle of the lounge that could seat twenty people. About seven that night is when all the big-time dope dealers arrived. You could tell them from the flashy way they dressed. The big diamond rings, the watches with the diamonds in them, the ladies with their rings, pearls, and beautiful dresses. They came from the IT club at Fifty-Fifty & Michigan. They came from the Crown Propeller on East Sixty-Third Street. They came from Forty -Seventh Street. They even came from Markham, Il., from Boots and Saddlers Lounge. They came from all over, giving respect to Karen on her Birthday. There were many presents given to her and to my surprise. There were a lot of police officers tat gave her respect, too.

A kind of fat lady with a yellow dress on was seated next to Karen with fox furs all over her shoulders, she kept winking ad blinking at me when Velma' head was turned from her. The women and men that were sitting at the tables were cracking jokes and having a good time. When Velma went to the bathroom, the lady in the yellow dress asked me, "Is

that your young lady that got up from the table?" "No," I said, looking at her. "Well, who do you belong to?" "He belongs to Momma," Karen said whispering. "And keep your hands off," she said, and they both laughed. "I'm glad you told me, girl," the lady in the yellow dress said. “I sure would like to take him back with me to Fifty-fifth Street.”

After a while, I increased my mother’s money from thirty dollars to fifty dollars a week. I guess she was splitting it with my father because I never had any more trouble with staying out late or all night. “You are a good boy, Al. This money helps me very much,” she would say. I was always happy when my mother was happy. I felt that she was in this big world by herself, and I loved her dearly although she had Uncle Heard at an early age he had to leave and who was left to find for herself, to be raised by cousins Lilly, then married to a man that was self0centered, selfish, and was not a supporter of his family. Every hurt that she felt from my father back down there in those lonely dark rooms of Georgia stays with me until this very day.

She would tell me about the hurt, and I could hear her crying way over in the night. But the next day, she would hold her head up high and go about her chores as she did every day. I knew my father, running around with different women, took a toll on her. For the next five months, I had big fun with Karen> I would meet her at the Glass Bar Lounge on Thirty -First Street, or the 114 Club. A new bar had moved around the corner on Thirty-First Street and Michigan called Two for One. We mostly spent an hour or two there every day. We would make plans for me to meet her at her house, or when she was busy at night, I would go home. iI was the nicest dressed fella around for those five months. I had made one mistake, though. I had left all the new clothes and shoes at Karen’s house. I would change as she told me to do.

She would get the suits cleaned, and the shirts starched and ironed. She had the women shooting at me with both barrels, but she dared any one of them to touch me. I was getting a big bng out of the whole situation, and I wanted to live up to the word that they had embedded in my head, Little Pimp. With two and three hundred dollars in my pockets everyday now, I thought there was no other pimp but me. Karen bought me the best food. I had my hair fixed every other week, and I would get a cond. She did my nails herself at night when she sat in the middle of the bed with her baby doll night gown. She would trim my nails as I stared at those big black beautiful thighs of hers. She would say, "I love you, baby," and lean over and kiss me on my lips.

It was on a Saturday morning at about eleven o'clock and as I turned the corner of Twenty-Ninth Street, I passed the Prairie Hotel. It sat to the right of me on the corner, and next door going north was the crazy house us kids used to call it. It was a red brick building that sat back from a huge yard. A big, huge wrought -iron fence stretched out in the front of it. It was a nursing home for the elderly. I walked kind of fast. The sun was shining down, and I was in the Bud Billiken Day Parade. Everybody was hollering and everybody was asking, "Are you going over to South Park Boulevard?" One lady said to another one, "Are you going over to South Park to see the parade? She said, "Yes, as soon as I lock my doors." They disappeared between the buildings.

I felt pretty good with my brown sharkskin vest suit on. Stingy Brim brown straw hat on, and tn shoes that sparkled. I had on a cocoa brown shirt with cuff links. I smelled good to myself from the expensive cologne that Karen jad sprayed on me, just before I left her house. The bankroll in my pocket was $6700 now. I sang "Chances are" to myself. Chances are 'cuz I wear silly grin the moment you come into view. Chances are you think that I'm in love with you; just because my composure sort of slips, the moment that your lips meet mine; chances are you think my heart s your valentine. I was so into singing that I barely heard the horn blow for me. Then I heard a voice say, "Al, Al," I looked over at the car. It was Dallas, a gambler, one of Wadell's and Tommy's dearest friends. He was a tall, light complexion man with long bangs that laid in waves across his head. Every now and then, his hair would fall onto his face like a ladies' when their hair is too long. "What are you doing, Al?" He called out. He was peeping around a younger girl named Elizabeth that I went to school with. She was about my age. Dallas was about 45 years old at that time. "Hi, Al," a voice came from the back of the car. It was James, another school buddy of mine. "Hey, James," I said. "Where are y'all on your way to the parade?"

"No, Dallas said peeping around the girl at me. "We are going to take these girls to the country and pick some plums. We are going to have a cold beer and plenty of fun, right girls." I didn't hear any response from the girls. And it was a girl in the car that I didn't recognize seated by James. "I've got nothing else to do., but first, I have to check in with my mother." Dallas took me to my house. My mother was in the kitchen cooking. My father sat at the piano playing his favorite song. "Laura." I eased up behind my mother and kissed the back of her head. She said, "I hear you when you came in, Bro Al." We laughed. She said, "You're looking awfully good today, and you smell good too."

I said, "Thanks mom," and gave her, her favorite money that fifty-dollar bill. I told her I was going to pick plums. She said, "dressed like that?" I said, "I won't be picking them. I'm just going for the ride." I was out the door and back into Dallas's car. Dallas pulled up in front of the liquor store. He said as he stepped out of the car, "Okay Al, how much you got o this beer?" James said, "I've got $5," and tried to reach it to Dallas. I spoke. "Keep your money, James. The beer is on me." I told Dallas "Get a case of beer," and I gave him a $50 dollar bill. Dallas was back with the case of beer, and we were on our way to the country. "Your cologne smells very nice," the girls named marina said, ho sat in the back with us. "What you call that cologne, lady catcher?" "I don't know what they call it, but it ain't no good." Sher said, "Why do you say that?" looking into my eyes. I said, "because it hasn't caught you." "How would you know that?" "Well, I don't," I said, "but if it proves out to be tree, I'm sure you'll tell me." I leaned back and closed my eyes and enjoyed the ride to the country.

Everybody was opening cans of beer and drinking, and talking about the cows they saw as were entering the country. "What is that green stuff out there?" James asked. "I know you know corn when you see it, but what is that?" he asked Dallas. "Damn James," Dallas said, "you ain't no city boy, you know damn well those are soybeans. Don't ryt to show off in font of these girls." "What is that???" Dallas repeated, "Like you don't know, as many damn soybeans you have picked." They were having plenty of fun now as they were tossing cans on the side of the road and opening other cans as we drove deeper into the woods. Every now and then, Dallas would reach over and pull Elizabeth close and try to get a kiss. She would say, "Look at those horses," and try to stop him. James would try the same thing as Marina, and Marina would say, "Slow down. James, I hardly know you. I only met you today." "You have known me long enough to give me a kiss," James said. She would snatch away and look over at me. I pretended that I hardly noticed them.

I had peeped at Marina one or two more times when James tried to pull her over in the corner with him. She had a small waist and big hips, lice legs, and a pretty face. I laid there with my eyes half-closed trying to figure out a way to beat James to that thing. It seemed to me that he was going at it in the wrong way. Dallas had parked now off the road and partially into a field. "This is the spot," he said, "look around you." We saw plums hanging from the trees, and blue and black berry vines hung around the road in spots. The sun was going down nw. I opened my door as Dallas once again pulled Elizabeth to him. She was kicking and laughing, telling him to stop. "You and I are going to get to know each other really good," James told Marina as he reached for him a beer. I reached over in the bag and got me a beer and left the car. I was way down the road, and I was throwing my beer can away into the field when a voice behind me said "Where are you going?" "No place in particular," I said. "I just got out of the car to give you and your boyfriend enough chance to do what you want to do." "That's not my boyfriend," she snapped, and if I was going to do anything, it wouldn't be with him!" "Good," I said, "do you drink anything else other than beer?" She said, "Yes, I love gin fizz." "Then you can tell me who do you want to do it with after we get our drink when we get back. Unless you don't want to have a drink with me, or am I rushing you? If this alright with you?"

I asked her. "Do you live in the same building Elisabeth lives in?" "No," she said. "I live next door to Elizabeth." "Then to not hurt James' feeling. Why don't you tell Dallas to drop you off at home. I'll be back to get you in half an hour after you get there." She said, "Good. And we both walked back to the car. Dallas hadn't gotten what he wanted. I could tell that when we got back to the car. Ames seemed pissed because Maring had gotten out of the car and walked up the road where I was. Before long, Dallas headed back to Chicago. There were eight or nine beers left in the bag. I reached over and got one of the beers and opened it, ad took one swallow. I broke the silence as I started singing "Chances are." Chances are because I wear a silly grin the moment you come into view; chances are you think that I'm in love with you. Just because my composure sort of slips the moment that your lips meet mine. Dallas interrupted me, "Give me one of those beers, James." "I'll take one, too," ''Elizabeth said. Then James got him one, then Marina. We were all drinking beers. Dallas took a sip of his beer. "Go on, Al, finish that damn song." Just because my composure sort slips the moment your lips meet mine; it seemed as if I got a choir because everybody started singing the song. Chances are you think my hear is your valentine; chances are cause I wear a silly grin the moment you come into view, chances are you think that I'm in love you just beasty composure sort slips the moment that your lips meet mine; Chances you are think my heart your valentine.

I could see that Elizabeth had moved closer to Dallas, her head almost lying on his chest as he drove up to Marina's house. Marina aid, "Well, I had a lot of fun." And yelled, "Aren't you coming, Elizabeth?" She said, "No, Dallas wants to take me to the Thirty-First Street Beach Don't you want to come?" She asked me. "No, not tonight," I told her. "I think I'm going to go upstairs and see what my auntie cooked, or maybe I'll go, and I'll go and get some BBQ." "Would you like to have some company?" James asked. "I still have my $5," he said jokingly. She said, "Not tonight, James, but I'll see you around." She said goodnight and closed the door. "Okay, fellas," Dallas turned around and balled his lips up as though he was mad. "Where do you fellas want to go, cuz' I'm going to the beach, just Elizabeth and me. Speak up, James, where are you going?" "I'm going home," I said. Dallas said, "just up the street." "Let me off at Twenty-Sixth Street. I think I'm going home," James said. Dallas said, "I'll take you home. Where is it, Twenty-Sixth, and Calumet?" "See you tomorrow, James," I said good-bye as I got to the house. He was in good spirits, so he said goodbye. "See you, Dallas and Elizabeth."

I went into the house at 2720 S Prairie. I walked through the vestibule, through the hallway past my door, then Paul's door and down the steps through the rear door. I was trying to kill half an hour, so I walked slowly across the alley to the vacant lot and to Indiana. I walked past Smitty's Shoeshine Parlor. I could see the curtain at the window. They were gambling. The restaurant was crowded as I passed the window. As I passed Sam's tavern and turned left coming back towards Prairie, I could smell the aroma of the BBQ. I looked over at the Alter Light Company that was dark and always looked deserted. Every now and then I would pass someone I knew, and I would speak to them and keep walking.

Before long, Marina and I were holding hands and walking to Thirty-First Street, to Redman's lounge. The moon was bright as we laughed and talked and began to get to know each other on our way to Redman's lounge. We reached Thirty-First Street. Why not get a half-pint?" I suggested to her that we could sit in my father's car and drink it because I might have trouble with my age in that lounge. "I'm with you," she said. We turned around and walked back to Henry's restaurant. Marina and I walked through the door. All the men's eyes were all over her. Drug Store Bob slid into me first. "Damn man, what tree did you pick this peach from" I said, "from the garden of Eden." He said, "I can believe that 'caus only angels are in the Garden of Eden, and you look like an angel, sweetheart." He directed his attention to her. "Thanks," she said with a blushing grin. "Look, Bob, take this $20 bill and get me a seven up, a half-pint of Seagram's gin and two cups. Get your favorite drink for you and Wadell." Bob left for the drinks. I gave Marina a dime to play the jukebox. She played Johnny Ace "Clock of the Wall." I looked at the face of the clock on the wall; it didn't tell me anything at all.

That face of the clock just stares at me; it knows I'm lonely and always will be. The record continued to play. Marina was back with me now sitting at the counter. We both were enjoying the music. When the door opened, and Tommy walked in dressed in beige and white Hawaiian shirt and beige slacks to match and a tan Panama hat, and real sharp sandals. Wadell was right behind him with a Panama black stingy brim straw hat, white and black shirt, black slacks, and black shoes that were freshly shined. “Hi, Al,” Tommy said, I said hi to him and Wadell at the same time. “This is Marina, “I told them both. “Hi,” she said and flashed her eyes up at Tommy, then to Wadell. I kind of felt an ill feeling there for a minute because I thought that she and Wadell held that stared a little longer than they should have. Wadell quickly directed his attention back to me. “Nice meeting you.” Tommy said to Marina. She said, “Nice meeting you, too.” “I’ll be over here at the booth. Wadell,” Tommy said. “So, Al,” Wadell said, showing that gold crown, “when will I be coming to your wedding? ‘Cuz I know this is going to be Mrs. Wynn.” “I hope so, Wadell. And if it works out, you are going to be my best man,” “You’ll be marrying a good man, Marina,” Wadell said. “Nice meeting you, likewise,” she said. Wadell made his way through e crowd to tommy.

Marina and I had made our way into the rear seat of my father’s Cadillac. We drank a third of gin. I still couldn’t drink much, so I sipped on mine slowly. Maria had thrown the first glass up to her mouth and kind of bobbled up the first drink with the seven-Up. The second drink, she sipped slowly as I did. I had learned from her conversation that she was having an affair with one of the neighborhood men, Joe Paulson. Joe Paulson was about six years older than I was. He had been in the neighborhood way before I moved there. I told her I knew him. She told me that he was married with two little girls and that he and his wife had broken up and she had taken the girls out to California six months ago. So, he said that he was going to check on his girls because they were having problems in California. He was only supposed to be gone one week, and it had been a month now that he had been gone. “I’m afraid that he won’t be coming back,” she said. “And at this point,” she went on, “he doesn’t have to come back because I gave up on him three days after the week was up and that makes tendays.” I said, “You mean to sit here and tell me as pretty as you are a nigger have left you for a month? You mean to tell me in a month you haven't hugged or kissed a person?" She said, "No, I haven't hugged or kissed anyone."

I poured a little more of the gin in her cup and refilled my cup. I said, "glass up," as I raised the cup to my lips. She followed the gesture. She drank half of her cup and brought the cup down with a frown. I did the same then I said "glass up" one more time. Shre blew and said, "Man, that stuff is strong." I said, "You can do it, baby." I took her cup and my cup and placed it in the front seat along with the gin and the pop. I scooted up close to her and kissed her softly on h ear and then the jaw, then I kissed her sft on her lips. She stared into my eyes as I leaned over and kissed her real hard in the mouth. My hands slid of her shoulders as I kissed her., and with that same hand, I cupped her breast. My hand went from the cups of her breast to her thighs. I rubbed her thighs softly on the top of her dress. She said, "Wait a minute, 'Al, move back. I'm in a cramp." She oved her body all the way around in front of me. Her left leg went up on the cushion seat, and her other leg stayed on the floor. Her dress was half to her stomach now and I could see her panties. She said, "Wait just a minute." She rose again and took off her sweater and laid back again and kind of scooted under me. We must have played, kissed, and hugged for half an hour or more before we slipped out into ecstasy.

CHAPTER 21

For the next three weeks, I saw more and more of Marina and less of Karen. I had to try and get myself more into Marina because Karen had hinted to me that her husband had written to her and said that he would be released from the penitentiary within the next two weeks. She had told me that she didn't know what she was going to do because she loved me so much. She had taken my wardrobe, shoes, scarves, and everything else she had bought me and given to her brother. She had given me a key to her apartment, but that particular day I gave it back to her. We sat at the Two for One table in the far corner. She took a drink of her Christian Brothers from her glass. I could see the tears in her eyes as she looked at me. "I don't know what I'm going to do when he comes back," she was saying. I know what you're going to do," I said, looking into her eyes, "You are going back to him as soon as he comes back. "I remember what Wadell said about him being a killer, having killed five people. "I know, baby," she said. "I can't stand the thought of losing you." I said, "I can't stand the thought oof losing you neither., but we both know that he is your husband." The thought came back to me about what Wadell said about easing out of the relationship gracefully, so I tried to give her the guilty conscience. "Things happen," I said. "And we both know it is wrong to commit adultery, and I above all other people should know it's wrong to mess with another man's wife."

"I know," she said in a low voice, sobbing, reaching into her purse getting a handkerchief to wipe her nose. I knew deep in my heart that she truly had feelings for me. I could feel it the way she touched me and the way she kissed me, but this was he end of a relationship, and someone had to take control of the situation and had to make sure that there would be closure today. I knew my words would hurt her more, but I had to put a wedge between me and her. I said, looking hard at her, "You know, I really don't believe that you care for me as much as you say you do. For instance, let's start with the clothes she bought for me. If you really bought them for me, why does your brother have them" "Because," she tried to explain, everyone knew I bought those watches, suits, and rings from Bowleg and the rest of the dope fiend bastards. Bowleg would never say anything, but you never know what a dope fiend would say." She looked at me and wiped her eyes with her handkerchief. "I didn't want my husband to come looking for you, so I gave the clothes to my brother." "You know that sounds very good for a square ass. You have used me up now, and you want to say good-bye." "No, that's not it, baby," as she started crying louder. "Well, if you don't want to say good-bye, I do," I said, staring into her eyes as if I hated her. "I don't want to see your black as ever again in life. By, Karen." I said as I rose from the table and walked out the door.

For the next month, Karen would show up on Twenty-Ninth Street. We guys would be in the restaurant talking. She would walk up looking as pretty as she possibly could. "Can I speak to you, Al?" She would ask. "We have nothing to talk about." I would answer. "Okay," she should say. "I'll be in Sam's for the next fifteen minutes, and if you want to say anything to me." She would turn and walk away. This particular night, just me and Leroy were in Henry's in their favorite back booths when Karen entered the door. "Can I speak to you for a minute, Al?" she asked. I looked at her for a long while, then asked, "Are you going to Sam's?" She said, "I always do, but you never show up." I said, "I'll show up this time. Go over there and order me some BBQ, and I'll be over there." She left for Sam's place next door.

"Damn, man," Leroy said, "who in the fuck teaching you how to pimp?" "Like Wadell said, "I don't know a damn thing about pimping., but I know you're doing this wrong." "What are you saying, Man?" I asked. "Damn, man. you just asked me to lend you twenty dollars, and here's a woman who came in begging you to talk to her and what the fuck do you say, 'Buy me some BBQ.' Man, you don't ever let a bitch know you're hungry, mother fucker. You have asked her to buy you some fucking food. When it comes to a hoe, you're either begging her out of her money or you're taking it. Now carry your ass over there and get then twenty dollars you were asking e for. And if you come back here with something less than one hundred dollars, I'm kicking your ass myself," he said jokingly. "And remember what I told you before, the name of the game is pimp or die. If you are a true mother fucking pimp, then prove that to yourself. If you're out here bull shitting, you should go and get yourself a job. Like I said before, that bitch ain't going to tell nobody that you're skinning her for her money."

I eased into Karen at the BBQ place, seated at a table. She had my BBQ waiting for me. She was sipping her favorite drink, Christian Brothers. I sat down in front of the BBQ, took a bone for the plate, and bit off of it. "Do you have any money?" I asked her. "I got a little. "What do you need?" "One hundred dollars," I said and looked up at her. She said, "Sure." She gave me a slight smile as though she had my ass hooked again, then she went into her brassiere. She came out with a knot. Sahe took her time and unpeeled one hundred dollars of the knot and handed me hundred dollars. I turned slowly around to observe the room to see who was looking at us. To my surprise, were alone except for the cook who was in the rear of the kitchen. 'That's when I snatched the rest of the money from her hand. and leaned over and said in a snappy voice, "You don't seem to understand that we are through. 'And when you get to understand this, you might get this money back, depending on how I feel at the time."

"Please, baby," she said, "don't do this. This is not my money." "What the hell are you talking about? How can you give me a hundred dollars if this is not your money" "That hundred dollars was mine, but the seven hundred and fifty dollars belong to Paul Will. I work for him. And he will kill his mama for a hundred dollars." "I'm gone," she tugged after my arm. "Please, Al, don't do this. I don't even have money to get back to Twenty- Fourth Street." "Walk back," I said, leaving out the side door, leaving her sobbing. I caught a jitney, and on my way to 31st street. I wanted to stop the cab and tell him to turn around because her words started to haunt me. "Pleas, Al, don' do this, this is Paul will's money, and he will kill his mama for a hundred dollars." But I had to go through with this. I wanted her to understand it was over because I didn't want to be the next victim of her husband's knife or bullet. So, I wanted her to think hard about trying to come and see me again.

The cab was approaching Leroy's gambling house, which sat on the Northeast corner of Thirtieth Street, across the street from the Harmonical hotel. My first thought was to stop and try my luck. The next was don't play like you are a damn fool with this lady's money. I was at Thirty-First Street now. I went into the Glass Bar Lounge, the 114 Club, and the Two for One club. There were just a few people in each one of them. I went over to the telephone booth and called Marina. She was home. She asked me to bring a drink. I stopped by the store and bought Seagram's Gin and Seven up., and her cigarettes, Pall Malls. I caught a jitney to 2813 South Prairie. It was six-thirty when I climbed the stairs to Marina's apartment. She and her aunt sat quietly in their living room watching T.V.

It was eleven o'clock when I stepped into Sam's bar. Billll called me over to the bar and said, "Wadell has been looking for you, boy. He's been to your mother's house. He is out looking for you now. I think Drug Store Bob and Tommy are next door, you better go and talk to them." I wasn't in the restaurant no more than a minute before Tommy and Drug Store Bob coaxed me over to the booth. They both sat side by side, and I sat in front of them with my back to the door. "What in the hell went on today, Al?" Tommy asked, looking at me seriously. "What do you mean? What are you talking about?" I asked, looking from one to the other. "Don't act like you no damn fool now, Al," Drug Store Bob said, "This is some serious shit. I mean, what did you do to Karen?" Tommy went on asking. Before I could answer, Drug Store Bob said, "Do you have all that Bitch's money? If you don't have it, how much do you have?"

After I told them I had all her money and I had it with me, they skinned the story down to me that Karen had come back alone and had run into Wadell and bought him a drink at the bar next door. She had told him everything that had happened in the BBQ house. She ran into a customer of hers named Henry in the bar and he took her back to Thirty-Fourth Street. It was not long after he reached Twenty-Fourth Street that Paul Will came looking for his money. The story she ran down to Paul Will is that she had recruited me two months ago to deal dope for her, to deliver some packages for her around Twenty-Ninth and Thirty-First Street. This particular day, she had met me to see how many packages I needed. She had all her money with her in one bag. I ordered some BBQ to go. We were sitting at a table. Both bags were on the table. I picked the wrong bag up by mistake. Wadell was lighting a cigarette when he left.

Will's reply was, "How long have you known him? Where does he live and hat little mother fucker better have all my money when you see him, and I'll be back here at twelve o'clock to collect my money."
"Damn, Al," Tommy went on to say, "I thought Wadell told you don't do anything suspicious with that bitch to draw attention to yourself, and I thought," he said, not giving e a chance to answer the first question, "that her husband was supposed to be out of the penitentiary a month ago. What happened tohis release or do you know?
"To answer your first question, I was listening to Leroy with that pimping and being hard bullshit of his before I met with Karen, and after that, I got into taking the money. I wanted to prove to myself that I was cold enough to go all the way with it. After I was out there in that water, I couldn't back up. Your second question is that her husband was supposed to be out a month ago, but he had trouble finding a job for his parole. Now I hear that Paul Will has secured him a job at the A & P and he will be out next week. This is why had to put a cinch on her not to be fucking with me to close too his release."

"I need a drink." Bob went into his pocket and brought out his little half-pint of gin. "Here, you can take a sip, don't take too much. Youhave a bigger role to play when Wadell gets here." Bob said, handing me the bottle. It was eleven-dirty when Sadell came into the restaurant. I quickly gave Wadell the rundown of what I told Tommy and Bob. "Well, this s is the way you are going to play your hand, Al," Wadell said. "You first apologize to her for not bringing her money back to her sooner." The reason for that is you had to go out to Harvey, Illinois to see an auntie that was very ill. When you reached into the bag to get your BBQ is when you discovered her purse. All the money is there, and she can count it if she wants to. Also, you can't run anymore errands for her on Thirty-First Street because you think you are going to have to go and live with your auntie, and that she is very sick and wants you to come and live with her for a while." We all loaded up into Wadell's car, me sitting in the front seat by Wadell. We headed for Twenty-Fourth Stret. I looked over at Wadell as he drove down Indiana, and he kept going over and over of what I had to say. I sat there starring at him and admiring him as though I was a bitch. I didn't know what Wadell was. Really, I tried to figure him out. He looked like three people in one to me tonight, he looked like a well-dressed gambler, a pimp, and as you looked closely at him, he looked like a handsome gangster. Rember, Al, he said, "be polite with Karen. Whatever she says, don't let her make you angry in front of Paul Will." "I'll Rember."

Wadell parked the Road Master Buick close to a big building on a side street. Tommy said, "We'll sit her ad wait on you." Bob said, "You got your piece, Wadell? If you haven't, I've got mine if you want it." Wadell said, "I don't think I'm going to need no gun as long as Al plays his hand and knows how to act." Wadell and I walked into the lounge. There were three or four guys sitting at the bar. One man and girl were playing the pinball machine, and Karen and Paul Will sat in the corner at her table. We reached the table and Wadell spoke to Paul. "How you are doing, Paul?" Paul gave a nod and a wave with a big cigar between his fingers. He was sitting, but you could tell he was about six feet tall with a white felt hat on and a white suit and black and white shoes. He was a big-boned stocky guy. His fingers were long and stocky. He had big hands. His eyes left Wadell and came back to me. "Hi, Karen," Wadell said. She said, "Hi, Wadell," "I'm sorry, Ms. Karen," I said that I didn't call you about your purse. My auntie got really sick all of a sudden and I had to go to Harvey to see about her and I took my BBQ with me. At the time, I didn't know it was your bag. When I went to eat the BBQ, that's when I discovered your purse in he bag. I'm sorry that I took so long to get back to you and I'm more than sorry that I had you worried. My auntie is very sick and Wadell is taking me back out there when I leave here, so I won't be able to run errands for you anymore." I handed her the purse. "You can count it, whatever was in there is still there." Paul Will said, "I'll count it for you, son," and reached and got the purse. He counted the money. It was seven hundred and fifty dollars. "What did you say your name is?" I said "Al," and looked at him dead in his eyes. He, in turn, threw a twenty-dollar bill on the table in front of me. "You are a good boy, Al. By yourself a beer for you and Wadell." I said, "thank you," and gave the money back to him. Isaid "I had Ms. Kaen's money, and I don't think you should pay me for bringing it back, I was going to do that anyway" I could ell that Kaen was pleased by the way I presented myself in the situation. I turned and walked away.

We were back in the car and Bob suggested that we go back to Leroy's place to see how well the game was going. I felt like one of them now because this was the first time that we all were going places and doing things together. I felt like I had grown. I looked at the guy at the wheel and admired him more. I guessed who he was when I was on my way down to Wtenty-Fourth Street, but now I really knew who he was from all the little things that he had done for me. Really, I knew in my heart who he was. He could be the pimp, the gangster, or the gambler, but tonight he was my true friend.

CHAPTER 22

There were about eight guys at the crap table at Leroy's. "Why don't you have a seat over there at the table," Bob said. I seated myself where I could see Tommy, Wadell, and Bob. "Fifty dollars I shoot," Wadell told the houseman. "The man is shooting $50," said the houseman who got him faded. he was shooting some guy on the other side of Bob. Bob spoke up, "I got him faded. Let him shoot." He threw out fifty dollars. Wadell shook the dice and threw them across the screen. "Eleven" Wadell said. The dice rolled on nine. "What you bar that nine for?" Tommy asked. "Fifty dollars.," Wadell said, "I'll bar that nine for fifty dollars bet." Tommy said as he threw the fifty dollars to the houseman. The dice came out again. Wadell threw eleven. "Eleven!" The houseman said. II was sitting where I could see Tommy's had slide out of his pocket and drop by his side. The way his hand was turned by his side, I could barely see the dice that he held. I saw his hand wiggling the dice to his thumb. Before I knew it, the dice was under his thumb. He reached over and caught Wadell's dice, and the switch came in the air as he slung the other dice back on the table. His hand fell to his side as he talked shit to Wadell and the other guy. He said, "I'm glad I caught them. That nigger looked like he wanted to throw nine." The other guy said, "I'm glad you caught them too." That's when Tommy slipped the other dice back into his pocket. "Nine points," the man said on the next roll!

"Come on, what are you shooting now? Goddamn, you that got me into this shit now, Tommy said. "I got fifty dollars. Are you still betting fifty dollars?" The man said, "Come on, I got him. Come on, let the nigger shoot." The switching of the dice went on and on from Wadell to 'Bob to Tomy. People came, and people left. At three o'clock in the morning, sitting at the booth at Henry's Restaurant, they split sixteen hundred dollars three ways and gave me the odd hundred. I said, "Man, you will have to teach me the dice switch. Man, how did you di that?" Bob said, "Shut up, Al. Walls have ears."

The next three weeks were like a training camp at Smitty's Shoeshine Parlor. Behind the curtain on the pool table, Wadell, Peter Rabbit, Tomy, Drug Store Bob, and even Leroy was practicing the third dice thumb trick. None of them were as smooth as Wadell. He seemed to put magic into what he did. He tried his best to teach me. That second week of trying, he said, "Al, I think your fingers are a little too short and stocky. I don't think that you should try to learn that third dice game because you only have one mistake to make. When all three of them dice hit the table, you won't have a chance to pray. What you should learn is the e lock. The secret of the lock is to see how fast you can catch the dice and lock them into the numbers you want to lock them into. For instance, you see the dice in the middle of the table." I said, "Yes." "You should see here's a six sitting up." I said "Yes." He snatched the dice as he said, "Thre's a one on the other side of the six and on the bottom of the six, there is the one. When you throw these dice across the line on the pool table, they call that pad rolling. Okay, now we know that's pad rolling. Okay, now we know that there is one under the six. We have the six on top," I said "Yes." "The lock for pad rolling when you are coming out is one on top of the six. Then watch me," he said, "I've got the one at the bottom in my hand. I'm looking for the six on the other dice. Just for your sake, I'm going to pick up the dice.

Now I'm going to place the one I've got in my hand on top of the six of this dice, making the dice have seven in the middle, six and one. The six and one are seven. In the middle now, if you look very closely as I turn the dice in my hand with six and the one, there's seven all around the dice, even in the middle. The whole lock is seven on the dice. As you fold your fingers over the cup of the dice in the fist, you give it just enough room to get the clicking sound no looser or no tighter. Then you shake them." He shook the dice and let his hand go down by his side. Then he swung his arm like a bird in the air. "When you can make the dice march like two soldiers, then you know the lock. Practice that, and then we'll go to the next phase next week. Practice how to snatch those dice off the table and make them stay in hat lock. I've got to make a run," he said, looking at his watch, "I'll see you at Henry's later."

The next week, we were at Smitty's once again practicing dice throwing. "Let me see what you can do, Al," he said. Right away, I went to the dice. Right away, he threw two dice on the table. I saw the five on the one dice. I started looking harder and I didn't see one or the six. I asked, "Can I pick he dice up and throw them again myself?" He said, "No You don't know here the six is, do you?" I said, "No." He said, "That's your lesson." I said, "What?" He said, "Learn what's on the other side of each number." Tant next week I was learning the lessons of the dice, trying to see Marina, and at the same time trying to keep my appearance up. With no money coming in, I was getting in bad shape. Not giving my mother any money, and not having the money to even buy beers for Marina. The way I used to look, and dress had faded. I had asked Leroy and Bob a couple of times to lend me a twenty or a ten. They had loaned me the money a couple of times, but I could see that begging and borrowing were getting on their nerves, and they began to shy away from me. Bob had made a crack once to me, "You're growing up now, Al, and you are not a Little Pimp no more. You better be trying to look for a job." I thought about going to Mr. Buddy at the shoeshine parlor, but now I had gotten used to real money. I wouldn't be happy there anymore. I had to do something because I promised my mother money this weekend and today was Friday. I just didn't know where I was going to get any money from. As I sat in Henry's sipping on a cup of coffee, the restaurant was dead. Only the fat waitress patrolled the counter.

There were no other customers in there but me and as I sat sipping my coffee looking out the windows at the drizzling rain hitting the window, I felt lonely and sorry for myself. I had to do something. If only I had a gun, maybe I could get a cab driver. No, that's too dangerous. I thought, and I had never done shit like that before. The only thing I was going to do as the thought built up in my mind was going to go and snatch a purse. After finishing my second cup of coffee, I walked out into the rain. I looked to the left of me and past the Alter Light factory, thinking about walking to Thirty-First Street. Then I turned and looked to the right and to the north of me. Thirty-First Street had too many hustlers and most of those hustlers had guns. So, I decided to walk to Twenty-Sixth Street where it was a little quieter and less dangerous. I walked rapidly down to Twenty-Sixth Street. As the wind tore at my jacket and the force every now and then kind of pushed me off the sidewalk, there was no one else on the street but me. Both sides of the street were empty. I had passed the drug store on the corner of Twenty-Sixth Street. I was almost in the middle of the block of Twenty-Fifth Street when I saw her coming toward me. It was a lady. Her head was bent down trying to block off the wind. I could see the long strap on her pocketbook. It hung from her shoulder. Hy heart started pounding in my chest. I held my head down to block out the wind but kept my eyes on the lady.

The wind was so strong that the lady didn't even notice me coming. We were side by side now. It was now or never. I reached out and felt the strap of the purse. I grabbed the straps and pulled it so hard I almost pulled the lady to the ground. She was stumbling trying to get her balance, straining, trying to see who I was, shocked at the snatching of her purse. I had that purse in my hand, and I almost reached out to turn and catch her from falling when she snapped me out of my daze. She said, "What are you doing? Give me back my purse." I took off running. She took off right behind me. I was near the corner of Twenty-Fourth Street. I could hear the heels of her shoes right behind me. She said, "You better not let me catch you, you little bastard." I seemed to have gotten a second wind as she started screaming behind me. "Help! He's got my purse. Help, somebody, help me." I ran almost half a block when I could hear her heels almost getting closer and closer. "Damn," I thought, "this wasn't an old lady. She must be as young as me." I looked to the right and saw the alley. I heard her shout once again, "Help! Somebody help me! He's got my purse!"

Halfway through the alley to the left of me was a big wooden fence about five and a half feet tall and ten or twelve feet long. I dove for the fence. Struggling, trying to stay on top of it. "That's all right, that's all right. Stay right there 'cuz I'm going to cut your ass everywhere but loose." I seemed to have gotten power as I fell on the other side of the fence into the yard. I saw a light when I was on the ground. It was on the floor. There was a dog behind the screen door on the first-floor apartment. He growled and eventually started barking as I ran through the side yad to the front gate, out the gate across the street to the second alley. And that's how I made my escape. Her screaming and hollering faded behind me. When I reached my house at 2720 South Prairie, I went into the hallway bathroom. The light was dim. I reached under my jacket and pulled out the woman's purse. I was nervous and anxious to know what was inside of it. I hoped it was a fortune because if it wasn't. I wasn't going to risk my life again snatching another purse. Only some old letters, a powder puff, lipstick, and an eyebrow pencil came out of her purse. Beneath all the rubbish was the coin purse. I opened it and it had $11.21 in it. You mean to tell me that lady nearly cut me and ran after me five blocks for eleven dollars? Well, at least my mother had ten dollars for the next day. The next day, I stood behind Smitty's Shoeshine Parlor. Four other guys and I were shooting craps in the dirt. I had turned that $1.21 into eight dollars by the time Smitty came and opened the door to the shoeshine parlor. When Smitty opened the shoeshine parlor, we all disbursed.

I sat in their favorite booths in the rear. Only a lady and a man sat at the counter. "What are you having?" the fat waitress asked me. "What is your name?" I asked her. "Carolyn," she said, looking at me while popping that gum. Her jaws and ears seemed swollen. "What are you having?" she asked me again. "You got bean soup?" "Yes." "I will have a bowl, muffin, and a pop." I sat there turning the dice. I discovered the four was on the other side of the three. The five was on the other side of the two, and of course, as Wadell had shown me that the one was on the other side of the six. I kept looking at those combinations and remembering them. I had finished my meal and was once again looking at the dice when Bob came to the door. "Hey, Al, Wadell is waiting for you next door." Once again, we had the curtain pulled, and just me and Wadell stood at the crap table. He threw a pair of dice down on the crap table. "Okay, Al, you know the drill. What is the lock six aces in the middle?" he asked. "Get me in the lock. I looked at the table and right away I saw the ace, it was sideways. I reached and got it and ran it into the six that was sitting on the other side of the table. I knew the swiftness of placing the lock together was the essence of the whole act. I did it with accuracy, locked my fingers back with the curve. As I curled the dice in my hand, I raised the dice to my ear just loose enough to get that click. My hand went back to my side as I raised it and let the dice roll evenly like soldiers across the line on the table. The dice stopped at seven, four, and three. "My man," Wadell said, "you got to practice that. This is the second thing you can practice when you are on the dirt or sidewalk. You shoot the navy spin, and the navy spin is six on top and the five in the middle making it one, five, two. And instead of letting the dice flow out of your hand on the dirt or sidewalk, you hold your hands sideways and throw the dice and pull your hand back like you do a spinning top, making it spin instead of roll. When you get them down pat, Al, you can make money. It's up to you how good you want to be, and practice makes perfect. As I have told you before, that third dice game is not for you. Don't ever step out into another person's game unless you can play it or master it. Learn your own game. A game you can master."

This was November 2, 1952. For the next two weeks, I studied the dice and practiced every day for two or three hours. While my mother and father were at work, I rolled the dice like soldiers across their bed. I would practice the spin on the carpet or on the floor. I met Bob, Wadell, and Tommy that evening. "How are you doing with the practicing, Al?" Bob asked me. I said, "How much do you want to shoot, Tommy?" "Do you think you're that goof to take on Bob?" "Give me a couple more weeks, and I will be ready for Wadell." They all laughed. "There is only one other thing that you don't understand. You don't know the bar. You got four numbers that you bar for, the nine-five-ten, you bar the twos under the bottom five. So, you know the five is at the bottom of the two. When you bar the four or the ten, you bar the twos under the bottom five. You know you have fives on top. You put the five, then in the middle, making the dice have a lock of ten and four all around. When you bar, you can lock up the four and five in the mddle or the three and six in the middle. You lock up that same lock six and tree or four and five for the nine and five locks. Well, you got it all," Wadell said, "the only thing you need to do is practice. I'm telling you, Al, a gambler doesn't have a life. He mostly starves all the time. Don't think you have a career in gambling. Me and tommy and Drug Store 'Bob do it for the fun of it, not for our full support in life."

CHAPTER 23

It was the 2 of December when all hell broke loose in my life. I had come home from Twenty-Ninth Street at about 7:30 in the evening. When I entered the vestibule, I could hear those old familiar voices of my sister and brother hollering. "Please, daddy, please don't hurt her!" My heart was skipping beats as I rushed to my apartment door. I swung the door open. My sister had tears rolling from her eyes. "Please, daddy, please, daddy, don't hurt her!" My mother lay on the floor. His foot was on herast. The chair was raised over his head. "No, daddy," I said as I snatched the chair from his hand. "What are you doing, boy?" he said as he raised his foot from my mother and grabbed me by my collar and held me in a choking position. My mother was on her feet now, and from the corner of my eye, I could see her go for the glass picture that hung from the mantle. My father didn't notice her as he tightened his grip on my shirt collar. "What you call yourself doing, boy?" I couldn't speak. "You leave him alone," my mother said as the picture came down and burst on the back of his head. I heard my sister scream again. "Oh, daddy!" She saw the blood and glass in his hair. My mother had grabbed her shoes and coat. She grabbed me by my hand and ran through the hallway and the vestibule door. We headed down toward Twenty-Sixth Street. "Where are we going, mama? I asked.

"I don't know. I don't have any carfare. I don't have enough money to call Heard. We can't go over to your Aunt Zaora's or

Queen's because he'll come there." I said, "Come on, momma, let's go the other way. I've got an idea." We ran bck the other wway past 2720 and up the street to Marina's house. After I rang the bell and explained to maringa What had happened, Marina's auntie welcomed my mother to the apartment. After four or five attemts of my mother trying to call my uncle Heard's house on King Drive, and she chalked it up to he was probably still at work at Pepsi Cola Bottling Company. "What do you really want to do, Mrs. Wynn?" Martina's auntie asked. We wer all sitting in her living room.

"Well, I could pay you tomorrow when I go to my credit union. What I really want is a place for me and Al to stay tonight." "You don't have to pay me, Mrs. Wynn," Marina's auntie replied. "Anything for my boy, Al. So, you're his mother, right? So, anything for you. So, what we're going to do is, you can have Marina's room for the night. Al and Marina can take the living room and sleep on some pallets for the night."

From the second-floor window we could see my father's Cadillac pull away from the curb. He was on his way to work. He left every day at five o'clock in the morning. My mother wanted to go and get a change of clothes, but she couldn't risk him coming back. So, Mrs. Kitty gave her one of her skirts and blouses that fit her to a tee. My mother seemed to like Kitty. They hit it off at their first meeting. I was supposed to meet my mother on Twenty-Sixth and Indiana after work at five o'clock, but she never did show up. I walked the alley to 2720 I cut across the backyard of the man's house. I saw Paul's car parked two or three columns from the house. I tried the back door of Paul's car. It was unlocked. I stepped in and locked the door behind me. I kept sitting there and scooting down to the floor when I saw a car light hit the window. I was going to jail for murder, I thought, if my father did anything to my mother. I knew that they were together because he would be at the house every day at three-thirty, and his car was nowhere to be seen. I waited there for what seemed to be forever. At about eight-thirty that evening, his Cadillac parked in his favorite spot. I rose and peeked through the front window. First, I saw my father get out of the car and go to the sidewalk. He waited and then I saw my mother get out on the other side. She had a bag in her hand. Maybe filled with food. They went to the porch and through the vestibule door. I jumped out of the back door of Paul's car and ran to Marima's house. I raag the bell. I waited for two or three minutes, then the door buzzed, and I went in. There were three apartments on the second floor. One was set by the stairs, then Mr. Kitty and Marina's apartment sat on the north side of the steps. An apartment was in the rear of the east side of Marina's house. Mr. Kitty had answered the door for me. I said, "Is Marina home, Mrs. Kitty?"

She said, "No, Al, I don't know where Marina is. She must have gone to the store. Did you see your mother? Where is she?" Mrs. Kitty asked. "She's at home, Mrs. Kitty. She's with him." "Well, they must have made up. I wish her luck," she said. "I don't know," I said as I watched the little girl down the hall with her thumb in her mouth watching me. I said goodbye to Mrs. Kitty. She closed her door and I turned to the steps. The little girl with her thumb in her mouth slid her back against the wall and followed me down the fall. So, I stopped her and said, "Have you seen Marina?" She said "Do you have fifty cents? I'll tell you where she 's at." I reached into my pocket and gave her the fifty cents. "Her in there." She pointed at the apartment by the steps. "Her in there with that man name Joe Baby." I asked her, "Are you sure she's in there?" "I saw her go in there with that man, Joe Baby." A knot seemed to be rising in my stomach. I felt nervous and angry at the same time. I knocked on the door hard. At first, there was silence. I knocked again and stopped myself from kicking on the door. "Who is it?" A voice answered.

I said, "Tell Marina, it's Al. I want to speak to her for a moment." "Just a moment," the voice said. I waited for what seemed like ten minutes before the door came open. Marina stood there as pretty as ever, with a slight smile on her face. "Hi, Al," she said. I looked past Marina and saw Joe baby sitting in the chair facing the door, staring at me without a smile. I said in a crappie voice, "I would like to speak to you." I got her by the hand. She eased the door closed behind her. We were down the on the bottom level of the stairs. "So, he's back," I said. "Yes, Al, he's back. But it's not going to do him any good. I love you," she said. "If you don't believe me, we can go upstairs, and I will show you who I love." I said, "No, I love you, Marina, and today is Wednesday. I want you to go back upstairs and I want you to do whatever you want to do for him. But next Wednesday when I come here and if it's still me you love, I don't want ever to see him in our lives again." It started raining. I stepped out onto the porch and headed to Twenty-Ninth Street.

I started to walk across the street and headed for Sam's Tavern. The thunder was loud as I pulled my coat collar tight around my neck. Why in the shit did I say that to her? Why would I tell her to do whatever she wants to do with another nigger? I was the stupidest ass that I know., or was I? At that point, I couldn't rationalize right from wrong. What the hell. I didn't have a job, was on the run from my father and got no place to lay my head. Maybe I need the weekend. This was my way of not telling her tat I was broke and didn't know where I was going to get my next meal.

CHAPTER 24

The rain was coming down harder now, almost blinding. I ran and turned the corner right in front of the Prairie hotel trying to make it to the alley to try and find some sort of shelter from the rain. As I ran, I saw the old raggedly Buick that sat in the vacant lot behind the Alter Light factory. It had been sitting there for one or two years abandoned and someone had taken the top of the trunk off. I headed for the car. I reached for the handle and the door came open with a squeak. The lightning flashed across the sky two or three times. The flash struck right in front of the windshield. I sat crossways so that my back was to the drover's door. I tried to convince myself that I wasn't scared, but I knew I was really scared. I closed my eyes and thought about my mother and her situation with my father. I wondered if my sister and brother missed me. I knew for sure that I missed them. I closed my eyes and tried to make myself as comfortable as possible. Before long, I was asleep.

It was one-thirty in the morning when I walked into Henry's Restaurant. There wasn't anyone around, just a couple of strange faces that I didn't know. The fat lady came to my rescue. "What are you having tonight, some more beans?" I said, "That's fine and bring e a pop." I had gotten through eating and made my way around to the fire barrel that sat in the rear between Smitty's Shoeshine Parlor and Henry's Restaurant. The wine heads and alcoholics had knocked holes in a drum barrel and placed it on four bricks. Early in the morning, before the restaurant opened or the lounge, they would build a fire and gather around it drinking and tell long lies about their everyday occurrences. Some swore that they were dynamite pimps in New York, some came from Philadelphia, some came from Detroit. Hearing it from them, they hit bad luck and had to regroup. So that alcohol gave them courage and hales hope that one day they would again be the forerunner with the baddest and prettiest hoe in Chicago.

Some claimed to be hustlers, some claimed they came from the medical world, other were con artists, but all of them had one thing in common, they were all alcoholics and were victims of hard luck. I eased over the fire barrel next to a familiar face that I knew. It was Lee. Whenever there was a crap game, in the shoeshine parlor, he would be the runner to the restaurant or lounge or tavern for he food ad drinks. He was one of Wadell's great admirers. He thought the sun rose in Wadell! He would say to Wadell, "You want me to shine your shoes, boss? You're looking very nice, boss. How many hoes have you done copped tonight, boss?" Wadell would smile and wave him off or sometimes when he was in a good mood, he would say, "Hey, Lee, take this $50.00 and get us a drink." Wadell drank Jack Daniels. Lee was also known by everyone around that corner as the world's greatest lover, he claimed to be the world's greatest lover when it came to women, he loved kissing them on their thighs or any other place they let him. He didn't mind an audience. Some people used to just come and get him for a show. I stuck my hands out over the fire and looked at Lee. "It's cold as hell out here, aint't it, Man?" He said, "Hell yeah, that's why I sent and got me a drink." I said, "What you send and get?" "Some Jim Bean," he said. I reached my hand into my pocket; I had three quarters left. I said, "can I buy in on it, I've got seventy-five cents." He said, "Sure, young blood, I'll give you a drink." He reached his hand out for the seventy-five cents. Before long, another younger fella was standing there with Le's drink. He took the pint of Jim Bean from the bag. "You mind if I knocked the poison off this whiskey, Lee?" he asked, "cuz' you know what you do Lee and I just don't want to be called secondhanded. "Yeah, go ahead, man. Knock the poison off and give young blood here the bottle when you get through."

The guy took a swallow from the bottle and passed it to me. I turned the bottle up trying to get my share because I knew when Lee drank it, nobody wanted any parts of it. Not being a drinker, I damn near choked myself with the swallow. I started gagging and it seemed as though the liquor had started coming out of my nose and mouth as I started coughing and trying to catch my breath. "Is you alright young blood?" Lee asked. Without giving me a chance to answer, he went on talking. "That's what will happen to you, young guys trying to hog all the whiskey. You'll fuck around and kill yourself." He turned the bottle up and took a long swallow. Two or three bottles of whiskey were bought that night. The young guy that was drinking with me and Lee looked at his watch. "Damn, it's four-thirty already. I had better get out of here too. I have to drive my mother to work." "I'm going, too," Lee said. There were three other fellas that left the fire barrel. I stood there alone watching the dying embers in the barrel. Well, there wasn't too much heat left around the barrel. the lounge and the restaurant were closed. So, I might as well go back to my hotel room; the Buick behind eh Alter Light factory. I had to remind myself to get some cover for my new bed. The next three or four days I would beg around in the streets for money. When I had begged up a dollar or two, me and a couple of more young guys would go to the Louis Theater on Thirty-Fifth Street or the Grand on Thirty-First Street and state. We would stay as long as we could, mostly sleeping. In the next three or four days I didn't see too much of Wadell and Tommy or Drug Store Bob. Our lives seemed to be drifting apart. At night, when I was in my hotel room, I thought about Marina and Joe Baby. One night I had a dream that they had moved together, and I woke up in a sweat as cold as it was in that car. I longed to see my mother, brother, and sister.

That following day I had just left the theater by myself and made a shortcut through the alley of Wabash where there was another vegetable barn similar to Fat's. The wagons were parked next to the barn. The barn door was closed and there wasn't anyone to be seen. Maybe I'll be lucky enough to find me a bunch of bananas I thought as I looked in each wagon. The last wagon on the floor under the seat was folded up neatly three blankets and a man's jacket. I ran to the front of the wagon and climbed on top and swooped up the blankets and jacket. I rushed out of the alley across the street to the next alley through a vacant lot across the street to the third alley, and then to the hotel. I took the heaviest blanket and wedged it from the roof of the car across the back of the seat cutting of the draft coming in from the trunk and making a wall between the opening of the trunk and the front seat.

It was the second night after I had placed the blanket in the car, about 3:00 in the morning when I was awakened by a noise from my visitor. The noise barely awakened me and as I strained my ears to find out what it was, the yawn came again from the trunk. I peeled the blanket open and three laid facing me a gray German Shepherd. He seemed to not be quite grown yet. He turned his head sideways to look at me. Just for a moment, our eyes met. He stretched his neck out back to the floor and closed his eyes. He seemed as though he had no fear of me. I stared at him for some time. He seemed harmless, I thought. The shock of him being in my presence seemed to vanish. I released the blanket that I had peeled back. I slept in the big jacket, so I pulled the other blankets over me and got in my sleeping position and closed my eyes. The dog was there with me every night for the next week. I looked forward to him coming or being there when I reached the car. Every evening I would stop at TJ's grocery store and go through the garbage trying to find some kind of food to give the shepherd. He seemed to appreciate it. I never tried to pet him. I felt that were both in the same situation. It had gotten to the place. When I would leave in the morning he would be there. He would jump from the trunk and wag his tail. It was seven-thirty in the morning when I met Wadell coming into Henry's restaurant. "Hey, Al," he said, "where have you be hiding?" I said, "here and her, but I've been around."

"You haven't gone back home yet?" "No," I said as we made our way to the booth in the rear. We were seated and Wadell ordered his breakfast of bacon eggs, and toast. "Give him the same," Wadell told the waitress. "Do you want grits or potatoes?" she asked. I almost said both, but instead I looked over at Wadel and said potatoes. The waitress was gone with our order. Wadell spoke in a low voice, "You are looking bad, Al. You should go back home. These streets can be a killer, especially to a young boy like yourself. I have been out here just like you. It can be rough, very, very rough. Some people get through it, and some never make it. I hope you will go back and face your daddy. All families have arguments, but love is still in the house. You are his oldest son, he loves you, and y I best he and your mother is worried to death about you. Who am I, Al? Who do you think I am?" "I think you are a pimp and lots of other things" I answered. "I have pimped every now and then. I take cash from those that want to just give up the money. The school of hard knocks taught me how to get a back up and get a cinch to win on the money and you don't have to beg for it."

"What is that cinch win?" I asked wide-eyed. "A job," he answered. "You didn't know that I worked, did you, Al?" The waitress had placed our food before us. "A job," I asked, reaching for the coffee cup. "Yes, a job," He went on talking. "Just you and a very few of my friends know that I work. I work from eleven at night to six-thirty in the morning. It takes thirty minutes for me to drive from downtown. A person would think that I am the last thing they see at night because they see me all day until nine-thirty or ten-thirty at night. They have no idea that I have slipped away to work and right in their face at seven o'clock in the morning, still talking shit and still clean. Appearance is very important. Sometimes or most of the time, it is deceiving. I like you, Al, I like a young brother. I could let you hold a C note, but deep in my heart I know that I would be hurting you instead of helping. Don't ever depend on anyone else when you are down. What the hell do they care? You can drown. They don't care, just as long as it's not them drowning. Hard knots will teach you that every rub must sit on its own bottom and every tongue must confess for its won soul. How you look this morning would deceive a person that doesn't know you. They don't know that three or four weeks ago, you were cleaner than clean, and your jacket pocket was swollen with money. You can do it again. Go back home. Light the fire again between you and your daddy. Geta jo, clean up your act and come back and surprise these niggers."

Wadell had me charged up. I was feeling very good and had confidence in myself before Bob came to the table. Bob was shorter than Wadell and 'Tommy, and the rest of his buddies, but he was built like a tank and looked like a wrestler. He wore nice acausal clothes. He had on a Steel Grey Dobbs hat, gray pants, and black shoes. He had on a black cashmere overcoat that was open showing the gray knit sweater, a silver buckle with his initials showing his waist. "Hi, Wadell, Little Pimp, or should I say Little Tramp?" Bob's voice was loud, and the whole restaurant laughter. "He's not lying, Al," a voice came from the front. Sitting on a stool was Peter Rabbit. "That overcoat, I know you can do better than this." They all laughed again at the size of the coat. "Why don't you niggers get off his back,'" Wadell spoke, "and how many of you are going to by him a better coat' "I will" Bob answered, "if he learns how to stand on hot bricks that I got for my bitches!"

Everybody laughed, even the cook and the waitress. I sat there, embarrassed. My blood had started to boil. I was mad enough to throw Bob out of the window. They kept laughing. I could see Wadell staring at me. I turned my head back in front of Peter Rabbit. He had stopped laughing and was waiting for action or a reply to Bob's brick joke. Standing on hot bricks in the wintertime meant if a whore is cold on any certain corner, a pimp would tell her to heat some brick and stand on them, whatever it took, he wanted his money. Bob had called me a whore in front of everyone. I fought to keep my tears back. I was sure if I jumped up at Bob, I would get a royal ass whipping. I reasoned with myself, and I was new on the block, and everyone seemed to like me, even Bob. So, the game plan was to embarrass me to run back home. Everyone around the corner seemed to be in on it. They were always on my back to go back home. I didn't have too much money when I left, but I was clean, haircut, and good-looking shoes on. To be truthful with myself, I was ashamed to go back in this condition. I looked up at Bob standing over me. I said aloud, so everyone could hear me, "the name of this game is cop-and blow, Bob. I just blew a bitch now and it's time to cop a whore and until I do, you can stand on your bricks. When I cop my whore and you are standing thee cold, I will give you this coat to keep you warm as it is doing for me." I rose from my seat facing Bob and said my goodbyes to Wadell and excused myself from the restaurant. 'As I was leaving, I heard Wadell tell Bob, "He got balls." Aa lots of them." Bob whispered. Peter Rabbit seemed to give me his approval as I went out the door.

CHAPTER 25

It was about eight o'clock at night when I reached the fire barrel. Four or five guys stood around drinking ad laughing and telling jokes. I didn't know them. One of the other guys walked up to the barrel behind me. I turned to look at him. It was one of Lee's friends. His name was Horace. "Hi, Al," he said, ruing his hands together and looking around at the other men throwing his hands over the fire barrel. "I'm glad to see you, Al. I got some gin. Do you want a drink?" "Yes, I need one," I said. He gave me the bottle from his inside coat pocket. It was an unopened bottle of gin. I cracked the top and took a big swallow and let the bottle down and then it went up again. "Thanks," I said, "I needed that," and handed the gin back to him. He took a drink and put the bottle back into his pocket. He leaned over to me, whispering, "Do you want to make some money?" "Yes," I almost shouted. "Come on," he said. We left to go to Sam's. We went around to the bar's barbeque and fish side. Horace peeped through the window, then stepped back from it. "He's still there. They are gagging his food. He will be coming out in a minute. Come on" While walking slow to Twenty-Ninth Street and Prairie, Horace ran the game down to me. One of his drinking friends that worked with just got a $3,000.00 dollar settlement from his lawyer. The money came from an accident he had in a cab. According to Horace, he had all the money in his right-hand pants pocket. "Now, this is the game plan," Horace said. "He's going into the basement on

Thirtieth Street and Prairie to his girlfriend's house. He went to buy her some fish and beer. He told me that he would not stay. He was going to put up the money and get some rest. I need that money; Al. Christmas is only four days away. I don't want to knock him out. I am just going to hold him. You get the money out of his pocket and run as fast as you can back to the fire barrel. If I can't get away, I will just knock him out cold." Horace went back into his pocket for the bottle. I said, "you better take it easy on that gin."

"Oh, I got it. I used to fight pretty hard in my younger days. So, if I have to knock him out, I will knock the fucker out as I said before." He was saying now in a drunken voice, "Shit, I will knock the fire from his ass. I don't want to hurt him, but I will knock his as off." He was saying and almost falling into me while trying to get his balance. Before long, Raymond, Horace's friend, had crossed to the other side of the street and had turned the corner walking to Thirtieth Street. We stood in the dark distance away from him. We followed him to his girlfriend's house. When we approached the basement there was a front and rear door. Both doors were propped open. There was a dim light in the ceiling, another of those 25-watt bulbs. Horsace stepped into the basement and screwed out the bulb. Inside the basement, you couldn't see the rear door because of the darkness. We stood by the front door close to the wall, waiting for Raymond to return to the gangway. After waiting for what seemed like an hour, the door came open, Raymond stepped into the gangway. "Okay, I hear you, Lucille," he said. "You want Pall Mall, gin, and BBQ. You just ate up five pounds of fish." The other voice came from the inside. "Just get them damn things I told you go get and get your broke ass out that door, the air is cold."

Raymond said, "the damn light has gone out, out here." He pulled the door locked. Horace eased the front door closed. You could see some moonlight, but now the gangway was pitch-black.

Now the damn door has closed." Raymond muttered to himself. You could hear his footsteps as he came closer and closer to the front of the building. He was not at the spot that Horace thought he was. When Horace let go with a haymaker that he thought would connect with that wild swing, Horace lost his balance and fell into Raymond. "What the hell is this?" Raymond asked. Raymond had reached out in the dark. He connected with Horace's neck. Horace tried to move back and straighten himself up. The fear of Horace falling into Raymond sobered Raymond up, and the fear of losing his money started to fight whatever intruder it was.

Raymond slung Horace up against the wall with one hand in his collar. Raymond's right-hand fist caught Horace in the stomach. Horace gave a grunt as the same fist caught Horace upside his head. "I'm going to kill your goddamn ass niggger whoever the fuck you are," Raymond said, slinging him to the other side of the wall. I opened the door and I was laughing so hard and loud until Horace confessed to Raymond who he was. "Hold it man, hold it. This is Horace. Hold it, what the fuck is wrong, man?" The more I thought about what Horace said on the way down here that he was going to knock the fire out of Raymond, the harder I laughed and he more Horace tried talking that ass whipping off himself. "This is Horace, man." They were both on the steps now in the moonlight. "Yeah, I see you nigger, "Raymond said. "You came here trying to get my money, you mother fucker. I ought to kill your ass." "Nothing like that man, Raymond," Horace said, wiping the blood from his face with his hand. "I came down here to try to get another drink, that's what I did."

"You're telling a damn lie. You thought I was drunk, and you were going to try to rob me, that's what you were going to do. That's the damn reason this goddamn light is out." He went over and screwed the light bulb in, and it came back on. Horace was sitting on the stoop. I stood over him, still laughing. The noise had brought the people out of the basement. His girlfriend and the people on the first floor were all looking on. "What's your name: Al, isn't it?" Raymond asked, and I was still laughing. "Yes," I said. He reached into his pocket and brought out a $20 bill. "Now, Al, I want you to tell me the truth, and I'm going to give you this twenty-dollar bill. Didn't this fucker bring you down here so he could take my money? just tell the truth, and I'm going to whip his ass again, and you can have the twenty dollars." Blood was still coming from Horace's nose as he held his hand up to his nose. He turned and looked up at me from a sitting position. At this time, the way he cocked his head looking up at me reminded me of the gray German Shepherd dog that I shared my hotel room with. I felt sorry for him just like I did that dog. I was dead broke, but secretly we were in this thing together.

If I told on him, I might as well tell the man to whip my ass too. I looked at the man dead in his eyes. "No, sir," I said. "He asked me did I wanted a drink after we had finished his bottle, and I said "yes." He said, "Come on my friend, Raymond will buy us a bottle and I know where he's at." And we were waiting for you when you came out. I told Horace that he was drunk already; he almost fell on me, knocking me down as we came here."

"I'm going to give you this $20 boy because I really don't believe that you knew what he was thinking. You take my advice and stay away from nigggers like this, he'll get you killed. As for you, Horace, I don't want you ever in my face again. Now get your ass out of here." I ran to the corner of Twenty-ninth street. After that night, I only saw Horace two or three times and then he didn't come around anymore. I learned that night that anything a drunk would say, you can take it with a grain of salt. The next day I went to Thirty-First Street to the secondhand store and bought some shoes, a sweater, and a cap. Later that night, I bought myself a bottle to droink all by myself in my hotel room.

CHAPTER 26

I was awakened from a drunk inside my hotel room. I peeled the curtain back to see if the shepherd was here. He wasn't. I left the car and headed for Henry's Restaurant. I peeped into the BBQ house behind Sam's. I could see all the people crowded up in line waiting for their orders and others sitting around the tables, drinking, and eating BBQ and fish. I could hear the song from the juke box playing "Merry Christmas." The voice was saying, "Merry Christmas baby, you sure did treat me nice; bought me a Cadillac for Christmas; now I'm living in Paradise." It was too crowdy in there as I went around to the front of Sam's and peeped through. the window. It was crowdy too.

It had snowed that day and a strong wind was pushing the rings of snow down the street. I went into Henry's restaurant. There were two or three people eating in the booths. I sat on a stool at the counter and ordered a cup of coffee. I didn't have enough money to order the beans. I was sipping my coffee when a nice-looking gentleman came into the restaurant and sat two stools from me by the window. He ordered him a Christmas dinner. "Chicken," he told the waitress, "The dark meat, dressing, greens, and he looked deep down on that menu that he held in his hands and said, "I want those lima beans and cranberry sauce." The girl poured his coffee and left with his order. He sipped from his coffee and looked over at me. "Merry Christmas," he said. I said, "Merry Christmas" back to him.

He said, "it's kind of quiet in here." I said, "Yes, but they're clowning next door." "Yes, I peeped into the lounge, but I thought I'd get me some food first. Yeah, I don't know why I'm stopping here or wanting to go to that lounge. Yeah, I work at Morrison's Hotel. I'm a chef there. Man, they have got so much food there. I didn't even want to eat in my hotel room, I got everything. Whiskey and beer, so I guess I'm just stopping to spend my money in the neighborhood. I stay right over there at the Havana Hotel, 29th and Wabash."

"Yes, I know where that' at," I said. The waitress was back with his food. The plate was so filled that the food was about to fall off. He started to eat, and as he ate, I sized him up. If he hadn't told me that he was a chef, I would've sized him up just as I had done Wadell. The way he dressed from the first sight of him, you would've thought that he was a hustler, a pimp, a big-time gambler. He had these three qualities. He was dressed in brown and tan shoes. Every now and then, the fork would go up to his mouth, and he would turn his head to catch me staring at him or at his food. I seemed to be swallowing with his every bite. "Have you had your Christmas dinner, yet?" He asked I said, "No" in a kind of whispering voice. The waitress was coming with his water. She placed it before him. "Give him the same meal, and put it on my bill, will you?" Water, she placed it before him. "Give him the same meal, and put it on my bill, will you?" She said, "Sure." the waitress came back with my food. We introduced ourselves. His name was Menard and he told me that he had a lot of whiskey in his hotel room and asked me if I would like to go with him to have a drink. He didn't have any family here, and he welcomed me. I had told him yes; I would go and have a drink with him! Not only was I going to drink with, but I was also going to steal all the heat I could for as long as I could. He was a very nice-looking guy, and my opinion of him was that he could pimp whenever he got ready. His room was like a little kitchenette apartment where there was a sink and a hot plate and a refrigerator in one corner. Next to it was a small bathroom with just a bowl and stool. On the other side of the sink by the door was the closet. The huge bed took up most of the room. On the other side of the bed was his table filled with fifths of whiskey bottles, about ten of them. Take off your coat and make yourself comfortable, and you can lay across the bed. Make yourself a drink." And he pointed to the table where the drinks were. He said, 'I'm going to grab something out of the closet. I'm going to go to the bathroom and freshen myself up. Make yourself at home.' I laid my coat across his bed. I walked over to the table. He had all old folks' drinks, I thought. Old Granddaddy, Old Taylor, Old Fitzgerald, etc. He had some gin and beer in the box. I poured some gin into a glass and sat in the chair beside the bed. I had taken a big swallow from the glass when Menard came back into the room. He was tall and he stood there smiling at me.

His chest was bare. M eyes fell down h he only clothes he had on, a pair of red ladies' panties. I couldn't believe my eyes! At first, he stood there smiling and posing in ladies' underwear. His long arms went up to the string that was tied to the ceiling light and headboard. The bed was iron, with iron ribs in between two iron bedposts. A big red light came on and the big bright light went out. Before knew it, he was lying across the bed on his stomach. He crossed his legs up over his head. "I like you, Al, I like you very much, did you know that?" "No," I answered. "Well, I do,"" he went on to say, "I was born with a lump growing in my throat and every now and then I need someone to help me push them to the other side. You know what I mean, Al?" "Yes," I said very quickly, not knowing what he was trying to say. Whatever it was, I didn't want any parts of it. My mother's words came back to me. "Be careful of who you smoke with and watch those sissies. Stay away from them. They will cut you." Her name for them was "she-male." He was looking at me now, dreamy-eyed. He went on talking, "You got the most beautiful brown eyes I have ever seen," he said, clicking his feet together over his head. He was very serious about whatever he was talking about. My voice had gotten very shaky. At one time, I started to just jump out of the chair and run straight to the door, but only a child would do something like that. I was out here on my own now. I had to outthink him and outtalk him. He said, "Al—"but I cut him off. I spoke. "Man, is that the only whiskey you have to drink over there? You don't have any vodka. Man, this heat is good, isn't this nice?" I said, "I could just lay down there beside you and go to sleep." He said, "would you like to get in bed?" "Yes, I would like to spend the night if you don't mind." He was on his feet now. He said, smiling at me, "Well, let me get you something to put on, darling," I said, "No, I'm not ready to go to sleep now. I want my drink. I drink vodka." "Oh well, I don't have any vodka and orange juice," he snapped. "I only have these drinks on the table."

"Well, I'll try to go and get some," I said. Standing and ready to run any minute. "Oh no, you don't have to do that," he said. "I'll get Betty from across the hall to go and get some. What kind do you drink, Smirnoff?" I said "yes," that's the only kind of vodka I drink with orange juice." He started towards the door. I said, "Say, Menard." He stopped and faced me. "Do you really want me to spend the night, man?" "You know I do, you cute little darling." His whole attitude had changed. His conversation was more ladylike than manly. I said, "You may have to go and wake her up. I'm here, and you can let me go. I can run so fast and be right back. Well, that's all right because she's going to be too long, and maybe tomorrow, I'll come back over here." I reached to get my coat. He walked over to where his pants laid neatly on the chair. I was buttoning my coat when he handed me the twenty-dollar bill. "Bring me some camel cigarettes back, will you, Al?" I said, "I'll be right back," and

I hit that door as fast as I could. For the next two or three days, I stayed off Twenty-Ninth Stret. I took that twenty-dollar bill and let it stretch out at the show at the Grand Theater and the Louis. It was the third night that I stepped into Henry's Restaurant. I had been around the fire Barrel looking for Lee or any other person I could get $2 from. I needed some beans, and I didn't have the money for them. Henry's was crowded, really crowded.

I walked toward the back where all the laughing and the talking was. Before I could squeeze through the crowd to the back, I heard Wadell's voice, and he told Bob he could stand on his won damn bricks. "Boy, that tickled the shit out of me." Wadell said, and everybody laughed. Bob said, "And he buttoned up that raggedy-ass coat and told me to kiss his ass and walked out the door." "I tell you" Wadell said, "that little nigger has heart. I stepped into the opening where they were standing. Bob said, "Here his Little Pimping mother fucker is now." "You can call me tramp if you want to, Bob, I'm not mad at you. Maybe one of these days I can lend you two dollars 'cuz that's what I need right now. Two dollars." "You know you can get two dollars Little Pimp, here's two dollars." I said, "my man, Bob" and turned and walked out the door. I went back around to the fire barrel. I was in luck; The two guys that I had been drinking with earlier in the week stood around the barrel with a fifth of white port. They gave me two or three sips from the bottle. I was feeling better now, and I had been gone for about forty minutes or so. Now, it was time for me to get those beans and Henry's was still crowdy. People were standing in the aisle and sitting at the booth. It was packed. I couldn't see Wadell, but I could hear Johnny telling jokes, this time he was telling the signifying monkey joke. Bob was saying, "The lion said I'm not going to whip your ass because the elephant whipped mine. I'm going to whip your ass about this goddam signifying. The monkey said wait motherfucker, you aren't raising no hell cauce the whole damn jungle see me when I fell; he said you let my balls out of the sand, I'll fight your big ass like the elephant, like a natural man, the lion jumped back on one knee and the goddamn monkey jumped to the top of the nearest coconut tree and turned his ass to the northeast wind. He said, you stupid hairy face mother fucker, I done tricked you again, who shall live to swing away, shall live to signify each and every mother fucking day. This is the future, not the past. If you think I'm going to slip out of this tree again it's your mother fucking's ass."

Everyone clapped and laughed. One guy said "damn, Johnny, you tell damn good jokes." I eased in and sat on the stool by the window. I was looking at the menu when a sexy voice asked, "May I help you?" I knew it wasn't the fat girl, so I looked up into the eyes of a beautiful young black princess. She had thick lips; she was really black. She wore her hair in a ponytail. The sides of the top of her hair were slick tight to her head. I looked at the arched eyebrows, the smooth texture of her skin, then back to her lips, then our eyes met. "How long have you been here?" I asked, "You mean today, or how long have I been working here?" she asked. I asked, "How long have you been working here?" She said, "About three days." I asked, "can I guess your name?" she said, "sure." I said, "You couldn't be nobody other than Bathsheba." She said, "Who is Bathsheba/" I replied, "a sweet African Queen." She said "I can assure you that I'm not her, but thanks for the gesture. Now, what do you want?" Little Pimp, or should I say little tramp?" I said, "Oh, you must have been in the conversation they've been having here." "No, but they have been talking about it for the last three days. I've been wanting to meet you to see what all this talk is about. Now, what will you have?" I said, "Give me a bowl of navy beans, cornbread, and a pop." She asked, "That'll be it?" I Said, "That's it." Everyone in the restaurant was talking among themselves and having fun. Some were having beer, whiskey, and pop. Others were eating. There wasn't anyone noticing me as I stared out of the window. Maybe I should go back home, I thought. Maybe all the guys were right. I wasn't proving anything to anyone. I need to get a job, that's what I need to do. Maybe, I was just like the guys from Detroit and New York that stood around that fire barrel. Maybe my pimping days had ended before they began. Maybe like those guys all I had was a dream, I would decide tomorrow.

The noise of the platter that she placed before me brought me out of my trance. I looked down at the platter, and it was chopped liver and rice with gravy, three side dishes, navy beans, candy sweets, and cabbage with the cornbread on the side steaming. "What did you say your name was?" I asked, trying not to attract attention to myself. "Loraine," she whispered back. "You got your orders mixed up, pretty." "I know," she said. "Are you hungry?" "Yes, but not hungry enough to wash dishes." "Eat up," she said, the treat is on me." She walked away back towards the kitchen. She hadn't said anything but a word. I damn near ate up the platter. Every now and then I would see her far off peeping at me and smiling as though she enjoyed looking at a hungry mother fucker eat. I finished eating, slowly enjoying every bite. Loraine was in the kitchen when I left out of the door. I came out in time to see Wadell, Tommy, and Leroy sitting in Wadell's Cadillac. The car turned the corner headed for Thirtieth Street. I knew where they were going and I wished I was there with them to watch the show, to hear those clicks of the dice. I regretted that I was not part of the team. I was back at the fire barrel. This time Lee was standing there drinking with his other three buddies. I soke to him, "Hi Lee." "Hi," he said. And he passed the bottle to me. I took a drink and passed it back to him. Then he asked, "Have you been inside the restaurant yet?" I said, "I just left man." "Did you see that good looking broad in here?" I said,

"Yeah, she bought me dinner." "You're telling a goddamn lie!" "No man, I wouldn't lie to you." "Well, it looks like you have going to choose again." "What you mean?" "The girl likes you. Nigger." "I said, "How you know?" "Well, what I do know is for two or three days now, all the so-called pimps and hustlers tried to talk to her, and they did not get her name. Now you jump up and say she has bought you dinner, what you think?" "Maybe you're right, Lee. I'm going in there and find out what's going on." "Yeah, why don't you do that. Here, you can take another drink." I took the bottle and sipped it a couple of times and gave it back to Lee.

I walked into the restaurant and there was a fortune-telling machine and weigh-in machine combined. It stood about five feet tall and at the top of it, it had a mirror on it. I stood on it and looked into the mirror. I had sandy hair, and it was standing straight up on my had. I had a baby face that didn't need a shave, but my eyes were slightly red due to my drinking and lack of sleep. I looked down at my shoes and all kinds of mud were on them, mud was all around the edges of my pants. The big heavy man's vegetable coat that I wore did not do me justice. I said hell no, she doesn't like me cause I don't like me, especially the way I'm looking. I stepped back from the machine, turned around, and faced her. She was right behind me, but behind the counter smiling at me. "Do you like what you see?" She asked. I looked around for the crowd, but only one old man sat at the counter in which he appeared to be drunk.

I walked dead up to her. That wine and gin and whiskey had kicked in and had aroused a false courage in me. I forgot about my appearance, and I walked straight up to her, looked deep down into her eyes, and asked, "what time do you get off?" She said "three o'clock. Why are you going to take me home?" I said, "I don't have a car, but I thought maybe you would have a drink with me before you go home." "Like I said, I get off at three o'clock. Will you be here?" I was right back out the door and back to the fire barrel looking for Lee. "You were right, I think that she likes me." "One of these days you are going to believe me. I didn't get to be fifty for nothing." "Look, Lee, I wouldn't do this for anybody but you. You and me going to both get the pussy." "How are you going to do that? Do you know we can get it?" "I'm telling you this because don't you do have a place to stay?" "Yeah, I got a place. I got a ig, big room around the corner." "I know we can get the pussy. Only one thing is wrong, I don't have any money. We need to get a drink." "I got some money," Le said. "I'm going to let you get the pussy first, so we need some gin and beer." "That ain't no problem. I got that." I said "Now here's what you got to do, Lee. We are going to start drinking and you lay across the bed like you're sleeping and as soon as I get her ready, you can wake up on us and she will be forced to give it up to both of us. "When is she going to get off, man?" I said, "Three o'clock. Hey Bubba." He said, "Yeah, Lee?" "Come over here for a minute. Hey man, do you want to do me a favor? Aren't you driving, Bubba?" "Yeah." "I need you to take me and that girl next door to my house when she gets off." "What time is it now, Bubba?" "Two-thirty." "Al, I'm going next door to get the drinks before they close. I'll be by the barrel when you get ready." I was back in the restaurant drinking coffee. All the other customers had left when Henry went to the door to lock it up. He turned to look over at me. "Okay, Al, last call for alcohol. I'm fixing' to close."

"He's waiting for me, Henry," Loraine said, "He's going to take me home.

Henry said, "On what? A bicycle?" I looked over at Henry and I smiled. He shook his head, turned and locked the door, and went back into the kitchen. Not long after, he went into the kitchen. He was back with his overcoat and hat on. The cook was fully dressed, too, and ready to leave. We all left the restaurant together. To my surprise, Lee and Bubba were parked right out front of the restaurant. He beckoned for me, and I opened the rear door, and we both got in. "I am not taking you home," I whispered to her, "we are going over to Lee's house for a stay. He lives around the corner." Bubba had let Lee and me off at Lee's address and we were in his apartment now. He and Loraine were seated at the table in his little kitchenette apartment. Lee had taken a big swallow from the bottle and had drunk a half bottle of beer before he laid across the bed. But to my surprise and his surprise too, he went to sleep for real. I looked over at Lee and said, "Damn, he's asleep. Let's sit on the side of the bed." We sat there. I laid her softly on the bed and kissed her. She said, "You know, Al, I like you, but I can't do anything because I'm on my monthly." We sat up and I said, "Let's have another drink." We walked back over to the table. Lee had started to snore. "By now, you know, Loraine, I like you too, and there is no sense in me trying to bullshit you. I'm up ere with Lee trying to steal some of his heat because I don't have a place of my own to lay my head. I guess as you have heard, I have run away from home on account of arguments and fights my parents had. I'm living in an old car with a dog."

That whiskey had kicked in now and maybe that drink had the truth serum in it. I went on talking. "I'm telling you this because I like you very much and I'm not even worthy of your company. I don't even have our carfare home. So, I'm not going to mess with you anymore until I try to get myself straightened out." "Wait a minute. Can I talk? In the first place, I like you too. Otherwise, I wouldn't be here, and I knew that you didn't have a job when I came up here. The only thing I didn't know is that you were sleeping in a car with a dog. I thought you might have been sleeping in a basement or something. And as for you being worthy of me, isn't hat for me to decide?" It wasn't long before the clock said nine-thirty. Me and Loraine talked for six hours. I enjoyed the conversation with her. We left Lee's apartment. I pulled the door closed just enough not to lock it. I left the outside door unlocked. I walked Loraine to the bus line in front of the restaurant and lounge. After she was on the bus, I walked swiftly back to Lee's house; but to my surprise, someone had locked the vestibule door. My only recourse was to go to my hotel room. When I reached the car, the dog was gone. I could see his tracks in the now. I opened the car door and climbed in. I awakened at about three o'clock that afternoon and walked to the restaurant. Bob, Wadell, and Tommy were in their favorite spot. Wadell said, "Sit down beside me, Al. Lee just left and told me that you had the new girl up to his house last night." I said "Yes, we had a drink at Lee's house." I kept looking over the counter at the fat girl. Our eyes met, the fat girl and me. "Where is Loraine?" I asked her. "She doesn't work on Sundays," she said. "She will be in tomorrow." "Man, I got a hangover. Do you have any gin in your pocket, bob?" He said "Yes," and went into his pocket and got the gin bottle. Wadell said, "Have you ate anything today?" I said, nope." He said, "Get what you want." I said, "I'll take some beans, muffin, and a pop, and I will have a piece of pie, to!" She was off to the kitchen with my order. "That's a nice-looking girl," Tony said, "that Loraine." I said, "Yeah, she seems to be nice." "Those kinds of girls will make you get a job," Tommy said. "She's not going to make me get a job. I'm going to get one anyway." "It's kind of rough out here," Tommy said. "Life is what you make it. You can make it hard, or you can make it right for yourself. It's all up to you," Tommy said.

I sat quietly with them and ate my beans and pop. Wadell said, "I want me some fish." Wadell asked, "Do you want to go next door with us? I'll buy a drink." I said, "yes." We were all seated at ta middle table. It was semi-crowded in the restaurant. People were talking loudly, playing the jukebox, some were singing with the jukebox. Tommy and Bob had a date at Leroy's gambling joint. They had gotten two orders of BBQ and left. Wadell was to meet them at Leroy's. We were sitting and talking while Wadell ate his fish. My back was to the door that led from Sam's lounge into the bar and BQ house. Wadell looked up as he was eating. He was facing the door, "Oh, oh, Al, don't look now but here she comes." Right away, my stomach started to get nervous and shaky. I thought it was Marina Wadell who was talking about. I really didn't want her to see me in this shape. I had longed for her and had missed her so much, but I wouldn't dare go around her house looking like this. I did see Dallas a couple of times and he had told me Marina had asked about me and she told him to tell me to come and see her sometimes, but I never did go.

"Hi Al," the voice said. I looked up at Loraine. She was dressed sharply in a fur jacket. Her lips were painted red, and she had on black boots that were designed like Mexican boots. "What are you drinking?" she asked as Wadell had finished his fish and pushed his plate aside. "We were dinking gin. Wadell had bought me a shot." She said, "Gin? What you are dinking, Seagram?" She reached over to the other table and got a chair and seated herself between Wadell and me. She said, "Wadell, would you mind going and get me pint of gin and whatever you were drinking?" "Okay, I'll go." She passed him a fifty from her purse. As I have said before, Wadell was dressed very clean and sharp. The white beaver hat with a big black ban made him look Hollywood. I was jealous and mad at Wadell for r the smooth black skin hat sat under the hat, made his look like a layer among players. I wondered why she gave him the money. Wadell was off for the gin. "What did you eat today?" she asked. "I ate some beans a while ago." "You love them damn beans, don't you?" And she smiled. I said, "Yeah, I was raided on them She said, "I don't know if I want BBQ or fish, which one ould you like?" BBQ". I spoke. She called the waitress over and ordered two

BBQ dinners. We ate and drank for two or three hours. Loraine was steadily spending. I said, "Do you work tomorrow?" It was about eleven o'clock. She said "Yes." I said, "I'll walk you to the bus." She said, "I'm really not ready to go home." I said, "I really don't want you hanging out with us guys." Really, I think I wanted her to go because everybody was looking so clean and I'm looking so damn bad. We were at the bus stop. She said, "You know I come to work at three o'clock tomorrow. Here take this twenty and buy your breakfast in the morning and every day that I come to work, you can come on my shift and get your dinner." The bus was coming. It stopped and the doors opened. "I'll see you tomorrow," he said as she kissed me on my lips softly. I waited until the bus pulled off. She waved at me through a side window and when the us was about half a block away, I felt sorry for myself, and I felt alone.

CHAPTER 27

The days that I saw Lorain, that next week, went very smoothly. I would come in at about three-thirty, half an hour after she was on duty, and get my dinner. Sometimes I would get $5 from her and go out and try to hustle with it, but mostly I would wind up drunk. It was on a Friday; her payday and we were sitting in the BBQ pit at a rear table. "I want BBQ. What about you, Al?" I said, "I think I want some fish." She told the waitress what we wanted, and the waitress was off to get our meal. My back was to the kitchen and the entrance of the lounge. "Here, Al," she said, handling me the money rolled up. I took the money. She said, "This is my salary and tips, $175, I want you tomorrow to get you a change of clothes and a haircut and an apartment where I can be with you, baby." I had eaten my food and Loraine was still eating hers when I told her that I had to go to the men's room. The men and women's toilets were in the hallway between the lounge and the BBQ house. I walked slowly out he hallway and after I had entered the hallway, I walked straight past the toilet to the front of the lounge where Wadell, Tommy, and Bob were seated in the corner in the front of the bar. They smiled at me, "What's happening, Little Pimp? We saw you when you passed."

I said, "Yes, but I have to ask you all a question. You all know that Loraine is a young girl and lives with her mother, and she just gave me all her money, $175. What do you think I should do?" Wadell and Bob started laughing. I said, "I'm serious man, all her money, man, and what the fuck should I do?" Tommy looked at me very seriously and said, "You don't know what to do?" "No, what's her mama is going to say?" I asked. That's when Tommy turned ice cold on me. He looked at me really hard without a smile on his face. "Fuck her mama!" You ain't dealing with her mama, you're dealing with her, and he gave you all her money, so therefore she wanted you to have it." "Take every dime." Bob said, "go back and see if she's got some more. Women know how to take care of themselves. So, if she couldn't afford to give it to you, she wouldn't have given it to you." Wadell said. "She dresses too nicely and looks too intelligent to be a damn fool. So, take the money and go straighten yourself up and do something beneficial for yourself. Hey Bill, bring me another drink!" Bill looked at me as though I had stayed a little too long. I looked back at him and went through that hallway and back to Loraine.

The next day I was up bright and early. I had pushed my money down in my sock. I wondered if the room was still vacant in Lee's building that I had seen on the first floor. I was going to get my hair fixed, and that was for sure. And I wasn't going to the Salvation army to get me any shoes or pants. I was going to the pawnshop; I saw a bad vest suit in then I peeled the curtain bac and for a long time, I watched the shepherd sleep. Then at 8:30 that morning I was on my way to Henry's Restaurant. To my surprise, when I reached the restaurant, there was Bubba, Leroy, and Lee drinking coffee. They all spoke to me. And I spoke back. "Say, Lee, I would like to speak to you for a moment, if I can." I sat at the front. "What is it little nigger, can't you see I'm trying to drink my coffee?" I said," Come over here, man, I don't want everybody to know my business, and it's important." He stood and picked up his cup. I said, "You can leave your coffee there, I just want to ask you a question." "Wherever I go, my coffee goes, I haven't had any this morning. Do you want me to come or not? I said, yes, come on.". He was seated beside me. "Lee, has your landlady rented out that room on the first floor, or is it still vacant?" "You mean the room in the front." I said, "Yes, I saw the sign in the window when I was over at your house." He said, "No, but the one in the rear is vacant." He said, "It is like mine. You have to buy a refrigerator and a hot plate, but the plate, you don't tell her about because she will put your black ass out." "Who do I see, and where does she stay? "Her name is Mary Fisher, and she stays in the basement apartment. The rent is eleven dollars a week and she'll ask for eleven dollars deposit. You need to give her $22.00 to get the apartment, you got that?" "Yeah, man, I got that." "When I get through with my coffee we can go and see her. Do you have enough money after you pay your rent to by my bottle, I bought you the other night?" "Yeah, I got that too, man."

It was one-thirty in the afternoon now as I looked at the young boy in the mirror of my bathroom. I had on a black Dobbs hat, that was rolled on one side and down on the other, black shoes and a still gray vest suit with a black shirt. The shirt stood open at the collar. I patted cologne on my neck as I stood for some time staring in the mirror admiring the transformation that I had made. The barber had done me justice with the conk and the chair cut. I still had $37.00 in my pocket. I went back to mt bedroom where the chesterfield overcoat that I had gotten from the Salvation Army lay on my bed. I felt ready for the would as I stepped out into the snow. That money was burning in my pocket. I hadn't had $37.00 in my pocket for a long time, and I knew what I was going to do with this money.

CHAPTER 28

I headed for Leroy's. There was a crowd there that Saturday afternoon. Leroy was the houseman. His shirt was pen at the collar and a tie hung loosely around his neck. He wasn't wearing a hat, and his hair was cut very short. He seemed to be sweating slightly and he looked tired from being up all night. But it was worth it because the money was stacked in front of him. "Speak up, my man,' he said to one of the shooters, "it's your shot." The man said, "I pass them." "Next shooter," he said, pointing the gambling stick at the next guy and tapping on the table in front of the guy. He said he passed, too! Meanwhile, I had wedged myself between a little, short bald-headed guy and a fat lady. She smiled and moved over to give me some room. Leroy's stick was now tapping in the front of the old-headed man. He said, "What are you shooting?" He said, "I'll shoot the fifty." He threw the fifty dollars to Leroy. "Fifty dollars, the man is shooting fifty dollars. Who's got him faded? Who's got him faded? Fifty dollars, he's shooting fifty dollars." Leroy spoke up, again.

"I've got thirty of them," the fat lady standing beside me said as she threw Leroy three tens. "I've got twenty," I said, as I threw Leroy my twenty. Then our eyes met. He said, "Al, Little Pimp. What the fuck man, looks like you threw a seven already." Leroy threw the little baldheaded man the dice. The man caught the dice and raised them up to his ear. "Come on, baby, throw a seven," the man said as he shook the dice in his ear. He slung the dice across the table. The dice landed on Snake's eyes. "Snake eyes and it crapped. The houseman said, "What are you shooting now, my man?" The little man dropped his head and walked away from the table. "What are you shooting pimp?" I said, "I'll shoot that forty I just won." "The man is shooting forty." The fat man smiled at me and threw forty dollars to the houseman. I could feel another transformation coming over me. When I was a little boy playing Superman or Roy Rogers, or Tarzan with Pap and Roland Lane, and the rest of the guys, "You think you are the people for real, now don't you man?" They would say. "Man, you aren't Superman for real." Now, tonight, I had transformed my mind into the mind of Wadell. I liked how he shot dice, and tonight, I was going to shoot them just like him.

The houseman threw me the dice. I caught the dice and jacked them off back on the table, one at a time noticing what each dice sat on. When they stopped like greased lightning, I had seven, the one sticking straight up. Then I saw five sitting up. I was looking for the dice to go with that one, but my mind was working so fast that it blocked me from finding the six as I wanted. So, I had to go with the five. Right away, I snatched up the one and placed the one on top of the five. I know that the navy spin was for dirt, but I was going to make it work on this table. So, I put my hand in an upward position, not a rolling position, it enabled me to do the spin. My hand went up as I shook the dice. You can hear the dice clicking together as I threw them out and snatched my hand back. The dice came out in a spin and danced around the table and came to a halt on two. Seven points! "I'm just getting started, Leroy." "Who's got eighty dollars, the man shooting eighty dollars? Who's got him faded?" The lady looked at me and said, "You aren't hot tonight, are you?" when she threw Leroy the eighty dollars. Leroy threw the dice. I caught them. I had seen where the one and six were. To my surprise, my fingers started doing the work. My hand went up again as I rolled the dice across the table like marching soldiers. I knew the combination was right. "Eleven" Leroy said, "Okay, we have got to get our cut, l. One hundred dollars we're shooting." "No, I'm drawing down a hundred." "Do we have a bet? Thirty dollars he's shooting. He's shooting thirty dollars. He's shooting thirty dollars." The lady said, "No, I ain't got him this time. He's too hot for me." "That's right." Leroy threw me back my thirty dollars. "I'll save my money. I'll see you back at Sam's."

CHAPTER 29

I got out of the jitney at Twenty-Ninth Street. I noticed Tommy and Wadell going to Smitty's. I noticed that they had gone into the back, but Wadell and Tomy were talking to Smitty. Without them noticing me, I climbed up in the chair and placed my feet on the shoe stand. I raised my pants halfway up my legs. My black silk socks were to the knee. "Phillip is in the back waiting on you, Wadell. His pockets are full," Smitty said. I said, "Can I help you get some of them, Wadell?" And they all turned and faced me. Wadell said, "MY man, Al, I knew you had it in you, Little Pimp. You look like a million dollars." "That's the way you are supposed to look for a hoe," Tommy said, "each and every day." "Have you been over to the restaurant yet, Al?" Smitty asked me. I said, "No." "Has Loraine seen you yet?" Smitty asked. I said "No." Wadell said, "Get your shoes shined, and then come on in the back." I said, "Okay." My shoeshine was forty cents. I gave Smitty a two-dollar tip. He said, "You got a pretty nice bank there," as I was putting my money back in my pocket. "You came a long way, Al," Smitty said, "the young boy that I met at the theater. Now you're stepping off into tall cotton when you're messing with Wadell and Tommy and with this gambling thing. You're on the fast track. Sometimes it can be a dangerous track so take your time. Go slow and try to learn everything you can. like you did on the shoes. Have fun along your trip ahead, but above all things, be careful." I thanked him for the information and headed for the back room.

When I got to the back room, there were about six guys back there, including Wadell, Tommy, and Phillip. Wadell and Tomy were having big fun. I watched them. They were like actors on the stage, switching dice and talking shit to their customers. I stood at the end of the table. I had bet one or two times and finally, after what seemed like half an hour had passed, the dice reached me. I felt good and I felt lucky, and most of all, I wanted to show off in front of Wadell. To let him know that his teaching me wasn't in vain I reached into my pocket and pulled out my roll and slung the $50 bill onto the table. "Fifty dollars, I shoot, houseman." The guys to the right of me anted up on my fifty dollars. Out of the corner of my eye, I could see Wadell and Tommy kind of laid back watching my next move. The houseman threw me the dice. I jacked them off, grabbed them up and jacked them ff again, one at a time. I was the two ones sticking up snake eyes. I knew under each one of those ones was the six, so as quickly as I could, I grabbed the one and stacked the six on top of the other one, shook them very slowly as I raised my arm up to my ear. I said, "Come on, dice, be nice to me tonight." I let them sail across the table. The soldiers marched again as I heard the houseman shut out. "Eleven, the winner!" "Don't get scared. A hundred dollars I'm shooting now. I'm just a young boy trying to make me some money." An older guy said, "You still got me faded?' He said, "No, well, I got the hundred. Let him shoot." I was rolling again. The dice stopped at six and three. "Nine," the houseman said. The man's point is nine. Get your bets down." I barred the nine for fifty dollars. "That's a bet," the old man said again and threw his fifty dollars to the houseman. I locked the dice on five and four and rolled them across the table and the dice stopped on five. "Nine," the houseman shouted, "the man's looking for nine." I started to sweat a little bit now. I was confident I could make that nine, so I licked them up again with six and three. This time, instead of making that roll, I came with the navy spin. The first dice stopped on four and the other dice spun for a second and stopped on five. "Nine," the houseman said. "Pay the man nine points!" The houseman took his cut and threw me the rest of the money. "What are you shooting now, young blood?" The houseman asked me. I peeled off a twenty and threw it back to him. "That's all you're shooting," one of the guys in the crowd asked. I wanted to go and see Maxine now, so I didn't give a damn about twenty. So, I just picked them up and threw them. "Eleven," the houseman said. I said, "Might as well let it all ride. Forty dollars, I shoot." Wadell said, "Let him shoot. I got it," and he looked at me. I threw the dice out. "Ten," the houseman said, "the point is ten." Wadell didn't ever try to catch the dice and I never tried to block the dice. I just picked them up and threw them. On the fourth roll, I sevened out. "Seven,' the houseman said and gave Wadell the money. Smitty had left the shoeshine parlor and had gone over to Henry's for his sandwich and coffee for the night. There were five or six people in the restaurant. Loraine was seated behind the counter smoking and Henry was standing by her at the register. Smitty struck up a conversation with Henry and watched Loraine's expression as he talked. "So, Henry," "Yeah," Henry turned back to face Smitty. "Did you see Al tonight, young pimp?" "That nigger was sharper than a razor tonight. Got a haircut, hair faded with brand-new clothes. Yeah, the nigger was greased lighting with them dice. Just won himself two or three hundred dollars. Yeah, he's very slick." He looked over at Loraine as he continued to talk. The game had come to an end as we all came out from behind the curtain, and passed Smitty as he was opening his coffee. His sandwich sat on the chair in front of him. The houseman gave Smitty the bag of money with the cuts in it. "I'll be back in about two hours, boss," he told Smitty. We were all outside walking toward Henry's Restaurant. "You handled yourself very well tonight," Tommy said. "Yes, Wadell said, you were really good tonight, but don't get too good that you stop practicing." "You got to keep practicing, and one day you might get to be as good as me." He patted me on my back and smiled as we entered the restaurant.

Loraine's expression seemed as though she was going to melt when she saw me. Her eyes were dreamy, and it seemed as though she wanted to just run and throw her arms around my neck. I spoke to her, "Hi." She spoke back, "Hi." All three of us sat in front booths. I sat beside Wadell, and Tommy sat in the booth on the other side of the table and watched me count my bankroll. It was about four hundred eighty dollars. Then Loraine was over at the table when I finished counting, she said, "Can I help you, gentlemen?" We said, "We're all ordering coffee." She went to get the coffee. I counted one hundred seventy-five dollars and put the rest of the money into my pocket. She was back with the coffee. I handed her the money and said, in a soft voice, "Thank you." She said, "What's this?" I said, "The money you loaned me." She said, "I didn't loan you any money. Yeah, I gave you the money to help yourself. You aren't in a position to pay me now. because you got a little money in your pocket." "I'm paying you while I got it so take it." She took the money and left. Tommy said, "You're a goddamn fool. You're a bigger fool than I thought. Here a woman gives you some money and tells you she doesn't want it back, but you are feeling so damn sorry for her that you make her take it back. You haven't listened to a damn thing that I and Wadell taught you. I don't know why Wadell calls you, "Little Pimp." It should be "Little Simp." Wadell didn't say a word. He just sat there and listened to Tommy scolding me and looking at the simple way I was looking back at Tommy. I sat there recognizing that they were my mentors and that I had fucked up again.

CHAPTER 30

The next three weeks, I would sit with Loraine in Sam's bar, and we would have two or three beers and take her home to fifty-Seventh and Wentworth. Our relationship was very good at that time. Gambling was good at that time. I didn't have to borrow any more money from Loraine. I managed to pay my rent on my own. It was the third week and she got off work. I said, "What are you drinking tonight" As we were walking out of the restaurant, she said, "I'm going to have one beer with you, Al. I have to go home early tonight. My momma is expecting me." I said, "Expecting you to do what at three o'clock in the morning?" "I don't know," she snapped back at me. "I'm just going to have one beer and go home." There was something funny about that. I felt like a rabbit was in my stomach. The nervousness in my stomach told me that she was lying. We ordered beer. I looked at the tall man coming through the front door of the lounge. It was Eddie. He was about six feet tall, dressed as the part of a player, dark-skinned like Wadell. He was about twenty-eight years old. He had only been here from Mississippi for three weeks. He had taken a liking to me, and I to him. He had a 1950 Buick, and we would it in there during the day. He would tell me about his dreams, and I'd tell him about mine.

He had taken Loraine. Home for me two or three times. I beckoned him over to the counter. "Hi, Eddie," I said "Hi, Al and Loraine," he said, smiling at her. I said, "Eddie, I know I told you that I wanted you to take Loraine home, but she just informed me that she wanted to take the bus." "So, what do you want to drink?" he said. "I'll take a beer," I told Bill to give him a beer. For about a week now, Bill had started letting me drink my beer at the bar. I believe it was because Wadell and Tommy asked him to, but he had always let me drink my beer in the BQ part of the bar. I said, "Eddie, if I buy the barbeque, would you go and get it" He said, "Sure." I said, "Get me a small end." He said OKAY, and he went to the BBQ part of the lounge with his beer. Loraine and I relaxed and were drinking our beer. I noticed she kept looking at the clock. I said, "Excuse me, but I got to go to the bathroom." She said, "Sure," I was through the hall, past the toilet, and was over to Eddie. He was seated at a table with some young lady in a booth across from him. I apologized to the lady for interrupting their conversation and blocked her view by pulling a chair up close to Eddie. "Listen, man, Loraine is on some bullshit. I believe she got another nigger or something." "Why did you say that?" Eddie asked. "I don't know, but where are you parked at?" "On the side by the paper stand." "Look, man, I'm going to give you five dollars, and when you get the BBQ, go out and start your car up. Stat tee, I'm going to go and put Loraine on the bus, and we were going to follow the bus." I was back with Loraine; she quickly finished her beer and sat with me for another fifteen minutes. We were out the door and crossing the street to the bus stop, I looked over my shoulder to see Eddie getting under the wheel of the Buick. "Is your mother sick, Loraine?" "No, Al, she just wants me to come home early. This is the first time since I've been seeing you that I had to go home early." "Is that bothering you?" I just stared at her, the bus opened the door and a lady and man stepped in before her. She said, "I'll see you tomorrow, Al." and kissed me on my lips.

It was snowing harder now as the bus pulled away from the curve heading south down Indiana. I ran back over to Eddie's car.

The light was in Eddie's favor. We turned the corner behind the bus, staying two or three car lengths behind the bus. 'We would stop and pull to the side when the bus stopped at each corner. It was not until we reached Thirty-Fifth Street at Redman's Lounge that Loraine got off the bus. "There she goes, there she goes," Eddie said. I said, "I see her." Eddie found a parking spot four car lengths from the corner. We waited. An hour had passed, and Loraine came back out of the lounge, but this time she wasn't alone. She was with a fat man who must have weighed three hundred pounds. They walked across to the other side of the street. The streetlight hit his face. I recognized him as Billy Bob, the BBQ man who owned the BBQ pit at Twenty-Sixth Street near Indiana, a big BBQ house. They waited on the corner there as though they were waiting on the bus and before long a jitney stopped in front of them. Loraine got in, then Billy Bob squeezed his fat ass in through the door and sat beside her. As the cab passed us on the opposite side of the street, Eddie and I scooted down in our seats. "Start the damn car up, Eddie."

The rabbit was getting bigger in my stomach now as I was mad and hurt at the same time. Mad because she had lied to me. Hurt because she was with another man. I didn't care if he was fat or skinny, he was still a man. Eddie swung the car into the street. The big car did a U-turn in the middle of the street behind the cab. When the cab slowed down, we would slow down, and when the cab picked up speed, we would pick up speed. It was a block and a half before the cab got wise to the fact that someone was following them. We were about half a block from Thirty-First Street when the light changed from red to green and the cab slowed down very slowly as we approached Thirty-first Street. The light was on caution now, yellow, when the cab accelerated quickly and went through it. When Eddie reached the light, it changed to red. Eddie put on brakes and slid into the street. Instead of going forward, he backed up. I could see the cab lights disappearing in the darkness. I was furious now. We drove down Indiana all the way to Twenty-fourths Street. Looking at every store, every tavern, every lounge, there was no cab in sight. I said, "What you got to do Eddie?" He said, "I'm with you." I said, "What time is it?" He said, "It's four-thirty in the morning." I said, "Take me to the bitch's house." Eddie drove to Fifty-Seventh and Wentworth. Loraine lived on the second floor. I rang the bell. Her mother came to the door. She was a nice, short, dark-skinned lady with gray streaks in her hair. She smiled at me, "Hello, Al." "Hello Ms. Lewis, is Loraine home/?" "No, she hasn't got home from work yet, Al. I thought you were er coming in. You didn't see her tonight?" "Yes, but I left early going elsewhere, but I think I know where she is. You have a good morning." We said our goodbyes.

I told Eddie to pull the car up the street. It was the sixth of January, and it was very cold. Eddie had cut the car off. We both had folded up in a knot trying to keep warm and try to get a nap while waiting for Loraine. I had dozed off. About a quarter to nine that same morning Eddie called to me, "Wake up, al, there's Loraine." I woke up straining my eyes and rubbing them. "Where is she?" "There she is getting out of that cab." We were about two doors north of her house. Her cab pulled in front of her house but was headed south across the street. She didn't see us. She got out of the cab and walked around to the front driver's window. She seemed to be laughing ad bullshitting with him as she laughed and walked away. The cab driver closed his window and drove away. She was halfway across the street when I opened my door and stepped out on the sidewalk. "Hey Loraine," she turned and faced me. "Come here." She walked up to me, and she was shocked to see me. "What are you doing here?" She asked. "I was very worried about you, baby," I said. "I told you it was nothing to worry about. I told you my mother just wanted to see me." "Eddie and I just got here." I opened the door for her. "Where are we going?" "Get in." She stepped into the rear seat. I stepped in behind her. "Smitty's restaurant, Eddie, I want to have some breakfast with Loraine." 'I really don't want no breakfast, Al. I'm tired and sleepy." I said," and funky."

"What are you talking about?" She asked me. I didn't say anything. I just sat there staring out the window. "Didn't you talk to my mother?" She asked. "No, I didn't, I told you I just got here." "She would have told you that she felt bad and that I had to go and get her these aspiring that are in my purse." "She has really bad headaches, migraines." "But I asked you distinctly before we left the bus stop was your mother sick and you said no!" "You know what I mean. She wasn't sick, she has like headaches." "Well, anyway, baby, whatever it was we going to have breakfast anyway, baby, just you and me." The car was crossing Indiana. "So, you came straight home last night and got your mother's aspirins?" "Yes, what is the big deal about aspirins and headaches if you would have gone up and rug the ell, my mother would have told you that she had a headache." "That's okay, baby, are going to have breakfast together at Henry's." Me and Eddie's eyes met in the rearview mirror. "Park by Smitty's if you can find a parking place." We were sitting on Twenty-ninth Street waiting for the light to change. The light changed and Eddie parked in front of Smitty's shoeshine Parlor. It was January, and it was very cold outside. All the trees that stood in the yard had ice cycles hanging from them. The sign on Henry's Restaurant and TJ's Grocery Store had ice cycles hanging from them. The old fire barrel that sat in between Smitty's Shoeshine Parlor and Henry's Restaurant looked lonely in the snow. I said, "I'll see you in Henry's, Eddie." He said, "Ok, Al,"

I said, "Come on, Loraine." She said, "What are we going back here for?" I said, "We're going back here because maybe you want to tell me of the truth about where the fuck you been all night." "Now, wait a minute, Al. I told you where I been, and you are not my daddy or my husband." "No, bitch, I ain't neither one of them, I thought I was your man," as that right hand came up and cracked her beside her jaw. It was a sharp right hook. I had never hit a woman before, nor a girl, but she shouldn't have been fucking with my feelings like that. I had great respect for her, she had almost taken Marina's place in my heart, but now she had ruined all that. I could feel the coldness in my heart for her lying to me and hurting my feelings. She had my heart beating fast as she sat here lying to me like I was a damn fool or something. Now the thoughts of how she had played me, even when Tomy and the guys told me that I was a simp, not a pimp for giving her back her money, I still gave her the money back. I saw her as my girlfriend, not a hoe. The blow shocked her as she fell backwards to the ground. Her legs went up in the air and her purse fell four or five feet away from her. It was open and all her lipstick, powder puff, mirror and money fell to the ground. There were tens and twenties scattered everywhere. I said, "What is this, bitch? Where did you get all this money?" She was trying to get up, but she was slipping back down into the snow. She was looking at me. I could see the blood trickling from her nose. I had grabbed a hand full of those twenties. I said, "what is this, bitch? Where did you get this money from?" And that right hand caught her again and she went back down for the second time. I went into that transformation again. I had seen a tree limb about five feet long lying there in the snow with ice cycles on it. She was lying on the ground on her butt trying to get herself situated. I could see blood still trickling from her nose. I said, "Answer me, bitch before I kill you with this tree branch. You're hoeing, ain't you, bitch?"

I was a good judge of distance as I drew the limb back. "You better answer me, bitch, before I bust your head." I swung the branch about two or three inches away from her head and hit the garbage cans and made large bang. I spoke. "Let me tell you what you did," speaking a little calmer, "You stopped at Smitty's Lounge, stayed in thee for an hour with that big fat elephant looking mother fucker, then you came out and caught a cab, and yes, the cab driver got wise that someone was following him. Yes, that was me and 'Eddie. At four-thirty this morning I was knocking on your mother's door, she hadn't seen your ass, but you came home at a quarter to nine telling me you went to get some mother fucking baby aspirins." "You done made me fall in love with your mother fucking ass, but you will put me down for a hippopotamus mother fucker like the barbeque man. Now, do you want to tell me what's going on or, are you going to make me bust your head with this tree limb?" "He doesn't mean anything to me, nobody means anything to me but you, baby. I'm a hoe, and I was a hoe when you met me." "You should 've told me this when we first met," I said, helping her from the ground. I dusted the snow from her coat, picked up her lipstick, powder puff, and mirror and placed all her things back in her purse except for the money. "Wel, Loraine, there's no sense in being a part-time hoe, so you can tell Henry this morning that you quit." "Okay, she sniffled.

CHAPTER 31

Loraine was fast, and she was smart. She didn't need me like a lot of girls needed their pimps watching her and being around her. Our understanding was that every night she met me between eight o'clock and ten o'clock at the 114 Club. The money was coming two and three hundred dollars a day. It seemed like I went shopping every day for myself. I bought shirts, ties, suits, and shoes. I remembered how sharp my father had dressed and everywhere in the back of my mind, I tried to out dress him. I had a nine-hundred-dollar bankroll as I sat in ''Eddie's car at Twenty-Sixth and Indiana, parked to the curb waiting on my mother to get off the bus. Finally, the bus that she was on stopped; four or five people stepped off the bus before she stepped off. She was happy to see me. Tears were in her eyes as she hugged my neck. We were inside of the fat man's barbecue pit at a table. I had ordered a slab of ribs for her dinner. I gave her the three hundred dollars and told her that it would be more money each week. I met her at the barbeque pit every Friday at the same time, about five-thirty. I told her that I was a waiter downtown and had a good job, for her not to worry about me. She told me that my father had forgotten about that night and that he was worried too, and he needed me home. She almost begged me to come back home, and I eased her mind by telling her that I would come back in time. I told her that I missed my whole family and missed them. "Oh, al, before I forget, she said, "have you talked to Maring?" I said, “No, I haven’t.” “She really has been worried about you. She’s been coming down to the house two and three times a week.” “Well, tell her that you saw me, and I’ll be by to see her shortly,” I said. Her food was bagged. I kissed her on the jaw, and she was on her way home.

It was another Saturday, and I had just finished my visit to the barber. My hair was trimmed nicely. My hair shined from beneath the brim of the tan beaver hat. I had on a patch flannel suit and brown shoes with buttonholes. It was time to go and see Marina. It was a sunny winter day as I turned the corner on Twenty-Ninth and Prairie. She was happy to see me. Here were a thousand questions and a thousand good answers. “Yeah, I was a waiter, and no, I didn’t live with no woman.” “Al,” she said, “it’s been so long without. I waited so long that Wednesday, but you never did show up. Joe Baby went back to California after I told him it wouldn’t work. I told him that I was in love with you.” She asked me to spend the night. I looked at the clock on the dresser. It said sic for-five. I knew hat I had to meet Loraine at the 114 Club at eight o’clock, so right away, I said, “Tis is one of my biggest night f or a party.” She said, where ae you are working?” I said, “The Palmer House. You should see those big rooms there.” She said, “I bet they are beautiful.” “The bathrooms are bigger than the rooms.” “They are?” she said “Yes,” I said, lying. I had never been inside of the lobby of the Palmer House, but I went on describing the rooms as if I had been in them. I looked at her as I got up from the chair to get my coat and hat. She was a real, smooth, and pretty girl. She had on a nightgown where the buttons were open form the tail of it and halfway up her thighs. I could tell that she was disappointed with my answer. If it were true that she told Joe Baby that night that it was over between them and if it was true that she was waiting for me to come back to her, then she had to be burning up and probably cursing me out inside her mind. And wondering was I lying about the other women. She knew how she looked, like a fresh peach and a nigger like me, that hadn't seen her in two or three months just couldn't walk away from her without a knot in his pants. She broke my thoughts. "Maybe tomorrow," she said, "maybe you can spend the night tomorrow." "Maybe," I said, and leaned over and kissed her on the jaw. It was a quarter to eight when I caught the jitney in front of Sam's and headed to Thirty-first Street.

The next day at about four o'clock in the afternoon, I sat at the bar in Sam's Tavern with a young lady named Blanch. I had tried to pull Blanch two or three times to be on my team, but she would always say "I don't want Loraine cutting on me. That girl looks like she would kill a mother fucker about you. But I tell you what, Al," she looked at me, "give me a little more time and I'll let you know." She sipped her beer. There were about seven or eight people in the tavern and I sipped my gin and orange juice. Once again, the same nervous feeling I had when I was afraid or in danger of something came over me. As I sat there wondering why I was feeling this way, I turned my head toward the door. My stomach shook as I saw danger standing in the corner by the door staring at me with daggers in his eyes. I said damn and dropped my glass from my hand. I quickly looked around the room, but everybody in there seemed to be strangers now except for Blanch. Even the bartender was a different bartender. He started walking toward me. Blanch was saying something, but I didn't hear her. I was watching him come closer and closer. Everybody around me, if they had been looking at him would have just seen a man approaching me. ''but to me, I saw a big ball-headed bitch with red panties on. "Hi 'Al," he said as he approached me. "Hi, I answered, sounding like the bitch I thought he was. "I'd like to speak to you for a moment, please, on the outside," he said. "Speak p," I said, "you can talk to me here." "No, honey, I said on the outside," sounding more and more like a drag queen. I was off the stool because I didn't want him to get any louder.

"I'll be right back, 'Blanch," I said. She said, "Okay, Al," and sipped her beer. I said, "We can go back to the barbeque pit if you want to." He followed me through the hallway to the other side of the tavern to the fish and barbeque house. I started for the booths or a table, but he said, "No, honey, not in here. I said outside," and headed for the door. I slowly followed him but hesitated to step outside when we got to the door. "Listen, Menard, if this is about your twenty dollars, I'm sorry I didn't bring it back to you. But the thing is that I went to jail that night." He was holding the door and facing me. I stood on the inside of the door, and he stood on the outside, holding the door. I could see the tears in his eyes as he said, "You're telling a damn lie! You just told a goddamn lie and took my money! I don't want to hear anything bout no jail!" "Well, I could give you your money back." "I don't care about no damn money; I don't like no mother fucker trying to make a damn fool out of me!" He was holding the door open with his right hand. I looked from his right hand to his left hand. He had the knife halfway up his sleeve, but I could see the shiny part of it as he tried to cuff it in in his hand. And he said, "I don't like no mother fucker to make a goddamn fool of me." And he began to get louder and louder. "Oh, here you are," a voice said from behind me, and I felt a hand on my shoulder. It was like God speaking from heaven and when I looked up and saw Eddie, his hand slipped off my shoulder as he kind of moved in front of me. "what's going on?" Eddie asked. I said, "tell him, Eddie, that I've been to jail and that I will give him back the twenty dollars." Eddie looked at me as I stared at his left hand. Then Eddie noticed the knife. Menard went on talking. He's not in the damn conversation. I'm talking to you and I don' t want no damn twenty dollars." "Then what do you want?" Eddie asked and looked hard at him and pushed me to the side. With one lift of his arm, he unbuttoned his coat, and there, tucked in his belt, you could see the black handle of a .38. Menard looked at Eddie and then at me, standing and looking from behind Eddie. "I'll see you again, Al. I'll talk to you again. "There'll be another day." "Come back and get your twenty dollars and let's all be friends,' 'Eddie said. He said, "I don't want no damn twenty dollars." I turned to see Blanch peeping out into the hallway. "Didn't I tell you, Eddie, that he wanted to cut him? I've seen him cut a guy on Twenty-Sixth Street. I told you to come back here." I thanked Blanch. "You ain't fucked that sissy, have you, Al?" I said, "No. That's the reason he wanted to cut me." We walked back to the lounge for another drink.

CHAPTER 32

I had just finished eating breakfast at Henry's. I was sitting on the stool looking out the window when an old lady came in and sat by me. She was Mrs. Reed, an elderly lady who stayed on the first floor across the alley from my hotel room, the Buick. She spoke to me. "Hello there, my you look nice," she said, smiling at me. I said, Hello, Mrs. Reed. Are you still throwing bones to my rooming partner?" I went on talking. "I haven't seen him lately." "No, you wouldn't have seen him. The dog catchers took him away three weeks ago. The people in the building called the dog catcher because he was hit by a car, and he would drag his back parts when he walked. There was nothing we could do for him., so we called the pound." I sat there listening to her with tears in my eyes, wondering if it was my fault that they were going to make soap out of him. I should've come back for him, but where would I take him: the landlady didn't want dogs in the house. I had to get up and go before I busted out crying in front of this lady. The waitress was there taking her order. "Give her what she wants," I said., it's on me." I placed a ten-dollar bill in front of Mrs. Reed and said my goodbyes and left out of the door.

It was a brisk and cool day as I walked the block to Leroy's. There were only four of five guys there at the crap table. We all wolfed each other. The big game had folded and when I got there. They were only shooting two or three dollars. I played around with them for an hour, then headed for the 114 Club. When I reached the club, there were only about seven or eight people there. Most of them I knew. They waved and bowed their heads. Black Sam came in after I had ordered m gin and orange juice. Zhe was s Thirty-First Street's famous pimp. He had on a big gangster-like felt hat that was rolled all the way around like a cowboy hat. The overcoat he wore was black and his black shoes sparkled beneath his pants. I sat there watching him as he drank his Tom Collins. I guessed his age to be thirty-six to thirty-eight years old. You could see an expensive watch and rings when his hands went up as he drank from his glass. The word was out that he had eleven girls on the street, and it seemed as though it was getting damned hard for me to get two.

After a while, he was gone; and as I sipped on my gin and orange juice, I thought about Loraine and Marina. Why did I think of Marina as the good girl and Loraine as he bad girl??? Was it because I knew what Loraine was doing? What about Marina? I had her on our first date, my first try. What made her different from Loraine? Why hadn't I thought about putting her on the street, or was Tony right? I was a simp, not a pimp. My heart was too soft. Anytime a man would damn near boohoo over a dog. He had to be soft. Oh, what the hell, I thought as I ordered another drink. I had drunk two or three shots when the bartender called me over to the phone. "Telephone for you, Al." I went over to the corner to the phone near the bar. It was Loraine. She wouldn't see me until twelve. I started back for the stool, but heard a voice call me from the booth. "Hi, Al, come over here for a minute please." It was pretty from Twenty-Ninth Street, Little Daddy's woman. She was sitting in the booth across from two real light-complexioned women, both of them were dressed really sharp. I approached the booths. Hi, Al, how are you doing?" Prett said, looking up at me. I said, "Fine," looking over at her girlfriend. She patted the seat beside her and said, "Sit down." I sat. "Al, this is my beautician, Mabel. See my hair. Don't I look pretty?" She shook her head and turned for me to see the back of it. "What are you drinking" Mabel asked.

"I was drinking gin and orange juice," I said. Mabel called out to the bartender and ordered drinks for the table. Mabel kept smiling at me as Pretty as I made small talk. "I sure would like to do your hair." She smiled at me. "In fact, I would like to do you period, so Pretty tells me you have that little girl, Loraine. Is that our woman?" Mabel asked. "Yes, you can say that. She's the only one I've got so far." "You're looking at a cinch winner when you look at me," she said, raising her eyebrows at me. "I can hardly wait," I said. She answered, well, you won't have to wait long. Just until tomorrow evening at about ten. What are you doing then?" "Having a drink at the Glass Bar Lounge, that's where I'll be at ten," I said, looking in her eyes. "We just stopped in here for a quick drink. I have more heads to do. Are you ready, Pretty?" She asked and raised from the table. I got up and let Pretty out the booth, and they were taller than me. Two tall stallions the men would say. They both were tall, had average-size hips but big legs and big buttocks. Their waists were small and with the big belts they wore, you could see the shape of their hips. I was stepping up in high cotton as Wadell and Tommy would say, and I knew it. Little Daddy was a topnotch pimp. When Pretty would go out of town hoeing, she would bring him back thousands not hundreds. Man, man, I wonder just how much money this beautician could bring back if I sent her out of town, I was thinking as I stepped into the cab. I had to find Wadell and Tommy now.

It was about three o'clock in the afternoon the next day when I caught up with Tommy and Wadell. Peter Rabbit had two tricks at the crap table. They were trimming. Peter Rabbit had the dice as I nodded to Wadell and Tomy. Peter Rabbit was saying, "Come on, dice, I've got to go and buy groceries for my house. My baby needs milk. Be lucky for me." He raised them to his ear and shook them.

His hands went up, and the dice sailed across the screen. "Seven'" the houseman said. "You've got two hundred dollars here, what are you going to do? Wadell said, "Let him shoot. We got him, haven't we?" Wadell said looking at the two strangers. "I've got thirty up here," Wadell said. Tommy said, "I've got twenty." And one of the strangers said, "We've got the rest, let him shoot," and threw the hundred fifty dollars of the table. Peter grabbed the dice, clicked them two or three times in his hands, brought them up to his ear and shook them. "Just one more time for hour daddy, baby, just one more time." The dice came out once again. "Eleven!" the houseman said. Winner! Pay the man!" tommy reached and grabbed the dice off the table. The two strangers watching Peter Rabbit count the money didn't see Tommy when he switched the fixed off the table. "We need a fresh pair of dice," Tommy said, "these are too lucky." The stranger grabbed the dice and looked at them and then threw them to the houseman. "Okay, Peter, what are you shooting now?"

"Shoot any part of the money." "Who's got him faded?" One of the strangers named James looked at his partner. He said, "I'm tapped man, you got any money?" "No, he got me on the last throw." The game ended. James and his partner headed ot to the front door. I followed them because I knew Peter Rabbit, Wadell, and Tommy would be splitting the money in the back of Smitty's Shoeshine Parlor. It wasn't long before Tommy, Wadell, and I were sitting in the booths at the BBQ house. I told them I wanted to be alone with them because I had some questions. We had brought our drinks to the back. Wadell was sipping his drink. I sat with Tommy facing Wadell. "So, what is it?" Tommy asked. "What's on your mind Little Pimp?' "I met one of Pretty's friends. Little Daddy's Pretty." "Yeah, we know Pretty," Tommy said. "What about her?" "She introduced me to one of her friends, a real fine chick and she hit on me. I mean really hit on me. She said she wanted to do me. So, when I meet her what should I do?" "What do you mean, what should you do?" Wadell asked. "I mean when I buy her drinks, should I try to take her to a hotel? What should I do, man?" "You can answer your own question on that, Al. How many weeks was it before you asked Loraine to the hotel The same rule applies to this girl. Just as it did to Loraine or to any other hoe. You don't let your little head overrule your big head. A pimp's job is to get money, not a pussy. When you start thinking about getting pussy first, then your dick is doing the thinking for you. And when a woman finds out that your dick is in control, you're not going to get a dime. Why did you ask us this, Al? What is the real reason behind these questions?' Wadell said, looking at me very seriously. "I mean, man, what I'm really trying to ask is what do I do? How do I fuck her to make her feel good? I'm telling you, man, this is a stallion, a big bitch. Big ass, big legs, I never had a woman this big before. What do I do?"

"Look, Al," Tommy said, "all women are the same from a fucking midget to a giant. First of all, you have to remember. When you admire a woman, you can feel the knot rise in your pants and that woman knows when you are aroused because she can see the knot. But you never know when that knot on a woman is aroused unless you touch her and feel that she is wet. So, my thing is I don't ever believe that they're ready until I make them ready, and how you make them ready is by caressing them, kissing them, squeezing them softly, rubbing their legs, kissing them on their tits, sucking them, sucking their navels." "Sucking their navels!" I shouted. "You mean kissing their navels?" "Well, Tommy looked at me and said that, will come in time for you. Let's start with the tits, then you let your fingers do the walking with the little man in the boat." I said, "What little man in the boat?" What the hell are you talking about?" Tommy looked at me seriously and said, "I'm talking about the lady's clitoris, that sits right at the top of her vagina and for you,

Al, right at the top of her pussy." Wadell said, "And when she starts begging you to fuck her, Al, that's when you know she's ready. Now that is it, Al, 'cuz I've got to go, I've got a date." He dropped the twenty-dollar bill on the table for Tommy. "Pay for the drinks and get you all another one. Don't teach him too much in one night. I have to go."

"You see, Al, the name of the game is to satisfy, not testify. Your main thing with your woman is to satisfy her. You got some dangerous tricks. And pimps to here. They will eat ten yards of your woman's shit but will never tell you what he's doing to his woman. So, you will have to stay on top of your game. Whatever you do to your woman, make sure you do it right. Stay on top of it. This is a muddy, shitty world out here when it comes to sex, but if you are a coldhearted stomp-down pimp, you can perform and absorb all of it. 'But if you are not down with the game, some of the acts will make you throw up." The next night I met Mabel at the Glass Bar. Had arrived there at nine-thirty. She got there at ten. She was dressed in pink, and it looked really gorgeous on the dress. Her hazel eyes winked at me. She sat on the stool beside me. "Hi Al, she said, passing me the money with a rubber band around it. "Can I have a drink?" she asked me. I called the bartender. "Give her what she wants," I said. I excused myself and went into the men's room. Inside the men's room, I counted her money. Five hundred dollars, I smiled to myself and thanked God and all the people responsible for the money. I had to think and think fast, while I was in that washroom of how I was going to ditch Mabel. I knew that she wanted to go to the hotel. I really wanted to go too. She was very pretty tonight, but I couldn't let her know this. I seated myself back on the stool beside her. She was sipping her drink as I ordered another gin and orange juice. "Did do all right for you, Al?" she asked, looking at me seriously. "You did fine," I said, looking back at her. "/

did do well enough for us to get out of her and go around to the Hermonia?" I said "No, baby, not tonight. I've got a couple of runs to make, and then I 've got to meet Loraine at twelve o'clock at the 114 Club. She's coming from Evanston tonight with a thousand dollars." I looked directly into her eyes and lied through my teeth. If her panties had the hots for me, I was going to damn near let them burn up before I soothed them. I bought her a couple more rounds of drinks. After I had whispered plenty of shit into her ear, I had her smiling when I walked out of the door. Mabel had dumped three other times to me before I took her to Hermonia. She was a big broad with smooth skin and all. I lay there and stroked her with caresses, kisses, and foreplay. She dug her nails into my back and whispered softly in my ear, "I need you, baby, I need you, baby, I need you now," as I penetrated her opening.

CHAPTER 33

For the next three weeks, during the day, I practiced throwing the dice for three or four hours a day in my room alone on my bed. Iwas getting better and faster as the days went by. I would eat my breakfast at Henry's Restaurant every day at seven-thirty. I would catch Wadell coming in from work sometimes during the weekends. Tommy and Bob would be in there after they had stayed up all night from gambling or whatever. We all would talk about the past events that we had the night before. The little breakfast event would break up at about nine-thirty and each of us would go our separate ways.

I would practice until one or two o'clock and then I would change clothes and go and see Marina. She was sitting on the porch looking very neat in blue. "You look very good today," she said, jumping up and throwing her arms around me and you smell good, too." I thanked her and sat in the chair beside her on the porch. Our thing each day would be to pick out the picture how that we were going to go to. We would hold hands and walk to Thirty-Fifth Street on our way to the Lewis Theater. We would buy hot dogs or hot tamales on our way to the show, and we would slip them into her purse before we went into the show. We would laugh about the food being in her purse when we ordered pops from the pop counter inside the theater. On other days we would go to Thirty-First Street Beach. She would swim so she would go way out into the water and kick up her feet and float half the back. She would leave me in the shallow water with the four-year-old kids because I wasn't going any further. I couldn't swim and I wasn't about to learn. She would come back to me and dash water on me and I would dash water on her, laughing and tickling each other. Then, we would go and lay on the towel on the sandy part of the beach, and I would tell her how much I loved her. And the serious part of it, this love affair, was that I did love her very dearly.

That Friday, I had met with my mother at the BBQ pit on Twenty-Sixth Street. She told me that my father was really ill. I got her favorite dish BBQ ribs, and we walked back to 2720 South Prairie. I was happy to see my father and he likewise was happy to see me. I could hardly talk to him for my sister and brother pulling after me and laughing and talking, glad and happy to see me. I told my father the same lie that I was a waiter at the Palmer House. He thought that we had something in common because he worked at the Stevenson Hotel on eight and Michigan in the linen department. We were both hotel men. I told him I really wanted to come home but there wasn't enough room here. And that I could be of more help to him on the outside that I could on the inside because sometimes the hours I had would disturb him cause he had to get up early in the morning and he knew that. He didn't want to give in, but he finally did. I gave him two hundred dollars and asked him if there was anything else he needed to send Francis to get me. I said hello to my uncles who were sitting at the table, kissed my mother and left. When I came out of the vestibule, two or three ladies from the building were seated on the round banisters on the front porch, including Mrs. Betty Rogers. I said, "how are you ladies doing today?" "How are you doing, 'al?" Mrs. Betty asked. I said, "I'm doing fine and how is Mr. Tim?" "He's fine also," she said. I gave another smile and nodded to the rest of the ladies and left the porch. Mrs. Betty seemed older to me. The whiskey was taking its toll. I wish I could have explained to her why I really stopped coming to visit. But what the hell, that was yesterday and today is today, and life goes on with one more roll of the dice. I turned on the sidewalk and walked toward Twenty-Ninth Street. When I reached Twenty-Ninth Street, Sam's Lounge was crowded. Music was playing and the people were talking, laughing, and drinking across the room. Gathered together, sitting at one table were Karen and her gangster-like husband. He was dressed really sharp and had a bulldog-like face with no expression. Little Daddy and Pretty, and they always dressed sharp, and Mabel sat next to Pretty sipping on her Martini. She saw me when I walked through the door. "here's my baby," she said, looking at me and pointing to the chair that sat on the other side of her. My eyes glanced at the table as I walked to the chair, but my focus was on Karen who threw daggers at me with her eyes.

I started for the chair. But before I reached the chair, two shots rang out in the back of the BBQ house. You heard screams coming from the rear, then two or three people ran from the back through the hallway into the lounge. Then there came Lee out of the back. Some guy hollered over to Lee, "What happened back there, Lee? "Some fellow got shot. Everybody is still in the back. Some went out the side door. Ralph is in the kitchen calling the police." "Let's get the hell out of here," Karen's old man said to Little Daddy. "It won't be long before the police will be here." Mabel looked over at me and said, "I'm riding with Little Daddy and Pretty. Meet me at the 114 Club."

CHAPTER 34

It was about ten o'clock when I reached the 114 Club. The lounge was crowded. Some people were crowded around the pinball machine. They had a nice game going there. Mabel was sitting in a booth near the rear with some man and woman sitting across from her. I sat beside her. I hadn't heard from Loraine and had really lost track of time. I was having a toast with Mabel when I heard the voice behind me. "So, this is what you be doing while I'm out here making your money and ducking the police. You are sitting here having drinks with this half-white bitch." I turned to look at Loraine standing there. She had daggers in her eyes as she stared at Mabel. "Who are you calling a bitch?" Mabel said, looking up at her and getting ready to stand. But the beer bottle that Loraine had snatched from the table beside us had smashed into her head. Mabel screamed out to me as the blood dropped to her neck. This was some really serious shit. I had never seen anything like this before. "You're next, mother fucker. I'm going to cut your ass everywhere but the bottom of your feet, motherfucker!" She was fumbling in her purse as I tried to slide out of that booth past her. One quick glance at Mabel holding her head and crying, I went past Loraine as I straightened up. Loraine said, "You ain't getting away, motherfucker." And I felt my belt snap in the back of my pants. The razor she had went through my suit coat and cut my belt in half in two but did not touch my skin. She drew her arm back again. I felt my pants falling from the rear, but I quickly gathered them up in the front with my right hand. I moved quickly out of the way of the razor as it came down again. I had opened the door now and was on the sidewalk. She said, "You'd better run motherfucker because I'm going to kill you when I catch you!" I tightened up my pants and headed for Michigan Avenue. I ran as fast as I could. I could hear those heels behind me. It reminded me of the lady when I had snatched her purse. I could hear Loraine saying, "I better not catch your ass!" I could hear those heels behind me, and I could hear the crowd behind Loraine cheering her on saying "Kill that mother fucker!"

My heart pounded as I rushed down Michigan Avenue. I had never been that scared in my life, not even when I was hiding in the space behind the stove naked. My life depended on me getting away and if I had to leave these pants, that's what I was going to do. I knew the neighborhood, an eight-foot tin fence ran about thirty feet, hiding a vacant lot. In the middle of the fence, a gate sat about five feet back off the sidewalk. You couldn't see the gate by just looking down at Michigan, but knowing the neighborhood, I knew about the opening and that was my advantage. Loraine had hesitated and turned to face the crowd holding the razor up overhead. She turned around and said, "I'm going to really fuck him up." She reached down to take off her shoes. She didn't see me when I turned and went through the opening through the vacant lot. The fence was down on the other side of the lot. I went through the alley to the next street and over through the next alley. Not seeing Loraine in the night, I took my time and walked home. Once in the apartment, I dressed rather quickly into blue jeans. I grabbed a sweater and a small jacket and headed back to Twenty-Ninth Street. It was about one-thirty now. Sam's closes at two o'clock. I walked past the Prairie Hotel. I stayed in the dark, keeping in the shadows. As I came close to 'Sam's, I could see the paper stand. Then I saw

Loraine. Across from Loraine was Wadell standing at the door of the lounge on the sidewalk. I was approaching the alley now. When I turned right into the alley, then I turned left into the gangway behind Smitty's Shoeshine Parlor. I was in the vacant lot now where the fire barrel was, although the fire barrel had nothing burning in it, but a two-by-four laid against it. I reached and got the two-by-four and walked around the corner by Henry's Restaurant. I hugged the walls of the restaurant until I got to the window of the lounge. I walked slowly to the corner of the building. I hesitated from that corner because the door was right on the other side. I heard Wadell say, "Well, why do you want to kill him, Loraine? Why don't you just leave him alone?" "Cuz that motherfucker is two-timing me with that half-white bitch and I'm risking my life out here for him. Yeah, I'm going to kill him." She was waving that razor in the air, showing Wadell her razor when I stepped around the corner. Her back was to me. 'Wadell could see me as I tiptoed up behind her. I raised the two-by-four and carefully aimed the two-by-four at the fat part of her buttocks. I shouted as the two-by-four connected to her body, "If I don't kill you first bitch. My voice and the blow from the two-by-four shocked her. I was careful not to hit her on the lower part of her back, but the two-by-bour connected right where I wanted it to. The razor slid across the sidewalk. The blow scared her and knocked her off balance. She tried to break and run. But in shock, she ran right up against the paper stand. I was right behind her with that two by four. It's my turn now bitch! I'm fixing to kill you." The two-by-four came over her head and hit the paper stand with a bang. "Don't kill me!" She screamed out. I said, "I'm fixing to kill your ass bitch," as she slid back down the paper stand wall. She tried to duck. She slipped to the ground in a sitting position with her hand in the air, begging me not to hit her with that two-by-four that I had drawn back. Other people had come out of the lunge now looking on. I could see Wadell with a smirk on his face. He knew I was on the stage again playing my part to the hilt. I hope he knew that I would never hurt her with the two-by-four. I went on with my bluff. "Bitch, I'm fixin' to bust your damn head 'cuz you will never pull a razor on me again you nappy-headed bitch!" I raised the two-by-four even higher. "Don't hit me," she said! "I'm sorry."

"Drop that goddamn two-by-four nigger before I blow your goddamn brains out!" "Drop it, "another cop said. I turned to see two black officers. They had their squad car to the curb and had their pistols drawn. I lowered the two-by-four. One officer put his gun away, while the other one kept his out. The one that put his gun away came and twisted my arms behind me and put handcuffs on me. When I was handcuffed, the other officer put his gun away and helped Loraine. The other one said, "Who are you supposed to be nigger, a pimp or something? I wish that was my sister. I'd blow our fucking head off. "They pushed me into the squad car and told the people from the tavern to break it up and go on about their business. The officer who helped Loraine told her that they were taking me to Prairie. The Prairie Police Station was across from the Prairie Hotel and if she wanted to press charges, she could come on over there. She said she did want to press charges. Once in the police station, I was put into the bullpen with two other fellas. One guy was in there for wife abuse, and the other guy had an accident in his car without a driver's license. We all took turns trying each other's cases. My case seemed to be the worst one, we thought because Loraine had said she was going to sign a complaint against me. The guy with the wife abuse was sure his wife would drop the charges when he came in front of the judge, and the guy without a driver's license would probably get probation. We were still kicking our problems around from one to the other. We had been there about two hours when he turn-key walked up to the cell and called me out by name, "Al 'wynn." I said, "Yes" jumping up off the bench, "You're going home, no charges have been filed against you." Loraine was waiting for me on the bench in the hallway inside the police station. I found out later that she had tricked with both officers, there was no charge and no trial. We caught a cab on our way to Thirty-First Street to Powell's Restaurant for breakfast.

CHAPTER 35

For the next two days, I sat on the BBQ side of Sam's with Wadell, Tommy, and 'drug store Bob. We all were talking about the killing that had taken place. It appears one man had come from Forty-Third Street to get some BBQ and caught his wife there with another man. An argument started, and the husband had drawn his gun and killed the boyfriend. Wadell was looking at Tommy now, "Wasn't there something that you wanted to tell Al, Tommy?" "Oh yes, Little Pimp. I used to have that girl that you got named Mabel three or four years ago. She will start off really nice to you with the money and all. She's a sweet girl at first until I found that her money was going into her veins and now, I found out she is a bigger dope fiend and she is trying to deal dope for Karen on 'thirty-first street." Wadell said, "She's big trouble, Little Pimp. You're fixin' to blow a star like Loraine for a nothing-ass bitch like Mabel. It's time for you to step away from her. When you are out there, you've got to get a clean hoe, clean of vices like Loraine. You have found a hoe who loves you. Not for your money, not for your dope, but you, like Loraine." "I'll tell you whom you should cop, "Drug Store Bob said, "She makes plenty of money on the quiet side. Little Daddy's trying to pull her, but she hasn't chosen yet. "Who are you talking about?" Wadell asked. "I'm talking about Blanch. If he can pull Blanch, then," I've been watching her myself. "Oh, I have put in a bid for her already," I told Bob. Putting in a bid is not copping her," Bob said. “I’ll give you two weeks. If you cop with her, I’ll give you two hundred dollars. If you miss it, you give me two hundred dollars.”

I said, “Bet.” Bob said, “You heard that, didn’t you, Wadell, Tommy, you heard that?” Tony said, “Yes, I did, too.” I hit Sam’s Tavern early that evening dressed in blue with a black shirt on, and a black Dobbs hat. I had put on some expensive cologne and had massaged my face with Noxzema, giving my face that powdery look. I was out to make sure that those hundred dollars that me and Bob had had bet. On. It wasn’t so much about the two hundred dollars, but it was the challenge. Bob had challenged me in front of Wadell and I didn’t like that very much. Then again, I wanted Blanch for myself. She has a nice smile and a nice plump buttock. She was quiet and very petite. I looked around the room and only saw Deloris sitting at the bar. I joined her. I said, “Damn, how are you doing, Deloris? Where is everybody?” I asked her, and at the same time told the bartender to refill her drink and give me one too. “A gin, a double shot,” I told him. “Where is Blanch at, Deloris?” “I haven’t seen her in two or three days.” “No, you wouldn’t have seen her because she’s off on Tuesdays and sometimes on Fridays. “She also works at the Bear Cat Lounge on Thirty-First and Giles. Didn’t you know that, Al?” she asked me. I finished my drink, and before long, I was in a jitney on my way to the Bear Cat Lounge.

I got into the booth and ordered a drink, my eyes searching the room for Blanch. It was a rowdy place. People were hollering and laughing loudly. The waitress came back with my drink. I paid her and asked her “Where is Blanch.” She said, “She’s in the kitchen taking a smoke.” I asked her to tell Blanch I was here, tipped her, and he was well on her way. I sipped on my drink and someone in the place loved Billy Holliday because I could hear singing.

Living for you is easy, living is easy to live when you’re in love,
And I’m so in Love, there’s nothing in life but you, to you maybe,

I'm a fool, but it is fun; some people say you move me with one wave of your hand; Darling that's grand they just don't understand that I am living for you.

"Were you looking for me?" Blanch asked me with a half-cut apron wrapped around her waist. She had on black pants and a red blouse. Her hair was freshly done, and she had a big, beautiful smile on her face. I said, "Yes, darling, I was looking for you. You and nobody but you." I asked her to sit down. I asked, "Can you have a drink with me?" She said, "Just one and it will be time for me to go back to work." I said, "One will be fine." We ordered a drink, and Billie Holiday was still singing.

"I'm a fool, but it's fun. People say you move me with one wave of your hand.

Darling that's grand; they just don't understand that I'm living for you. It's easy to live when you're in love and I'm so in love; There's nothing in life but you."

I grabbed Blanch by her hands and rubbed them softly as I looked deep into her brown eyes and asked, "Did you know that I was in love with you, Blanch? And did you know that I need you so much in my life it hurts? You know how long I've been out here and I'm not in love with Loraine. Although she's a good girl, but I need you." Why do you think you need me, Al?" She asked me, looking back at me. "I just told you. I'm in love with you and it's hurting me to not let you know this, but most of all, I need you. You don't have anyone else, do you?" I asked her while staring her right in the eyes. "No, I don't have anyone. Me and my boyfriend had broken up about two weeks before you had that argument with that sissy. You picked a hell of a time to tell me, and I'm leaving tonight on my vacation going to Memphis for two weeks." The barmaid was back with her drink placing it before her. "If and when I come back, then my answer will be yes. I can see myself getting with you. What are you going to do with the little wild child, Loraine?" "That will be entirely left up to you, Blanch. Like I said before, Loraine is a sweet girl and she makes enough money to help ad you, but my heart is here with you. Do you know my address, Blanch?" "No, write it down." I got a pencil and paper from the waitress and gave her my address. I bought me another drink and told Blanch that if she will be gone for two weeks to drop me a line and remind her of my love for her. I smiled to myself as I walked out the door heading for the 114 Club. I thought I did pretty good, short yet right to the point, and I hoped that I had given her the impression that I was sincere, but only time would let me know that.

`I was in the 114 Club about fifteen minutes before the phone rang for me. The bartender told me I had a call. I went to the phone, "Hello," I said. "Hi babe," a voice said. "I'm lonely for you, do you know who this is?" I said, "Yes, baby, I know who this is. You are Mabel, my sweet peach." "Can you see me, baby? It's been four days, and I haven't seen you. Can I see you tonight, baby?" I said, "Where are you?" She said, "I'm in the Hermonia Hotel in room 213." I was knocking on the door of room 213. "It's open," she said. I was kind of leery of going there by myself because of the four brothers she had. I still didn't know how she felt about that lick on the side of her head from Loraine. I stepped into the room cautiously. There was just one big room. The bathroom was in the hallway. She was sitting on the bed facing the dresser. Her skirt was raised to the middle of her thighs. I saw the bandage on her head and neck. "Are you ok? I asked. She said, "Yes, just a little cut. It's nothing. I miss you baby. I miss you so much." She went into one of those long deep nods that reminded me of Bobby. I was standing in front of her. Now, she kind of jumped and snapped her head back and looked up at me. I could see her eyes half closed as she mumbled her words out to me. "I want you to make love to me, baby."

I said, "How much money do you have, Mabel?" "Damn," she said, going back into a nod. "That's all-you mother fuckers think about is some mother fucking money. I ain't got no damn money," she said, snapping out of her nod and rubbing her fingers across her nose two or three times. She snapped her head back to look at me and said, "It's hard out here, baby. I don't make a dime. I didn't work since that bitch of yours hit me with that bottle. When I get well, I'm going to kill that bitch," she said with her mouth half open. Then she started to nod for the third time. She quickly snapped out of her nod and looked at me and said, "Come on baby, make love to me. Make love to me," as she laid back on the bed and kind of opened her legs. I looked at her in disgust as my eyes scanned her whole body. I saw the knot inside of her stockings on the fat part of her thigh. I started to snatch her whole dress off and take all of the money. But Wadell's voice came to me again, "She's trouble, Al." And in so many words, he had said, "ditch the bitch." He said, "whatever you do with a woman, do it smoothly because they are some dangerous characters. Especially when they think you are trying to drop them for another woman or just quitting them period. Especially when they have given you some of their money, they think hat you owe them." I looked at the unmade bed, the two towels that lay on the floor. Maybe the trick that she had had just left, or maybe he was on his way back. I had to play her like I did that sissy that night. I said, "Yeah baby, I'm going to make love to you. What you got here to drink?" "I ain't got nothing," she said, "nothing at all." She lay there with her eyes still closed. I said, "Well, I need something to drink." I'm going to walk over to the liquor store. What do you want?" "Anything, just get what you want and hurry back, baby." I cut out the light and locked the door behind me. I could hear her almost whispering, "Hurry back, baby," as the door closed behind me.

For the next week, I hustled hard at Leroy's and Smitty's and any other crap game that I could get into. I made money and I lost money. Onne day as I reached my apartment, the landlady called to me and gave me a letter. The letter was from Blanch. She was telling me that she missed me. She thought about those things that she talked to me about. She didn't realize how much I meant to her, and she couldn't wait to see me. She will be in Chicago next Tuesday at eight o'clock in the evening. The day was Tuesday. I had another week to get my act together with Loraine. We all were sitting in Sam's, Wadell, Bob, Tommy, Leroy, Eddie, and myself. We were seated at a long table in the middle of the floor. We all had drinks. Bob was telling jokes. Everyone was laughing, and all at once, the place went silent as Emma stepped through the door. She was about five ten, small waist, middle-sized hips, big, beautiful legs, and about a size eight shoe. She was extraordinarily sharp, in a brown tweed-like suit, brown high-heeled shoes, long hair that fell on her shoulders. She walked with grace to the bar. Bob whispered to Wadell, "that's her, man, that's the broad I told you that came back from Detroit with Pretty and Little Daddy. She's living at the Havana Hotel over on Twenty-Ninth and Wabash. They say she's a moneymaker." I watched Wadell and Tommy kind of ease their way, slowly working themselves up to Emma. My money would be on Wadell, or maybe in my heart, I was hoping that she would be the one to cop her. Tommy had three or four women, but Wadell didn't have the main one that I know of. A whole lot of women like him, but I didn't know of one that he had chosen. He was very secretive. Bob had kind of backed up out the race, maybe because of her height and him being five six, and the woman being five ten. Me, I felt that was really high cotton for me and when was another bitch. I wasn't really used to big bitches as so I just kind of laid low and smiled every time she looked my way. In the next couple of days, Bill introduced Emma to Wadell and Tommy.

I had bragged throughout the week to Wadell and Tommy and Bob for Bob to get his money right because on Tuesday, they would see that I had won the money. I let Wadell read the letter to them. Bob said, "There was no doubt in his mind that you would win the money. I'm just trying to teach you Little Pimp hat wishing won't do that, you have to move on something and when I see her in your arms, little nigger, I'm going to give you your money." It was Wednesday, about twelve noon when I went into Smithy's restaurant. I had just got through practicing my dice and wanted a sandwich before I took Marina to the show. Tommy, Leroy, and Bob were sitting in the back booths. Henry was sitting on the stool across from them and they were all talking. As I entered the door, everybody stopped talking and faced me. "Say, Al, come over here and sit by me," Drug Store Bob said. "I'm going to sit by your nigger, but you don't owe me yet. I waited for her, but she didn't come back to Chicago," I said, looking over at Tommy. "Yes, Al, she was coming back," Drug Store Bob said, looking over at me wide-eyed. "She had left St. Louis, but she never did make it. She had an accident," Drug Store Bob said. Tommy said, "She's dead, Al. They had a hell of an accident. her auntie just left here going to get the body." That night was the first time that I got drunk! I managed to go and meet Loraine. I had called Marina and cancelled our date for the show.

CHAPTER 36

For the next couple of weeks, I stayed away from the 114 Club. I tried my best to keep out of contact with Mabel. When she called the tavern or Sam's Restaurant, the people would tell her that I just left or that I wasn't there. But on this particular day, I wandered into Powell's Restaurant. I didn't see Mabel as I slid my tray down the counter and told the cook "I wanted those scrambled eggs that you took from a pan some bacon, toast, and an orange juice." I made my way down to the cash register. I had just finished paying for my food when she confronted me. "First, your itch hit me with a bottle or whatever. Then you're going to lie to me and leave me alone in some fucked up room, and now you're playing hide and seek with me. Ain't no little punk-jive ass nigher like you going to get away with this bullshit." Before I knew it, she had hit the tray and the food was on the floor, and the food was all over my suit, shirt, and tie. I was shocked by her action, looking down at the food on my clothes. I didn't see the haymaker that she threw from her hip, knocking me against the next person in line behind me, knocking at least three of us down to the floor. All the pimps and hoes in the place were getting their thrill. I got on my feet quickly. I had to do something fast on account of this bitch knocking me on my ass in front of everybody. I said, "Bitch, are you crazy? What the fuck is wrong with you? You silly dope fiend bitch!" I was steadily getting louder and louder with her. "If you weren't a sick dope fiend hoe,

I would kick your mother fucking ass." I reached down to pick up my hat which was between her feet and my feet. "Kick my ass now punk," she said, reaching toward me. She made her mistake when she lounged out at me. From the floor, my right hand caught her in the stomach. She gave a holler, "Oh god," she said as that same hand caught her up beside her head. She went over two tables. She lay on the floor looking pitifully up at me. I looked down at her. "If you ever put your hands on me again, bitch, I will kill your ass. And stay as far away from me as you can." I reached and got my hat from the floor. I walked out the door. The news had reached Twenty-Ninth Street. Twenty-Sixth Street, and Twenty-fourth Street about that fight. Wadell and Tommy's only remarks were to watch my back when I'm around that bitch and watch those big silly ass brothers of hers.

When all the hustlers and whores around Thirty-first Street had told Loraine about the fight and had told her how I had knocked her across two tables, she was pleased, and she was extra nice to me for the next two or three days. Especially when she had heard the part about me telling Mael to stay out of my face and don't fuck with me anymore. She knew that I was through with her. The relationship between Marina and I had really gotten tighter and more serious now. I was at her house so much and it seemed as though I was staying with her. I tightened up on Loraine too. I made love to her more often than I used to. I would whisper in her ear. "I don't need anyone but you, baby." "I'm not looking for anybody else. You are all that I need." She was licking it up all gracefully. Mostly, instead of looking for women, I was looking for gambling games. I started running with Tuck, Wadell, Leroy, Bob, and Eddie. We started running to the West Side, and Markham, Illinois to Boot's and Saddles, to Gary, Indiana, to Forty-Seventh Street. Anywhere there was a crap game. Bob, Leroy, Wadell, and Tommy would switch those dice so good that neither one of them could detect what the other one was doing. They would throw me the passing dice and when I hit three or four licks, they would throw me back the regular dice and no one detected that they were being cheated. I would see Emma from time to time. Sometimes in Henry's Restaurant, and other times on Thirty-First Street. She should just see me and with no expression, she would go her way and keep doing what she was doing at the time. To put it in a nutshell, she would ignore me as if I wasn't there. That would really get to me. Damn itch, I would think to myself. One of these days I will walk on top of you with your fine ass. T thought as I kept doing what I was doing. Sometimes she would sit there in Henry's sipping on coffee as I would play copycat to Bob while telling jokes that I had learned from him. Sometimes she would be sitting with other people in the bar inside Sam's. She would laugh at the jokes of whoever was telling them. I was one of her secret admirers. The way she dressed, in different colored ladies' suits and the latest of shoes. She beat Loraine dressing, hands down.

CHAPTER 37

The year was 1952, and during that year, my mother had convinced my father to move out of 2720 South Prairie. They had moved next door to my aunt Zora on Twenty-Eighth Street and Prairie, second floor rear with two bedrooms, a bath, kitchen, and living room. My mother was very happy to have just her family in an apartment once again. My uncles had moved out into their own place. Everything seemed to be going smoothly for my family and me until a month after they had moved into the place. My father and mother had christened the new place with another fight. My sister had run up to Twenty-ninth Street to get me. I ran ahead of my sister back to the house. When I reached the apartment, there were two officers there asking my mother if she wanted to press charges. "No," she said again, looking at the officers "I don't want to press charges." He said to his partner, "Let's get the hell out of here. If she wants to get her damn brains knocked out, I don't give a damn. Let's go." The partner followed him out the door and down the steps. By the time the officers had left, my sister had made it through the door, still crying. I looked around for my brother, Robert. He was sitting under the table with his thumb in his mouth, sniffling. "You hate me that much. Francis," my father asked, "that you would call the police on me?" I looked at my father and kind of stepped in front of my sister at the same time. I had experienced a fight with the opposite sex and deep down in my heart and mind, I didn't believe that I was the cause of the fight, and maybe, just maybe my father wasn't the cause of this fight.

This time I reasoned with myself. I noticed that I wasn't as mad with him about this fight as I was when I wanted to kill him. Maybe now I'm beginning to learn there are two sides to every story. Maybe if we heard his side of the story, we would feel sorrier for him than we did our mother, but feeling my oats at the age of eighteen, I thought I was a man now, so, I answered for my sister. "No, Daddy, we don't hate you. We love you as much as we love our mother, but we don't want you hitting her anymore. The fighting has got to stop." My mother had laid across the bed and my father kind of looked sideways at me from where he was sitting on the couch in the living room. I went over to my mother. She was lying on her side. I patted her on the back. "Rae you alright?" I asked her. I bent over and kissed her on the jaw. "I'll see you tomorrow," I said. Said my goodbyes to my sister and brother, looked over at my father who had turned on the television and seemed to be lost in his favorite cowboy show, Bill Elliott. I went out the door. Thereafter, from time to time, my uncles would say that night, my father said that he was proud of me, and he said that he thought that I had grown up. After that night, they didn't ever have another fight again.

CHAPTER 38

Ron Slick was as slick as the name, "Slick." He was from the Big Apple, New York. But as a boy coming up in the streets, Ron Slick lived in Detroit where Father Divine, Elijah Muhammad, and Daddy Grace originated from. These men rose up out of the streets, changing the minds of some people and crushing the minds of others. Their knowledge, quick thinking, and talking ability raised them above common men. Ron Slick grew up around most of these men. He learned the scriptures, the drag game, the two-card molly, the dropping of the wallet game, and switching off the handkerchief. All these games he learned as a boy, he was good at all of them. He went on to New York to bigger games and larger prey and there in New York is where he earned the reputation of one of the youngest and most daring con men to come out of Detroit. Now, today, he was part of us, a part of the crowd, a part of the wine-headed pimps and gamblers that hung around the fire barrel, reminiscing about the past.

Slick had just gotten out of Joliet prison and was staying with his uncle Lee. Lee was proud to introduce Slick to the crowd because Slick had a reputation and Lee wanted everyone to know this was his famous nephew. Slick had done three years in the penitentiary for beating a white woman out of ten thousand dollars in Philly. "Yes it should be," Slick said, and raising the bottle he took a big swallow from it. "I need one more good sting and I'm off to California." "I'll drink to that," Lee said as he took the bottle from his nephew. That next day, I came to Henry's Restaurant at about 11:00 am. Slick was sitting in one of the booths by himself just finishing his coffee. I sat in the booth across from him. "Hi, how are you doing, man?" I said to him. He said," I'm alright. I've just got a hangover. This coffee will fix me up." He beckoned for the waitress to come over to the table. He ordered a refill of his coffee. "I'll take some coffee and bacon and eggs," I told the waitress. She said, "Potatoes or grist?" I said "Grits" "Slick" he sipped from his coffee and looked over at me. I said, "How much would you charge me to teach me the con game?" I didn't give him the chance to answer. I said, "I could hardly sleep last night thinking about that guy you called the Yellow Kid. Man, it sounded like a movie. For a guy like the Yellow Kid to go down to City Hall in Chicago and they say he tried to sell it. Man, I wonder where he got all the paper and the false deeds. And also, then he sold the Brooklyn Bridge and showed the man how to make a fortune just by charging ten cents a car. Man, is there such a man as the Yellow Kid, or did you make him up?"

"Naw, there's such a man. He's a very smart man and to your other question, he was something like an actor because he could play a part like an actor. He could play the character of a wealthy person or a vagabond. Whatever situation he might find himself in, he could talk his way out of it. As for the question, "how much would I charge you to teach you how to con? I could never teach you the short con. Nobody can, and you would have ot be born with it. In time, if you were born with it, you would know this. Because you will find yourself getting out of situations that nobody else can. Short con artist is a quick thinker. Very swift in his planning and execution of a plan. Oh, I could show you some tricks of the con game like the dropping of the handkerchief or the finding of money by the bank. A whole lot of other tricks that go along with conning. But a true short con artist works by himself." No, Al, can't anyone teach you the con game, but let me tell you this, the slickest person in the world is not the one that can cheat, bt the one that can keep the cheaters off them. "The one that knows the game and doesn't get caught up in it. If you are true to the game, thee game will be true to you."

Slick finished his coffee and rose from the table. He stood and hesitated for a minute, looking at me. "You know, 'Al, you are a young boy out here in this game. I like you. My uncle likes you, too. He talks a lot about you and Wadell. I wish I could have taken your money and laid on you what you wanted to learn about the con game, but remember the words I told you, if you are true to the game, the game will be true to you. Don't ever try to play a game you don't know. Always stick to the games you know."

That was the last I saw of Slick. Someone said that he went down to Union Station and beat some old man out of a lot of money. Lee sears that he is in California. I wondered why he didn't take my money anyway. He was a boss con man. I had two thoughts. Of course, my ego spoke up first, thinking a hustler respects a hustler, so because I was on my game, he didn't go any further than the offer to each me some tricks even though he already told me he couldn't teach me to con successfully, but he could teach me some tricks that could have possibly gotten me killed. My second thought came to me that he was living with his Uncle Lee, who was my good friend and had respect for me and maybe if he had taken my money, it might have caused a problem with him and his Uncle Lee. I don't know. I just know he was a boss con artist, and I still wished him well. I never put too much thought into becoming a con man anymore, but I was always looking for an angle in the streets to help me to make big money quickly. Being on the streets, you always take a little risk. I wished him well wherever he was. I will never forget him. He was a slim, brown-[skinned, neatly dressed fella and I imagine thinking of him that he could get just as sharp as one of those wealthy characters shat he played in his cons.

CHAPTER 39

On this particular day, Smitty had sent for me. I reached the shop at three that afternoon. He met me at the door. He was dressed very neatly with a long-sleeved starched blue shirt, navy blue pants, and his half-folded apron wrapped neatly around his waist. He spoke to me. I nodded and he pointed to the chair. I climbed up on the stand and seated myself. He reached over and grabbed the wash brush and started to wash my shoes and then he dried them, not saying a word. Then he stopped and looked at me and as he batted his eyes, I could see the tears that had rolled up in them. "Our buddy is dying, Al, and he wants to see you." I said, "Who?" getting excited, thinking he meant Wadell or someone. He said, "Mr. Buddy. He's dying of cancer and the doctors say he doesn't have too much time to live. He's at the old folk's home on Twenty-Sixth and Calumet. You can visit him until eight tonight." He finished shining my shoes. There wasn't a word spoken there. It seemed like for fifteen or twenty minutes. "Does he know he is going to die?" I asked. "Yes, he knows, but he wants to see you right away." I was off the stool and back to Sam's Tavern where I had left Eddie having a beer and talking to a young lady. When I came to Sam's, Eddie was alone. I ordered me a quick drink, drank it down real fast, paid the tab for Eddie's bill and we were off to see Mr. Buddy.

The lady at the nursing home took me through a dingy half-lit hallway. I was back in the twenty-watt bulb factory, I thought as I looked at the ragged lamps and pictures that hung from the walls. Different colored rugs lined the floor. It wasn't a well-kept building at all, I thought as we reached a rear room to the right of us. The lighting wasn't good in that room, either. He sat there, kind of drooped in the wheelchair as though he was asleep. He had on some house shoes that seemed to be too little. His feet and ankles were swollen. His whole head of hair had whitened. When we were working, I used to tell him how black his hair was and how he didn't look his rightful age, but now his head of hair was pure white and as his head was bent towards the floor, you could see the bald spot in the middle. The lady said, "You can wake him if you want to. If you need me, just pull the cord there, that is right above his bed." I wondered what was on the other end of that cord, a cowbell, I thought. I had pulled the chair up close to Mr. Buddy now, I gently shook him by the shoulder and called out his name, "Mr. Buddy," in a low voice. It took a couple of shakes before he responded. He opened his eyes and looked at me. His eyes seemed to have gotten smaller and set way back in the sockets. And it seemed to me from the way I was looking at him in the dark. I said, "Mr. Buddy, it's me, it's Al." He said "I know," and smiled, "You hink I've gotten too old to see." And I smiled. "I didn't know where you were, Mr. buddy. It's not that I didn't think about you every day, but these streets grab a person and it takes you so fast, Mr. Buddy, that you can hardly stop on your own, Me and Smitty talk about you all the time."

"Well, that day on the bus, I knew I had lost you. But knowing that you were there with Smitty comforted me because I knew the situation with your daddy, and I didn't want you out there in them streets and you get swallowed up and or in the wrong hands or in the penitentiary. I knew if Smitty would see you from time to time that he would try to guide you on the right path." He spoke in a low voice. I pulled myself close to him and strained to try to hear what he was saying. "Do you remember, Al, when I used to read the bible to you? There is a God you know," he said, and kind of looked directly at me. "Always remember that zero from zero leaves zero, you can't take zero and make something out of it. The world could not have come into existence without a maker. It had to be a world maker to make the world. You will not know the time that it is now unless there is a watchmaker. Are you listening, Al? Thre are no hinges on the sun and there is no chain that holds the moon in its rightful place. There is a God, Al," He looked at me directly in my eyes again. "Do you remember the books that I read to, Al?" I said, "Yes." "What is the main thing that I told you to remember?" "Do you remember that?" I said, "Yes, sir." "And what is that," he asked me. "What I told you to remember?" I said, "The first one was to honor thy father and thy mother, and your days will be longer on this earth." "What was the second thing that I asked you to remember?" "First, get wisdom, but above all things, get understanding." "What was the third one? He asked me, looking back at me again. "Believe in God with all your mind heart, and soul. Seek, and you shall find, knock, and the door shall be opened unto you, ask and you shall receive." "If you really believe this, Al, in your heart, there's nothing on this earth that God won't do for you, and if you seek it, whatever it is, in the name of Jesus, it will be given unto you. I had lived a dangerous life in the game in New York when I was younger, married to four wives. Then I got sick after all my wives were dead. I asked God to let me live. I started applying these things to my life that I just told you, and here I am now, eight-six years old, and Al, I am content to meet my maker. The reason I told you to honor thy father and mother and your days will be longer, Al. It's not only your mother or your father, but remember, this. It's any elderly person that talks to you in the right manner and lays on you ancient wisdom, or we can say ancient advice that's been handed down to them from their mothers and daddies and so on through generations that helped a person direct their future and the right paths. So, do not ignore the elderly people, because when you throw them away, you are throwing away your wisdom. So, when you do what your father and mother advise you to, it's that ancient wisdom that keeps you. So, Al, I'm not saying I'm fixing to die now, it's just that I want to leave ho with this prayer."

The Lord is my shepherd; I shall not want.
He maketh me lie down in green pastures.
He leadeth me beside the still waters.
He restoreth my soul; he leadeth me in the path of
Righteousness for his name's sake.
Yea, though I walk through the valley of the shadow of
Death, I will fear no evil;
For thou are with me; thy rod and thy staff they
Comfort me;
Thou prepare a table before me in the presence of mine
Enemies; thought anointest my head
with oil; my cup runneth
Over
Surely goodness and mercy shall follow me all the days of
my life and I will dwell in the house of the lord forever.
Psalm 23:1-6

"Al, don't ever forget this prayer!" I went to see Mr. Buddy one other time about three weeks later and two months after the first visit, he was gone. I talked to Smitty about Mr. Buddy. We both loved him. The day after his death, the nursing home called my house, where my mother and father lived, and requested my presence. My sister, Francis, came and told me at Henry's Restaurant. I had Eddie take me. He had left me his watch, ring, and an older ring that looked like a Masonic ring and a note. The note read: "Well, Al, I have no other family. I have grown to love you as my son and I hope you appreciated the things that I was trying to tell you. I saw some things in you that maybe your father never noticed. You have a kind heart and maybe your gift is to help people. I could see how careful you were with that blind man when you would bring him down to get his shoes shined. I appreciate the time you took with me and the time we spent together. Always look out for your elders, as I have told you before, that's your wisdom. Take care of the old people and God will take care of you. You know I told these people to cremate me, and I hope you and Smitty will be at the service. I have taken care of the arrangements with the people already. And the balance of the money I had left four hundred dollars, I hope you do something really nice for yourself with it."

Signed

Mr. Buddy

The following week, I sat in the shoeshine parlor with Smitty, he broke down and told me about Mr. Buddy and himself in New York. "Yes," he said, "Mr. Buddy did live a rough dangerous life. He was a gun and dope runner for one of the black mobs and me. I used to tell guns for him. We knew each other from a young age, from shining shoes to robbing people doing the average thing that young people were doing at that time. Mr. Buddy grew really big in the mob until he shot three people in the lounge. He beat the rap in court, but his mob boss liked him very much and cut him loose from the mob. And I guess that's why he ended up here in Chicago. First, a waiter, then as he got older, a busboy, and then he met Thurman and started running the shop for him. Yes, Al, I, and Mr. Buddy were lucky to get out of that thing in New York. When he left, I left, then I went back to Detroit, and then I came here, and when I first met up with him again, it was in that very show where I met you. Buddy was a good guy." Smitty said, reminiscing about the past. "Yes, he was," I said," he was a good man." Smitty rubbed my shoes, looked up at me, shook his head, and reached for the brush.

CHAPTER 40

When I got to Marina's house that Friday night, I was met with the bad news that one of her aunts in St. Louis had died and that the aunt she was living with was not only going to the funeral, but she was going to stay and run the family home. All the cousins were there too. They were also going to go to St. Louis. Everybody's attention was on me. They wanted to know what my intentions were. Was I going to marry Marina or what? It was like a husband-and-wife relationship between me and Marina now. Eddie met me while I was drinking a beer at Sam's. I had just finished talking to Leroy about coming to his dice game tonight at about twelve. Wadell and Tommy were going to be there and were expecting high rollers. Leroy was just leaving the bar when Eddie approached me. He spoke to Leroy going out of the door. "What are you doing, Al?" I said, "Nothing, nothing until about eleven, I've got to meet Loraine." "I need you to go with me," Eddie said. "I'm supposed to meet my first woman. I pulled her out of Smitty's at Thirty-Fifth Street Lounge last night. Man, she said, she wants to do everything under the sun for me. I'm supposed to meet her at the114 Club."

I said, "Hold up, Eddie, you know I don't hang around the 114 Club too much." He said, "Why?" "On account of Mable." "Man, don't worry about Mable, or her brothers, I got my thing with me." We left for the 114 Club. The first people we saw when we entered the lounge were Mable and her two brothers sitting in the back booths. I kind of flinched when I saw them. Eddie said, "Let's sit down in this front booth." I sat facing Mabel and her brothers. Eddie ordered a dink from the floor barmaid. There were about ten customers in the place scattered. Some guy had played Lena Horne on the jukebox. I had taken my eyes off Mabel one minute while talking to Eddie, "What time is your girl supposed to meet you here?" He said, "She's supposed to meet me at about eight-thirty." I said, "What time is it now?" I looked at my watch. It was seven-thirty. We had to wait damn near another hour. After the floor barmaid had delivered our drinks, I looked up to see Mabel headed for my table. I whispered to Eddie, "I think it's going to be trouble, here comes Mabel headed to our table." He said, "That's okay," and we snapped the button on his coat and reached around to his side took the .38 caliber pistol out and stuck it down in his belt in front of his stomach where everyone could see it. Mabel was at the table now. "Hi, Al," she said, looking at me and then at Eddie. We both spoke to her politely. I knew she had seen the .38 in his belt. She turned her attention back to me. "I've been trying to catch up with you. Do you mind if I just sit here with you for a minute?" I said, "I don't mind." She said, "I don't have any animosity in my heart against you regarding that little scaffold that you and I had. But you see," she went on, "I cared about you baby, and it hurts me how you dumped me in that hotel room. I understand why the habit I have is that you didn't want to get caught up in a mess like I get caught up in. I explained to my family that it was all my fault. Even calling Loraine your lady a bitch, I should have never done that. That was wrong." "I'm glad that you feel this way," I said. "I am glad too," Eddie said. "Because your apology stops a lot of shit." Eddie continued to say. Mabel had seen Eddie a couple of times knock people out in front of her. She said, "Well, now that I've got that off my chest, can I buy you two a drink?" I said, "No, the drinks are on me." I called the floor barmaid back over to our table. I bought a round for my table and drinks for her brothers. We were all happy family again. It wasn't too long before Eddie's healthy stallion walked through the door. Eddie was grinning from ear to ear. She approached the table, "Well, big daddy, did you think I would make it, or did you think I was lying?" He said, "I believed you, baby," standing up to make room for her to slide into the booth. She said, "I don't want anything to drink. I'm tired. I just want to go somewhere and lay down." He looked at me. I said, "Take me back to Twenty-Ninth Street, man."

CHAPTER 41

Leroy's crap table was filled with high rollers, five of them. I had never seen so many hundred-dollar bills stacked on the table before. Wadell stood on the side of Leroy, and Tommy stood on the other side. Bob was in one corner of the table. I kind of squeezed myself between two of the high rollers. I had come in late so as not to appear like I was in the crowd. Bob had got there fifteen minutes before I did. Leroy was the stick man. Tommy and Wadell were there when the high rollers arrived. The other customers had kind of drifted in. "It's your shot, my man, "Leroy said to the high roller by me. Five hundred I shoot" he said. Some guy over by Tommy said, "Let him shoot." The houseman got the dice. The high roller cupped his hand. Leroy threw him the dice. The shooter lifted the dice to his ear. "Eleven," Leroy called out. What are you shooting now?" He spoke. "Throw me back eight, shoot the two." The dice came out again. This time it caught ten. He shot ten four times before the dice seven out. It was my shot now and the show began. We had practiced these moves at the gambling house on the west side, and Boots and Saddles in Markham where I would hit three or four licks, pull the money down then shoot a small amount. Then they would switch dice on me, and I would crap out and so on to Tommy, Wadell, Bob, and even to Leroy if he shot, the dice.

"Okay, my man," Leroy was tapping the stick in front of me. "How much are you shooting?" I said, "Shoot three hundred." "I got him," Wadell said. The high roller said, "It's my turn to fade my man. You're not going to take my fade, are you?" Leroy said, "Go ahead," and the high roller, the one that missed the ten-point, threw his three hundred up. Wadell kind of looked at me in disgust like you have to go on your own. I can't switch the dice for you. Leroy grabbed the dice, sat them in the middle of the table, picked them up, and threw them to me as I cupped my hand to catch them. When the dice hit the palm of my hand, I had learned from Wadell who had been teaching me how to detect the numbers the way they were when they reached my hand. I had practiced this for so long that it came naturally. And as I rolled the dice slightly in my hand and went up in the air with them, my thumbs snapped the five under the one. The dice felt good and fell in place when I threw them across the line. "Seven!" Leroy said. "What are you shooting now?" I said, "Shoot it all." I said, "No, throw me three back, shoot the two." The high roller said, "I got you for the six." "I'm ghosting two." He said, "Someone else can have him," Wadell said, "Let him shoot, "and he threw out the two hundred. Leroy threw me the dice again. I cuffed them. I knew the routine. I didn't try to do anything to the dice because I knew 'Wadell was going to catch them. I went up and shook them to my ear and rolled them across the table. Wadell caught them and started talking shit. "No, not this time, young man, you are not going to hit me in the ass like you did my man over there." Wadell was so fast and smooth that no one at the table saw his switch. Not even me, as he threw me the passing pair of dice. I wound up again and swung the dice across the screen. "' Eleven," the houseman said. There were four hundred up there, and the houseman said, "I'm getting my cut, you've got 350 up here now. How much are you shooting?"

I said, "Throw me that fifty, houseman." And I reached in front of me and threw two hundred more on the pile. I said, "Shoot the five hundred." Wadell said, "Someone else can get him. I don't have that. The nigger's too lucky for me." One of the high rollers looked at his partner and said, "Do you want to go half?" "Yes, I got it. Let the nigger shoot." And I came out again. One dice spun while the other dice sat on the one. When the dice stopped spinning, it was a six. "Seven, pay the man! "It's time for another cut! You got 950 here, what do you want to shoot I said, "Fifty dollars." The high rollers said, "What kind of shit is this? You shoot five hundred and then you shoot fifty? I don't want that." Wadell said, "That's my kind of bet. Let him shoot fifty." I came out again, knowing what Wadell was going to do. He grabbed the dice and threw me back the regular dice. Shit, I had made my money. So, I didn't try to do anything to the dice. I just shook them and threw them out! "Eleven," the houseman said. "What are you shooting now?" "Shoot that hundred," I said, really wanting to miss out to get out of the game. "Let him shoot, the first high roller that bet me the first time said. Leroy grabbed the dice to throw them to me. But the high roller said, "Man, can I see those dice?" Leroy threw the dice to him. He picked them up and clicked them around his hand, looking at them. Set them on the table, took his index finger, and turned the dice over and over about three times. Leroy looked at him and said, "Is there anything wrong, my man?"

"No. The way this little nigger has been hitting through you would think there was. I want to buy a new pair of dice. This little nigger is just lucky." Leroy got the dice that were wrapped in silver foil from the little box on the side. He took a cigarette lighter and burned both dice on each side, making the dice useless. He said that will be $5, my man." The high roller threw him the five dollars. Leroy picked up the dice and said, "You've got a bet for the hundred, let's go." I raised the dice to my ear and shot them. I said, "Just one more time dice, just one more time for me," as I shook them and turned them loose across the screen. Snake eyes," Leroy said, and he's a loser!" When the game was over that night, and I had given the houseman a percentage of my money, I left with twelve hundred dollars. We all promised to meet each other for breakfast at Henry's. The next day as we sat eating with Leroy, Wadell, Tommy, and Bob, we all were grinning from ear to ear. The way he had made those dice dance around those high rollers, we all made a nice piece of money. "You're getting very good, Al. Yes, that practice has paid off for him—" Wadell said when Bob butted in, "Practice makes perfect. What are you going to do with that little money you won?" Bob looked at me. "I'm going to buy Marina an icebox, a dresser, and a bed. Then I saw this bad cocoa brown overcoat with a cape in the back. I'm going to buy it for myself and maybe a hat and a pair of shoes. Get kind of clean for Loraine, and party with her tonight when I meet her at the 114 Club." "If you fellas are going to be around here, I might be back this way with her and we'll all have a drink together." "Don't count on it, Al," Wadell said, "we're all planning to go to the west side and double our money." He smiled at me. I looked at each one of them and smiled back.

CHAPTER 42

It was a cold November evening on Thirty-First street, and the wind howled as bits of paper blew from one side of the street to the other. A middle-aged woman got out of the cab before me. As I stepped onto the sidewalk, she smiled at me admiringly, then she turned and walked eastward to the Glass Bar Lounge. I, on the other hand, walked straight ahead toward the 114 Club, about six doors down from the corner. The club was crowded. There was one empty stool at the far end of the bar. As I passed the drunken customers, I recognized the faggot and the whore seated at the bar. They gave me a slight smile of recognition and I returned the gesture with a nod as I seated myself on the stool. Joe, the bartender, was in front of me now fixing my drink as he told me that Loraine was being held hostage on Thirty-Ninth Street by two fellas. I drank my drink and paid Joe. I stopped a jitney, and then asked the driver if he turned off the line. "Sure, Buddy, if you got the money, I'll take you to New York," he said, jokingly. I made a deal with the cab driver to wait for me at the Pitch Pub Lounge. The cab pulled to the curb. The lounge looked like it was closed for the night but as I moved closer to the plate glass window and peeped in. I could see one man seated at the far end of the bar with his back facing the window. Loraine sat on the other side of him with her back to the bar. The second man stood on the other side of Loraine, facing her. They seemed to be in deep conversation. Suddenly, from the corner of my eye, I could see a man coming from the left of me inside of the lounge with a flashlight heading my way. I swiftly moved from the window to the door, not really noticing my movement. I muttered softly, "Help me, God." With those words, my left hand went into the patch coat pocket. My right hand knocked on the door like a log of wood. The flashlight turned toward me. A man came to the door, peeped out at me, and said in a low voice, "We ae closed." "I came for Loraine." What?" he asked. The door became ajar. "Who did you say?"

At a young age, I could always act a role that should be acted in any given situation. Now, tonight, without noticing my own movements, I was once again on stage playing a role. My left hand was still in my pocket, I stepped with my right foot blacking he door and with the same movement, my right hand had pushed he door open. I said, "I came for my woman, Loraine." Everyone at the bar faced me. The old man stood the as if in shock, watching my face and left hand in my pocket. "Bitch," I screamed at her, "get your ass off that stool and let's go!" She rose to obey, but the guy who was standing pushed her back on the stool. I made two steps and asked, "Did you her me, bitch? Get off that damn stool before I kill every mother fucker in here!" She rushed to me. With my right hand, I slapped her hard across the face. Then with the same hand, I grabbed a handful of her hair and pulled her slowly out the door. The jitney pulled off from the curb and headed back to Thirty-First Street. Loraine was still crying and wiping tears from her eyes. "I don't know why you hit me. I called you all night to come and get me." The crying continued louder. As we reached Thirty-First Street, I told the jitney driver to pull into the front of Powell's Restaurant that had stayed open twenty-four hours. It was three doors down from the 114 Club, going west. It was a buffet-like restaurant where pimps and whores.

Hung out at night, sitting round the tables gossiping and bragging about their actions that night, what went on in other neighborhoods, what dangers they had escaped and just general conversation. Loraine stood by the ladies' bathroom with three other whores. She was bragging about the way I came and rescued her from two thugs on thirty-Ninth street. she had the ears of the whole restaurant. Everybody kept looking and cutting their eyes over at me. Loraine said, "He said, 'Get your ass off that stool before I kill every mother fucker in here,' and I jumped off that stool because I didn't want my baby shooting me." I felt pretty good that night and so did Loraine. So, at about six that morning, I treated her to a bottle of champagne and a hotel room. Before I went to the hotel, I called my house. My sister answered the phone. I told her to tell Marina I was gambling at Leroy's, and I'll be home at about one o'clock.

We were up at twelve, dressed, and walking through the door of the 114 Club. I kept noticing all the whores, pimps, and hustlers looking at me, smiling. Three or four girls had pulled Loraine to a back table and were talking to her. It was crowded in the 114 Club that Saturday morning. I walked over to the bar and spoke to Joe. He handed me my double shot of gin. He said, "I took the trouble of pouring you one. I heard you had a rough night last night." I said, "Rough is not the word." I turned to face him, and in a low voice, I said, "Just between you and me, I damn near pissed on myself." "Yeah, I know, kid. It can be pretty rough sometimes." He threw up both his hands and said, "What can a person do?" He still had his rag in his hand. He started wiping in front of me. Paul was at the pinball machine talking loudly. "Come over here, All. The pot is $10." "I ain't hard to beat," he hollered over at me.

"What the hell," I said aloud, "your money spends like any other tricks. I might a as well take it." I had won three games straight on that pinball machine. I broke Paul and bought him a drink. He had sat down, cooking off. I tried to get someone to bet me seventy-five dollars. I felt lucky, but no one would bet me. I tried to pull down the fifty. One man in the front of the bar said, "I got twenty-five." 'And as he walked toward me, I could see the Indian-looking fellah with a ponytail down his back staring at me. As I stared back, he turned his head to face the bar. I stood there looking at him for a while, sizing him up. I didn't like that look that he had given me. I had seen him before several times. To my recollection, he stayed in the Prairie Hoel. He's a very neat dresser. I had seen him in Henry's and 'Sam's bar, but he never did hang out with the crowd. One day, I saw him in Sam's in a green-colored suit, and I asked drug Store Bob, "who is that guy, Bob? I've seen him in a lot of places, but he doesn't seem to hang out with anybody." "Well, that's a lady's man, Al. We were just bullshitting when we were talking in our crowd, but the nigger here is a sure enough pimp Look at the nigger's hands. His nails are longer than a woman's. The nigger wears the best of clothes," Bob went on talking. "He lives in the Prairie Hotel with four women."

Tonight, he was dressed in black with a big black Dobbs hat on that was rolled like a Texas cowboy hat. I could feel his eyes staring back at me in the mirror. That nigger had made me nervous and mad at the same time as I went back to concentrating on the trick that had walked up to this pinball machine. The machine was going off like a chime bell. The jukebox was playing, and the niggers were talking. It was very noisy in that lounge that morning. It didn't take me long. Two games, and I had the trick broken. I looked over and saw Loraine sitting with the other girls, laughing and talking. The trick had left me standing at the pinball machine by myself and Paul had disappeared. I felt as if I had to go to the bathroom. I had almost forgotten about the Indian looking fellah, but as I began to pass him, he turned his stool and almost blocked me. "How are you doing, young fellah?" he said, looking at me coldheartedly. He kind of shocked me the way he stopped me. I swallowed, "I'm okay," I said. "I see," he said, "with your chest all stuck out like a rooster. I guess you feel pretty good." I kind of leaned over to him and asked, "What the fuck is it, man? Why ae you fucking with me? And why do you keep staring at me?" I was pissed off now because he was getting to me with those stares and boastful talk he was giving me. I knew that the switchblade knife was in my pocket, and I had been practicing opening that, too. So, if he had made one move, I was going to knock his ass off that stool and cut his goddamn neck.

"Don't get offended, young blood," he said, smiling. "I'm just like the rest of these tricks around here. I kind of like you, too. I said, What the fuck you mean, you kind of like me? I was thinking about the sissy on Twenty-Ninth and Wabash. He smiled again. "My name is Travis. Let me buy a drink." "Maybe when I come out of the bathroom. I've got to piss right now," I said, kind of rolling my eyes at him as I left. "That nigger is a faggot, not a pimp," I wanted to tell Bob as I went into the bathroom. I was back at the bar, and he was waiting for me. Joe was pouring him his Christian Bros. he said, "What do you drink?" Joe said, "I know what he drinks. The same Al?" I said, The same." Joe poured me my double shot of gin. As I sat, the stranger said as he lifted hi glass to toast," I like you as a man, as another player in this game of chess. Sometimes a man will make good moves and sometimes just one wrong move can cost you your life." He took a swallow from his glass, and I did the same. He went on talking. "Like I said, no offense, but you are walking around here with your chest stuck out like a rooster. Or can you understand that last night you could have gotten killed? Going in someone else's neighborhood to get your woman is very, very dangerous," he said, looking at me straight in the eyes. "I'm sure that you've got an honorable lady, Ms. Loraine, isn't that what you call her?" I looked at him. "Yes," I answered. "I'm sure she loves you," he said, "but the question you should've asked yourself last night is, what if she didn't. She could've had two or three niggers waiting to cut your mother fucking head off and put it in one of those garbage cans." He was looking coldheartedly at me. Driving his message deep down in my head like he was using his eyes for a hammer. "Then you wouldn't be walking around here with your chest stuck out like a rooster, and like I said, no offense, but I've been out here fucking with these hoes fifteen years, and you don't see no scars or nicks on me, no place. You've got to know the game to play it. Just like she dropped hat dime in the telephone to call you, you tell her the next time to call the police. They're the ones that protect and serve. They get paid for it, young blood." His message had gotten to me like a ton of bricks. And if those guys had called my bluff last night, maybe this morning I could've been lying in an alley. I ordered another drink, hies time I paid for it. I sat there sipping a I kind of looked at 'Travis out the corner of my eyes. He was a nice-looking guy with a smooth tan face. The texture of his skin was similar to that of an Indian or a Filipino. His ponytail lay at the top of his shoulder blade, black and shiny. You could smell the expensive cologne on him. He said, "Yes, young blood," as he finished his drink in his glass. He was standing now facing me. He set the glass on the bar and pulled a twenty from his pocket and threw it by the glass. He said, "Yes, young blood, I kind of like you." I said, "I kind of like you, too, Travis," looking him in the eyes. "And thanks for the advice." He said, "No problem. Take care of yourself." He then walked away.

CHAPTER 43

After a week or two, I got Marinna an apartment on the first floor of my mother's building. Her rent was $12.50 a week. It was a nice big room with a closet, and with a bathroom near her door. Everything was going smoothly for the next three weeks; her auntie was gone to St. Louis. I stayed with Maring every night. It was two weeks after we moved into the apartment that she got a job up north. I never knew what the job consisted of. I just found out that she was working, and I didn't have to babysit her during the day. On her first payday, we enjoyed dinner with my family. I was sitting around my family's table with my woman by my side. I was nineteen now and thought that I was on top of the world.

It was in August and the sun had gone down and the night was hot. Me and Marina had stepped out onto the sidewalk when I saw Loraine coming from across the street. I damn near shitted on myself. I hadn't told Maring about Loraine. She thought I was just a gambler. She was closer now as she crossed the street to us. "So, this is the bitch you are living with?" Loranne asked. Al, who is she calling a bitch? Who in the fuck is this?" Marina asked. "Who in the fuck are you?" Loraine asked. Mariano was big boned too, But I knew Loiraine was fast with that motherfucking razor. So, I kind of stepped in front of Marina. I said, "It's not what you think, Loraine. You see, her family left her, and she rented a room under my mother, and I am kind of watching over her." "What are you lying to this bitch for, Al? Who is this bitch you're lying to? Hell, yeah, we're staying together. You don't have to lie to this bitch." She tried to shake herself loose from another tenant named Ruby.

The crowd had gathered around us, edging on a fight or whatever was going to happen. I stepped closer to Loraine, watching her hands. I caught Ruby's eyes. She was standing behind her, holding Marina's shoulders. I nodded my head and said, "Ruby and Frances, take Maring into the house. I said, "I got this" as I was watching Loraine's hands. Marina was dragged off to the apartment kicking and screaming. I got Loraine by the arm, "Come on, Loraine, Let's have a drink." Surprising to me, she walked very close to me, not cursing or anything, very cool. We were in Sam's tavern on the barbeque side. She said, "I got off early because I have something for you." She handed me an envelope. Three hundred and seventy-five dollars was in the envelope. I counted it. I bought her a Bloody Mary, and me, a gin fizz. There were no words spoken until she took a few sips of her drink. "She is pretty, Al." "Huh?" "Marina, that's her name, isn't it?" "She's not as pretty as you, baby." "The only thing I want to know," she asked, "is, are you in love with her?" I said, "I'm in love with you, baby." She said, "I know. Do you remember when we first met?" I said, "Yes." She started to smile and sipped from her glass. She said, "You were sleeping in a car with a dog, but now, you're grown up with two apartments." "I told you that her auntie left her." "Yeah, I know." We ate barbeque and drank some more. I tried to trick her to a room, but she said she couldn't remind me of when I first met her, when she told me her mother had a headache. My stomach had tightened up on me. zI guess the rabbit had raised his head. I knew something was wrong, but zI couldn't put my hnad on it. I walked through the hallway to the front, and got Eddie, and he took her home.

I got back to Marina about twelve-thirty that night. I had to go through the whole night with her crying, telling me she wished she would have known about Loraine before her auntie had left. She would have left with her auntie. She told me she wasn't going to put up with this Loraine bullshit. She was going to write to her auntie and tell her to send her some money. I turned my stomach on the bed and tried to block out the whimpering and crying that Marina was doing. I laid there trying to figure out my next move. I didn't give a damn about Marina's crying. It was Loraine that was bothering me. She was too cool, and she didn't raise any hell. It was way over in the night after Marina had gone to sleep that I lost consciousness. It was about ten thirty when I woke up the next morning. Marina was in a good mood; she was sitting at the little table with the middle leaf folded down sipping coffee. "Do you want me to go to the store and get some eggs or something? We are out." I said, "No, I can take a bath and run up to Henry's and get us both something. And when I get back, we can take Frances and go shopping." I was dressed in a matter of minutes after taking a bath. She was still at the table, watching the tiny thirteen-inch television. I gave her a hundred-dollar bill. "I changed my mind. You and Frances can go shopping. You and Frances can stop at the Turnover Restaurant and get yourselves some breakfast. I've got to go and see Thurman at the shoeshine parlor and get some papers that Mr. Buddy left. You can buy yourselves something pretty out of the hundred dollars." I pulled her up close to me and kissed her on the forehead. She was a young girl, and she was infatuated with me. I smiled at her, and I knew in my mind that I had gotten through Phase 1. But it was Phase11 that I was worried about, Loraine.

I walked swiftly to Henry's Restaurant. Eddie was sitting there with Tommy and Leroy. "Come on, Eddie, I got to get to Loraine's house right away." "What's wrong?" he asked, walking really fast to the car. "I don't know what's wrong until I see Loraine. Then, maybe this knot will get out of my stomach." We reached Loraine's house. Her mother invited us in. "Hi, Eddie," she said. He said "Hi" back to her. "Do you want some coffee?" she asked. I said, "No. Where is Loraine?" She said, "I thought you knew. She packed her bags last night and this morning at six-thirty some car blew for her, and she told me that she was on her way to Minnesota and that she would be gone for a week." "If she calls you, tell her to call me at Sam's or Smitty's." "Did you all have a fight, Al?" "No," just a misunderstanding." She said, "I guess she will call you," as we walked out of the door.

This particular night, I left Mariana watching the television with Frances, my sister, who was her company keeper when I was away at night. I walked around to Sam's. It was filled with people back-to-back. I drank one beer and left, going next door to Henrys. Three weeks had passed since I had seen Loraine. It was about two-thirty on a Wednesday afternoon. The October sun was hot. The rays from the sun were almost blinding me as I sat right there in front of the window drinking a gin fizz in Sam's. I saw the Road Master Buick pull right to the curb in the front of the window. I could hardly believe my eyes as Loraine stepped out and onto the sidewalk. The driver got out of the car too and met her at the door. I looked around the room quickly for Wadell, Tommy, Leroy, or anybody. "Now, I'm sure enough in a jam." I thought to myself. I realized then I didn't know all the moves to pimping. In fact, I didn't know shit about pimping. "What should I do now, just knock her ass out when she walks through the door. What about the nigger, should I knock his ass out too, or fuck around and get cut? What am I supposed to do?"

I looked around the room again. Bill wasn't the bartender today either. It was an old man, a perfect stranger to me. An old man and woman who seemed to be lovers sat way at the end of the bar and some lady was leaning over the jukebox. You could hear Billie in a low voice, "Smooth Road on a clear day. Oh, why am I the only one traveling this way?" I turned back to face the bartender as Loraine and her friend were coming my way. "Give me another gin fizz would you, my man?" The bartender came to fix my drink. I heard her voice behind me saying "Hello, Al. I've been looking for you." Trying to keep my sanity and my coolness, I turned around on the stool and said, "Hi, Loraine." They both were dressed very, very sharply. The guy' watch and ring damn near blinded me. He was a nice-looking guy about twenty-six years old. At that precise moment, I knew that I was a damn fool. Loraine had been a standup lady for me as the gospel singers say, "She had brought me out of the muddy clay" and look what I did to her. I damn near busted out in tears. I wanted to beg her to forgive me right there in the front of everybody, but somewhere between my pride and trying to be a man, I held the tears and the hurt out of view.

She said, "I want to you to meet Freddie, my husband." He said, "Why don't we take a table over here and sit down." I got my glass and followed them to the table. We were all sitting. He reached into his pocket an said, "I don't really have to do this, but out of respect for Loraine, I'm showing you this license." She said, "We were married a week ago in Minnesota." She said, "I didn't mean to hurt you, but it's almost been a year since Freddie first asked me to marry him. I tried to help you get on your feet and do some of the things you dreamed of. But you helped me make up my mind when I met Marina. I can only wish you well and hope that we can remain friends." I looked at her, holding back tears, and cutting my eyes over at Freddie. He had put the license back into his inside coat pocket. And he was kind of laid back, staring at me. Looking like a real Mac man, and to hem, I must have at that time looked like a damn fool. I ordered them a drink. They drank it kind of quickly, made an excuse that they had something else to do and was happy that I could accept the situation as it was, and wished me luck and they were gone. She said before she left, "By the way, Al, I might not see you very much because in the next couple of weeks I will be moving my mother. We are going back to Minnesota. And be aware of your associates that you call our friends, especially James." The saddest thing about this whole matter was that I recognized Freddie as being the guy who was sitting with his back to me on the stool when I went to get Loraine from the bar on Thirty-Ninth street.

1952 had been a good year for me. As the days turned into months, January brought in the new year, 1953. I promised myself that this year would be a better year for me. But two disasters came right in a row. I was lying in bed with Marina, sleeping late from a hard night of gambling when a knock came at the door. "Who is it?" I hollered out. "It's Frances," she said. "Open the door. Something has happened to Daddy," she cried out, "and some man is here from his job." I quickly jumped into my pants and rushed to the door. I invited the man into the room. "My name is Peacock. I work for the Steveson Hotel. I understand that you are the oldest child that Estell has. How old are you?" "Nineteen," "Theres been an accident. Your father is no longer with us. I guess you will let the rest of your family know." I said, "Yes." "What company does your mother work at? Do you know?" he asked me. I said, "Bradley Lamp Shade Factory. It's near Ohio and Orleans streets." I had to go through with the screaming, hollering, and crying for the next week. The funeral home was crowded, and it was a sad service. The funeral saddened everyone, and I guess it hurt me the most, losing my father because I really didn't get to know him, and with the third-grade education he had, maybe he didn't know how to express himself to me or teach me the things that an educated father would have taught his son., There was never any carfare to go to school from Twenty-Seventh Street to Thirty-Ninth Street. Ther was never lunch money for anyone of us, me, or my brother or sister. We all went to Phillips High School. The carfare, clothes, food, and all other concerns that a child needed, even the love came from my mother. Maybe she understood that care and love much better than anyone else in the family, because he had been lonely and alone, and had no one to care for her but her Aunt Lil. And that's why, I loved her so much. I wanted to try and show her all the love that she missed as a child and as a young lady. After she had met my daddy, the burdens of the kids were on her.

My mother had given me all nineteen of my father's suits, tailored made from Forty-Seventh Street, Dan Douglas Tailor. I went back to the tailor shop and had the suits altered to fit me. She gave me the car, a ten-year-old Cadillac. But after a couple of weeks of going to Forty-Seventh and King Drive to get my drover's permit, I pulled out form a parking space too quickly. A Buick car hit me near the Regal Theatre on the left front side, busting the springs or breaking the axle. Whatever it did, the wheel was bent outward. I junked the car. I wondered why my mother only got ten thousand dollars for my father's death. Maybe it was due to being black or maybe because we had a real estate lawyer that didn't know anything about accident cases. Whatever the reason was, I thought that ten thousand dollars was little money for falling seventeen stories in an elevator while at work. After she had cashed the check, my mother gave all of us kids five hundred dollars. She gave Marina two hundred and fifty dollars. She gave her sister-in-law and brother-in-law some money. She paid all of my father's debts. The day before she had given us, he money, she told me of her plans. This was the first time I had raised my voice to her. "Mommy, you don't owe me anything. You dure don't owe Aunt Zora, Uncle Prince, or Uncle Willie anything. Spend that money on yourself. Pay a down payment for a building and let other people pay your rent. And when it's time for you to retire, the building will pay for itself." "Yes A, that sounds very good, but I don't know how to run a building." She was sitting on the piano bench and looking up at me when I was standing by the window. "No," she said, "I have made up my mind. I'm going to pay his bills and give his family a little piece of the money. I think this is the right thing to do." I looked back at her and said, "you're right. That is the right thing to do." "Yes, I believe it is." She smiled, she had a giving heart, she always been like that even from a child.

CHAPTER 44

For the next six months, I was hard to get along with. I didn't come around the familiar clubs. I went to strange clubs because I didn't want te frustration of the old crowds. I had kind of pulled myself away from Wadell, Tommy, Leroy, and the rest of the crowd because Marina had lost her job and I was losing my coordination of the dice because I couldn't concentrate., and it was all about concentration., There was too much happening to me at one time, and it seemed that all of it was being piled up on my shoulders at the wrong time. I couldn't keep my appearance up to par, either. It was hard struggling. It was much harder to cop another hoe, and to be truthful to myself, I really wasn't trying to cop another hoe. It was late on a Saturday afternoon that I had decided to go by Leroy's gambling place. I walked to the door when some guy came down the stairs and met me in the lobby. "We are closed, man. The police just took two wagonloads of niggers to jail, including Wadell, Tommy, and Drug Store Bob. Come back tomorrow. I know we'll be open."

At a slow pace, I walked home. I had been gone for six hours and I had the same forty dollars in my pocket that I had when I left. It was about nine o'clock when I reached my building and I saw my little brother in the yard. He said, "I've been waiting on you, Al cuz' Maring is gone." I said, "Gone, where?" I said, "Gone where?" He said, "She caught the bus. She called a cab, and they took her to the bus station, and she said that she was gong back to St. Louis."

For the next five days, I laid in the house. My mother was worried about me. She was asking me every day when she got in from work was, I ok. I would say, “Mother, I’m alright. I’m just trying to get my thoughts together. I’m not sick. It ain’t nothing wrong with me.” The hurt and pain from losing Loraine and Marina had my stomach in a knot and I had that rabbit jumping. I was suffering from loneliness because of separations. My mother used to cook for me and send the food down by my sister.

It was on the third day, as I lay in the bed looking at the ceiling when Wadell’s advice came back to my mind when he told me I should go back home and makeup to my father, and then he told me he had a job. I didn’t know that he had a job. He said, you should find a job, straighten up your act and surprise the shit out of these niggers. So that’s when I decided my next move was to get a job. It was two days later that I landed a job on Elston at a powdered egg company. I had worked a month straight, saving everydime, other that what I gave my mother and my rent money.

This particular night, I cleaned myself up in one of the finest suits my father had left me. I was dressed in gray, with a light gray Dobbs hat that sat on the top of my head. The shoes were black and shiny. I wore a black shirt to blend in with the black band around the gray Dobbs. I stopped at Henry’s first. The old gang was there. Everybody was happy to se me. Johnny reached on the inside of his coat pocket and brought out he gin bottle and hand it to me. “Man, where you’ve been?” Leroy asked. “We all thought you had run off to Minesota, going to get Loraine.” I looked at Leroy sitting in the booth by Tommy and said, “Loraine’s a dead horse.” “I’m looking for a live one.” I gave a little laugh, as Emma came through the door and all eyes were on her. She told the waitress to give her a coke to go. She looked around the room, hen at me. I kind of cut my eyes in an ignoring manner at her.

She paid for the pop and was back outside the door. It was about two weeks later when I entered the Harmonia hotel. I went to the basement to hear the Combo band. I had bought myself a drink and kind of wandered in front of the band, popping my fingers to the beat. I heard a woman cry out from the rear of me in the crowd. "Hey, daddy, daddy, daddy." I kept popping my fingers to the rhythm. Some guy touched me on my shoulder. The lady's voice kept ringing out, "Dad, daddy, daddy." I turned to face the stranger. "That lady over there at the table is trying to get your attention," he said. I turned around with a frowning stare because I never had anyone to call me daddy before, and I wasn't old enough to be anyone's daddy. So, I thought they had the wrong person. I turned to the table where the voice was coming from, and to my surprise. It was Emma.

She was dressed very conservatively. There were three guys and two white girls sitting at the table with her. They all seemed to be high and having a god time. "Sit down," she said as I approached the table. "The fellah that was sitting with me is gone. He seems to have had too many drinks," Beverly said. "Did o see how he was walking? He might not make it home." One of the guys named Rick said, "Don't say that." She introduced me to the people at the table. I sat beside her. She said, "Pretty daddy, "smiling at me, and showing the gold in her mouth. "Tell these girls about the signifying monkey." One of the girls that was named Beverly, said, "please do tell us about the little ole monkey." Then the party began and as I told the jokes they were steadily buying the drinks. One of the girls laughed so hard she knocked over a fifth of Cognac on the table. "My goodness, how did you learn so may jokes?" Crystal asked me as she laughed at the last joke. The bartender said, "last call for alcohol, you don't have to go home, but you got to get out of here." The band was packing up their gear. People were leaving their tables, heading for the door. Emma told Crystal. you guys go ahead to the car. I want to tell Al something. I'll catch up with you."

"I want to let you know, pretty baby, that you were always the chosen one as far as I'm concerned. But you had those little chic's following up behind you." When I choose a man, I like him to be my man and m man alone. I heard that you are free now." I said, "Yeah." "Maybe, you are ready to deal with me now?" I hurried up and said, "very much so." She said, "Do you want to make some money with me in the morning?" I said, "Sure, I do." She said, "Do you still stay at Twenty-Eighth and Prairie?" "No, just a couple of days ago, we moved to 2901 South Prairie, right across the street from the police station. My apartment is apartment C." She said, "I know the place. I'll meet you there at eight-thirty." I had gotten up at six-thirty that morning and had taken a bath at about seven. I was dressed and ready for her at eight. She got there at about eight forty-five. I saw the cab when it pulled up in front of the building. In minutes, I was in the cab. She told the cab driver to take us to twenty-eighth and Michigan. The cab stopped in front of a factory, a one story long white building. She paid the cab driver, and we walked up to the door, and she knocked on it real hard. She must have knocked on the door for at least five minutes. We had almost gotten ready to give up when she said, "Damn, I bet he's gone. I was supposed to have been here by nine." By the time she had gotten those words out of her mouth the door had come ajar.

"Hi, Ema," he big fat white guy said. I thought you weren't coming. He seemed to be six feet tall with a stomach that hung out like Santa Claus. His hair was sandy brown as he led us through the waiting room. He stopped at the door to the right of the hallway, and he opened the door to a big spacious office where pictures of plants and horses hung on the wall. A big desk and chair sat in front of a picture window to the rear of the room. A leather couch hand lounge chair facing the couch sat by the door. A night lamp stood by the lounge chair. "I'm sorry I was late, Jake. She started taking her gloves off and laid them on the coffee table where a silver horse head sat on the other end of the table. He sat down in the lounge chair. His breathing was loud like rustling noise. She turned to me, "Take off your clothes, baby. Lay them right there on the table." I said, "WHAT?" I kind of looked at the fat boy's eyes. They had gotten big. Then I turned my attention back to Emma, and my eyes got big as I looked at those long curly hairs and the long nipples that had gotten hard. I forgot about the fat boy and inserted that warm area. I was young, inexperienced, and excited, so I started to buck like I would do on Roy Rogers' horse, Trigger. As I got faster in my motion, the fat boy said, "That's right, whip that pussy, whip it, whip it, whip it." Immediately as I climaxed and rolled off Emma, the fat boy handed me a towel and pointed to the bathroom across the hall and the door locked behind me. I forgot about the bathroom and kneeled down. I wanted to see what was going on, so I peeped through the keyhole of the door that they were in. The only thing that I could see was the long legs of Emma and the fat boy with his arms around her legs.

After a while, we were dressed and out of there. Two hotels sat at Thirtieth and Michigan. She asked when we were inside of the cab, "do you want to go to breakfast in the hotel, or do you want to go to Powell's?" I said, the hotel would be fine." We were in front of the hotel. Emma said, "You can pay for the cab, and I'll go and register for the room." She handed me a roll of money. Emma ordered our breakfast at the desk. We were in the room now. She said, "Do you want to take your bath daddy before the food gets here?" she said, "You can take off your clothes and I'll run your water." She reached into her purse and took out some kind of lotion or water solution and put it into the water. While I heard her playing with the bubbles in the water I tried my best to take my clothes off and count the money at the same time. She had given me six hundred dollars.

CHAPTER 45

Emma gave me a bath, and after we ate and drank the chilled Morgan David wine, she pulled two refers from her purse and placed one of the table by he bed and lit the other one. She smiled at me when she took a puff from the refer. She took two more pulls and passed it to me. I knew that refer made me kind of paranoid. I didn't want any, so I grabbed the refer and started puffing on it like it was an everyday routine to me. After I had finished puffing on the refer, I passed it back to Emma and kind of laid back and relaxed. Her voice seemed to be far away now as she was saying "Do you like me just a little bit, baby? Do you, daddy?" Her voice sounded like she was five blocks away. She was rubbing my legs now, then my feet. She was saying some words that I couldn't make out. She was nibbling at my big toe. Before long, the whole toe was inside of her mouth. I kind of relaxed more. Then her tongue was racing up and down my leg to my thigh, and then to my belly button, and back to my nipples. The little knot between my legs had stretched out now as he slowly started to swallow it. I said, "Yes, baby." I said, "Everything I have is yours." I had plenty of fun that night with Emma as I lost my cap. Emma had a vast clientele. Whereas Loraine was giving me three hundred or four hundred a night, in a matter of three or four hours, Emma had six hundred. For the next year or so, Emma rested and dressed me. She wouldn't dream of me having job. She made me quit the last one I had when I met her. It seemed like everywhere we went, she tried to show me off. She would get louder with that daddy, daddy, daddy shit."

It was one night in October that Emma had taken me to a lounge called the Esquire. She said, "Daddy, would you have a drink here? I have a client I need to see. Would you wait for me a couple of hours, sweet daddy/" I was looking around for the barmaid. Some guy was sitting at the bar and said, "if you're looking for the barmaid, she is in the bathroom. She'll be right back." I was listening to music on the jukebox. The voice was saying, He heard the rooster crow for a day, when a voice behind me said, "Can I help you, sir?" I turned to face the prettiest girl I had ever seen, I thought. She was really light-skinned, with freckles on her face with red hair, natural red hair, with a beautiful smile and dimples. She smiled at me again and said, "May I help you?" I said, "Yes, give me a gin fizz. And can I ask you a question?" She said, "Sure." "Do you have a husband with a shotgun or does your boyfriend carry a hatchet?" She said, "Neither one, I don't mess with characters like that." I said, "then fix yourself a drink and come and join me." She was back with the drinks. I gave her some money to put in the box. There were about five other people there. She was taking care of them, but then she would come back to me. For the next six months I would enjoy the evenings from about twelve to five, and I would stay with Candy. She had to be at work at six. Cand was a young girl, twenty-two. She never gave me any cash money, but he would buy me gifts. Sometimes she would buy me a nice sweater or shirt here and there, and even a tie. Emma was a late sleeper, so she would never get up until around five or six in the evening. I never had any trouble out of Emma about Candy until one day we were sitting in the Glass Bar, a guy named Jasper said, "Al, you know that little sweet dish named Candy that you were drinking with in the 114 Club? "I said "Yeah, what about her?" He said, "Man, I know where that broad works, and I'm going to go there tonight. She works at the Esquire Lounge on Ninety-Fifth Street." I know of have seen Emma's lips tighten up out of the corner of my eye when she looked around me. "What were you doing with that little bitch, Candy from the Esquire? She asked me. I said, "Eddie and I were together last week. We stopped in for a drink. Eddie started talking to her and he invited her down to the 114 Club." She said, "Eddie, my ass. If I find out the little bitch is down here to see you, I'm going to knock all the shit spots of her face. Bring me another drink, baby, and bring me some dimes for the jukebox." She signaled the bartender. Emma got her drink and went over to the jukebox. I wasn't thinking about Emma too much. I was thinking about how to clear this up between her and Candy. I had ordered me another drink when Nat King Cole was singing on the box.

"Bought you a Cadillac for Christmas and diamond ring a beautiful fur coat, and everything love iw shat mekes me do the things I do, Gee baby ain't I good to you."

Emma was sitting at the table near the jukebox, sipping on her drink with her head low and shaking it from side to the other side. I sipped the last of my drink and looked around for Jasper. I wanted to slap the shit out of him for making that mistake with Emma, but he was gone. I walked over and pulled a chair beside Emma. I said, "What do you want to spoil our night for?" You know I don't want any punk-ass bitch like Candy. It was hard enough for me to cop you. You know I don't want to lose you now, you're my everything. If you want to, I'll go out to the Esquire with you and we'll clown together, or we'll find Eddie and he'll tell you the same thing. I just told you." She looked up at me and tears were in her eyes. She said, "You do love, don't you, daddy?" I said, "With all my heart, soul, and mind. You know this so. I don't know why you are sitting here thinking that a little punk-as girl like Candy could possibly take your place. Come on, baby, let me go to your place and show you who I love." She said, "Okay." Almost falling into me from the drinks that she had drunk. I held her up and helped her to the cab. Once at her house, the taking and love making that we did erase any concerns about Candy out of her mind.

CHAPTER 46

It was July 1954. We had moved to Sixty-Fifth and Langley. We lived on the second floor with three bedrooms, a living room, dining room, and a kitchen. My Uncle Willi had moved with us to help my mother with the rent. Candy and I had gotten tighter than ever. I would take her away from the neighborhood. We hung out in Chuck's Sea and Sea lounge on Sixty-Fifth and Cottage Grove. Someone tipped Emma off. Emma took a cab the lounge where Candy was working and called her all kinds of bitches and told her if she caught her with me again that she would blow her goddamnhead off. She left without being arrested or anything. She then caught a cab and went home. Emma had scared the shit out of Candy. She called me the next day and told me that she never wanted to see me again in life. I told her I could fix it. She just needs to give me a chance to fix it. She told me we could never do anything again while I was with Emma.

On July 25, I sat in my living room reading a draft notice that they had sent me. The letter told me that I would be classified the following week. The letter also said, "Uncle Sam needs me." I had just finished reading the letter when the doorbell rang. Everyone in my house had gone to work. I answered the door, and it was Emma. She came upstairs. She was dressed neatly today with her sunshades on, looking like a million dollars. But I was thinking about Candy telling me I could never touch her or see her again as long as I was with Emma. And my heart hardened as I spoke ot Emma in a snappy voice. "I guess our playtime was over," I said to her. "What you mean, daddy?" she answered. "I mean they're fixing to send my ass to the army, that's what I mean." "That's good daddy," she said. "I can go with you wherever you go to, Fort Bragg, Texas. We can get married. Look how much money we can make on the army base." "Who said any goddamn thing about marriage> I never said I was going to marry no damn body!" "I thought we would get married. I love you. Don't you love me, daddy?' I thought about Candy. If I was going to let it go, I had to ice it here. "I don't love no motherfucking body, especially your motherfucking ass." "You don't mean that, daddy. I know you love me cause I love you, she went on. "What I'd love Emma, is for you to get out of my motherfucking face and go and find you a man your age and get married." These words seemed to have burned through her. She seemed to have sunk back into the chair when I said that. I felt bad after I said that. But I couldn't show any emotion. She got up from the couch slowly and got her purse.

Well, you certainly told me. It's that bitch, Candy, isn't it? When I see that bitch again, she will never look at another one of my men again." I said, "It isn't Candy, Emma. It's this lifestyle. I'm tired of this damn lifestyle, but this man's army is going to have something for me. So, what I am really trying to tell you is find someone that you can settle down with cause I'm not ready to settle down, not with you or Candy!" She had her purse in her hand and tears in her eyes as she smiled at me, turned, and walked down the steps and out the door. Two weeks later, the army classified me as 1F, meaning that I didn't have to go to the army. I didn't miss Semma at first until my mother started needing help with carfare, part of the rent, the light bill and gas bill, etc. I had lots of clothes, but they were all piled up in the closet like dirt linen. I was twenty years old. I didn't shave and my hair was long, and I needed a haircut badly. Two or three months had passed since I last saw Emma. I was coming out of Dudley's Lounge at Sixty-Fifth and Cottage grove when I saw this pretty El Dorado pull up in front of Chuck's lounge across the street from Dudley's. The lady that got out of the car was Emma. I kind of stepped back into Dudley's, peeping through the glass window as Emma took the driver's arm and went through the door.

CHAPTER 47

I would never tell anyone That I could kick my own ass the way I played myself with Loraine, and especially Emma. It was true that I had gotten tired of that "daddy shit" and her all over me, smothering me, not giving me the chance to breathe. With Loraine, I could get around and do my thing with gambling and joke with the guys. But after fine in the evening, it seemed like I was in jail when I saw Emma. Although I hurt myself when I let her go, but now it was time for me to snap myself out of this bullshit about Emma. I had to go get me some money because I really thought I was the best hoe I knew for myself. That Friday night, I begged my mother out of one hundred dollars, promising her dearly that I would bring it back that Monday. I went and got a haircut and Noxzema for my face. I put on a starched white shirt, black pants, and a black summer cap. I found myself walking on Sixty-Third and Cottage Grove up the stairs to Ann Hues Crap joint on the second floor over Ann Hues Lounge. I got to the bar gate that they had up at the door. The door was closed. A guy named Jimmy answered e door. I knew him from Leroy's. "Well, I'll be goddamn. Here is Lil' Pimp," he said. "Where have you been, man?" "I've been chasing hen dollars like you have," I answered him. He said, "Charels in in the other room, Chales from the Sea& Sea Lounge on Sixty-Fifth & Cottage Grove. They are shooting big cash in there. Another one of your partners is here, John Levi, from Twenty-Sixth and Prairie."

The crap table was crowded. You had to fight your way to the table. All kind of niggers, broke niggers, niggers that lost their money, nigger's that still had money, crowded around the table and I squeezed my way to the table. The stick man said, "Hey man, hey you there," he said hat to a guy that was full of whiskey. The drunk guy said, "Are you talking to me?" "Yeah, man, get back from the table. Let his man come in that's got some money. You aint got shit." I looked around the table. It seemed that every hustler in Chicago was here. All the guys could shoot. I knew John, and he could switch those dice damn near faster than Wadell. Charles from the Sea & Sea Lounge was John's partner. I started to back up and just leave. Then I thought I would stay around to see how it would go. The dice finally worked their way to Charles. Charles hit about three licks, doubling, and tripling the hundred dollars that he shot. Then as the old game went, he dropped down and played twenty-five dollars. The old guy said, "I ain't got him." Of course, John said, "That's my kind of bet," just like Wadell and me, John came out for the twenty-five dollars. "Snake eyes," the houseman said, "pass the dice." The guy next to Charles was shooting now. He said, "I'll shoot fifty dollars." He came out and caught a ten. He came back and made two fives. "Ten points," the houseman said, "what are you shooting now?" I'll shoot one hundred dollars." Charles said, "Let him shoot." The guy was out again with the dice. "Two sixes," the houseman said. He crapped out and passed the dice. "Next shooter." It was John's time to shoot the dice now. John hit about three good licks for one hundred dollars and missed out shooting fifty. It seemed like forty-five minutes had passed before the dice reached me. I really didn't want Leroy or Charles to fade me. If they had, I would've passed the dice on the next roll.

I needed some money. Tonight, I had to shoot it. All or nothing, ten or fifteen dollars weren't nothing. And once again, that rabbit kicked up in my stomach from being afraid of missing on my first throw. I went back to the Bible like I always did when I was in trouble or feared something. It might have been wrong, but, once again in the crap house, I said, "God, please help me." I needed to help my family. I wanted to once again bring something to the table for my family. I cuffed my hand, stood there with confidence, not shaking or trembling, very alert. I saw the dice when it hit the palm of my hand, it was on the twos and the five, one pair on the bottom and the other on top. Right away, I knew that the two were under five. I had to roll them twice in my hand, let one of the twos catch up with one of five. Like clockwork, I shook the dice. And with my thumb, I clicked the dice twice to make the two catch up with the five, making the dice read seven in my hand. I shook them to my ear again. "Come on pretty dice," I said as I slung the dice across the table. I saw Charles kind of smile when the dices marched like soldiers across the screen, "Seven," the houseman said. "What hyo shooting now?" I said, "Shoot the two." Again, right away, I cuffed the dice and clicked them on eleven. The dice sailed again. "Eleven," the houseman said, "You have four hundred dollars here. We cut fifty. You have three hundred and fifty dollars left. What are you shooting now?" I said, "Let it roll, all of it." I had enough confidence. And I was sure that I had my coordination back as I sailed the dice across the screen. "Six and four, you got a ten," the houseman said. I cuffed my hand again and caught the dice. I clicked the dice on deuces because I knew the two fives were under the deuces. I sailed the dice out again across the screen, the one sat still as the other dice spun and landed on the three. "Four," the houseman said, "you are looking for ten." "Come on, Al, you are shooting at it. It is under the bottom, bring it to the top. A hundred dollars, he bars the ten," Charles was saying. Some guy in the crowd said, "bet," and threw the money to the house guy.

I came out again across the screen and this time caught a six. The houseman threw them back to me. I saw a deuce and six. I blocked it with the two and the six in the middle of the dice, throwing a kind of navy spin. "Two times," the houseman said, "ten". You have seven hundred. what are you shooting?" I said, "Shoot he hundred." I put the six hundred in my pocket. I missed out trying to make a four. I stayed here for the next two hours going up and down, and I left the crap game with six hundred dollars in my pocket. I had met some friends who were trying to be pimps, so I sat in several Chili Parlors and Lounges on Forty-Seventh Street, Forty-Third Street and even Sixty-Third Street trying to pull any lonely or forgotten whores out there. I made a few pennies off a couple of girls, but they were on the run from the whorehouse, or they jumped into a trick's scar, and I never saw them again. They were little street hustlers. They didn't have a change of draws. Nasty bitches, I should have put them in the clinic. I talked to a whore in a bar around the corner from the Crown Propeller Lounge. After talking to her, the dope must have come down on her. She was so incoherent that I winded up giving her ten dollars to go and get her some food. I knew at this time that it was time for me to go back to Elston, to my old job at the Powder /egg factory. I had established myself on /Sixty-Third Street, Sixty-Fifth Street, the Douglas Longe, and the C&C Lounge of being a half-ass pimp and a husler. Now I'm going to use Wadell's tactics of getting a job as a backup and not let anyone know that I was working, not even my closet friends.

As the months passed, I used the money wisely, buying clothes, and keeping my hair done. Every two weeks, I got my hair done and a manicure at he house of Nelson on Sixty-Fourth and Cottage Grove. I would change at least twice in one day on the weekends. There was one guy we called shug. He was kind of neat. He wasn't a player or anything, just an average guy. We sat together at the

Douglas Lounge. He said, "Man, I'm not trying to be funny or anything, but how many suits do you have? I said, "About twenty." As we talked and I bought him another drink, a pretty blonde-haired lady walked to the bar. I recognized her as being the lady hat sat in the Art Movie house booth when I went to the picture show. I admired her. I used to go to the show just to see her, watching the same movie three or four times a week. I didn't know if he had noticed me when I went to the show. She had nice pretty legs. The hair on her legs excited me. I like hairy ladies. She wore an ankle bracelet. Some black women did not look good with blonde hair, but her blonde colored hair fit her face perfectly. She was a very pretty young lady. "What's her name, man?" I turned to the guy that was sitting with me. He said, "I don't know. I just know that she works in the booth of the art show, and she lives in the Mansfield Hotel. I would see her here every now and then walking a white poodle. I said, "Yes, I have seen her waking a poodle also. Man, I like this bitch," I told the guy sitting next to me. "Man look at the hairs on her legs." "Yeah, man, I had noticed that, too." I got up from the bar and walked over to the jukebox and put fifty cents in. Al Hibbler came on singing.

> ***As the light do down low and baby you know there will be no reason for teasing and when we huddle up near without any fear, I got some sweet talk that you want to hear, and I'll be loving you so you after the light go down low."***

I moved back to the stool where I was sitting with Shug and called the bartender over and ordered me and Shug a drink and told the bartender to give the lady whatever she was drinking. There were about eight other people in the bar, but they were laughing and talking and doing their own thing. The bartender was back with the drinks, and he gave the blonde lady her drink. She raised her glass to give me a toss and thank me. I had played five records including Al Hibbler's record, Nat King Cole, and Dinah Washing. Wen Al Hibbler's record came back on, I went over to the young lady and introduced myself, "My name is Al." She said her mane was Sydney. "I kind of like this record would you like to dance?" She said, "Yes." And put both of her arms around my neck. I kind of pulled her close to me as we danced. I had the bartender to bring my drink next to hers. We sat and drank three more shots. We were feeling pretty mellow then. I looked about to see Shug throwing up his hand as he left out the door. I said "We will have one more dance and then we can go across the street to Chuck's for a nightcap. And then maybe you might invite me to that hotel room of yours." She said, "I'm with you, baby." We were dancing again to Al Hibbler singing,

> ***I got some sweet talk that you want to hear, and I'll be loving you so, after the light go down low."***

I kind of pulled her close to me and lightly bit her on the neck. She laid her head on my shoulder. As we stopped in the middle of the floor and grinned, she said, "Oh, baby, don't do this to me." I started to take her straight to her hotel room, but I wanted everyone to see me with this fine bitch. So, I went over to the C & C Lounge across the street from the Doughlas Longe. We had two drinks there. We sat in front of the bar. I wanted everyone to see me. She had the most beautiful smile I had ever seen, I thought. I was smiling to myself as she would lean over every now and then and kiss me on my jaw. That little knot in my pants was smiling too. I could really go for this girl, and I knew that. She had the looks and the personality. I looked around the room and the bar where I was sitting, everyone was laughing and talking and appeared to be looking at me with envy. The telephone in the rear of the room rang. About two or three seconds after the phone was answered, some guy hollered from the rear, "Is there a guy named Al, in he house?" I said, "Al?" He said, yes, are you Al?" I said, "yeah," He said, "telephone," I said, "Baby I'll be right back, and kissed her on the jaw. I went to answer the phone. "Hello," He said, "Hello Al, this is Ray, the bartender. I can't talk loudly. Man, you know who you are kissing and talking to?" He continued, "That's why everyone is talking and laughing. Everyone but you know that she is a man." I damn nearly fainted. He said, "I'm telling you the truth. I don't want you to keep sitting there looking like a fool. Look at his Adam's apple and his hands, Al, you will know." I came back to the table. The man could see in my eyes that I knew. He said, "What's wrong, baby?" I said, starring at his Adam's apple, "My mother I sick, and I've got to rush home now." "Maybe tomorrow." After paying the bill, I said "Meet me at the Douglas Lounge.: and I was out the door. I stayed away from around the Douglas Lounge. I didn't come around for a while.

I was sitting in the Douglas on a Sunday afternoon in a brown polka-dot suit. I thought I looked jazzy that night when Nella walked in. She was about five feet three, nice hips, hairy legs. You could see the fuzz on her arms beneath the short-sleeved dress she had on. It was in August, so she was dressed in summerish. Her skin color was a soft caramel color. She had thick black hair that hung down the middle of her back. I was sitting with a gentleman friend named Lewis. We had just ordered a drink. I kind of nudged him in the side. I said, "Goddamn, man, I never seen her in here before." He said, "She's a newcomer to the neighborhood. She lives on Sixty-Fourth and Drexel. I don't really know her personally but while driving, I have seen her going in and out of the building." She walked to the rear and took a stool at the bar. She ordered a Budweiser. Every now and then she would catch me staring at her. She kind of gave me a smile and sipped off her beer. She drank two beers before she walked out of the bar. I watched her leave. That Friday night, I went into the Douglas Lounge hoping to see her. I was again dressed in blue and trying to look my best in case she came in. I had only twenty dollars. But before long, talking and drinking with the guys, I had already spent my money. At about ten o'clock, I had one half of the beer, and I was broke. There were seven people in the tavern, two women and the rest were men. One of the men was sitting by me. A fair looking brown skinned woman came into the door at about ten fifteen. We sat across from the jukebox, which was in the middle of the room. She walked past us and gave me a little smile. She went to the far end of the bar and ordered a shot of Hennessey. I found a quarter in my pocket and went over to the jukebox and played "What a Difference A Day Makes," by Dinah Washington, "After the Lights Go Down Low, by Al Hibbler, and "Living for You, by Billie Holiday. The record by Al Hibbler was playing when the bartender asked me what I was drinking. The lady wanted to buy me a drink and he said, "I'll take a bud," and he said, "I'll take a Bud." I said, "I'm going to put it by her. She wants you to join her. I winked at my friend. He gave me a smile. I walked over to the lady who bought the beer and I seated myself beside her and I introduced myself. "Thanks for the beer, "I said. She said, "You are more than welcome." She went on explaining how hot it had been that day and tonight was the first night that she was starting her vacation from her job. She said, "My name is Gloria." I told her my name one more time, Al." "I know." "So, you are on vacation?" "Yes, I am." "Well, Gloria, you have caught me in an embarrassing situation. The truth of the matter is, I am in between jobs and as much as I would like to buy you a vacation drink, I'm really broke. I sure wish I had some money, and I could show you lots of things on your vacation." She smiled and said, "Like what?" "I can assure you all of them would be good things." She poured the rest of her beer into the glass and drank it down. She asked me, "How long are you going to be here, Mr. Al?" I said, "I was just about to leave before you saved my life with that beer." She smiled again at my joke about the beer. She said, "I'm going to buy you another beer. Do you think you can stay around for another hour or so? I need to run home." I said, "Sure." She ordered the beer and left. There were about four men in the bar when she left. It appeared that they all had their ears peeled to my conversation. One guy sat with another guy by the jukebox. They called him Uncle Bud. "Boy, you are a slick fucker. I heard you over there talking to that girl. You got another one, huh?" I said, "I don't know yet." "Yeah, I think you are going to have company tonight, so just stick around." "I've got to go t work tomorrow." It was twelve-thirty when Gloria left. There were only three of us left along with the bartender. The clock said one forty-five. I said in a loud voice, "I guess I've had it. She's not coming this late. I guess I'll go home." Then I heard a voice behind me say, "She's coming into door now." She said, "Had you given up on me?" I said, "Oh, no." She ordered us a drink and she gave me thirty-five dollars that were wrapped with a rubber band. She said, "Can you work with that and show me some of those good things?" I said "Yeah." We wound up in a hotel where we wrestled, and it seemed like it was all night. We got up the next morning at about ten o'clock and we went to Dale's Restaurant and ordered breakfast. The morning crowd had left, leaving only two old ladies sitting on the sidewall of the restaurant, and old man with a mop pail was sitting in the back. Gloria and I sat in front, at a side window looking at the people walking by. She said, smiling at me, "You are a very neat dresser. I kind of like you a little bit." She said smiling at me. I said, "You know I like you, too baby, the way you handled me last night." "What time will I see you tonight? We agreed to meet at the Douglas Lounge, or do you want to meet me back here at the Daley Restaurant?" I said, "It doesn't make me any difference, whatever you say."

She told me "Go ahead and spend that little change in your pocket." That was all the money I had in my pocket. "And if you need any more, just give me a call, and I'll bring whatever you need. Don't be afraid to call. I live with my mother." We had agreed to meet at the Douglas Lounge at seven o'clock. I had told all my partners about her. They helped me to drink up the few pennies by praising me and telling me the things they thought I wanted to hear until the money was gone. It was about six-thirty when everybody left me sitting there half high and broke. She had said to tell her if I ran out of money, so I'm about to tell her. I was going to be lights on her, or so I thought as I heard the phone ring. I wasn't going to ask her for four hundred or five hundred. One hundred dollars would be sufficient for me. I heard a voice from the other end, and it sounded like an elderly woman. Hello, hello." I said, "Hello, may I speak to Gloria? Is Gloria available?" I asked as I crossed my fingers. She said, "Yes, this is Gloria's mother." I said, "So, may I speak to Gloria?" "I don't know who you are, mister. When was the last time you seen Gloria?" I said, "Last night." "Well, if you see her tonight, tell her that this here baby, her baby has no milk for three days. Would she please come home and let me know that she's alright and see about her baby? It's wrong to stay away from this baby for so long." I heard the baby start to cry as the old lady tried to mumble more words into the phone. I felt bad. The rabbit had knotted up again in my stomach. The nerve of that bitch to give me a fucking sixty-five dollars and hadn't bought her own child a can of milk. And who knows? She didn't say it, but her mother might be hungry, too! I said, "Is Gloria married, or is there a boyfriend that she is living with?" she said, "no, that girl is in and out. She hardly stays here. She leaves that baby on me all the time." "Where do you live?" "Why, what do you want to know that for?" "I would like to try and get the baby some milk." "that's all right. The baby and I will make it. Just tell her if you see her what I said."

I had a lot of goddamn nerve asking the lady where to bring the baby some milk, and I didn't have fifteen cents in my pockets to catch a jitney. How in the fuck was I going to buy some ilk? But is she had told me where she lived and asked me to bring the milk, I would have brought it, even if I would have had to stick up a motherfucker because there were two things that I was weak for, old ladies and babies. Or maybe I was just feeling guilty because I had drunk up all the money and then last night, I was jumping up and down on that bitch's nasty ass with her baby mild money.

For the next three or four weeks, I worked at the Power Egg Factory doing some time twelve or thirteen hours on some weekends. I would go out with some guys to the Chili Parlor's on 43re, 47th, and 55th Street to try and catch some bar hoes. We would beg and rip them off for whatever we could, sometimes we would get something and sometimes we wouldn't, and it was a good game for us. Sometimes you would find an exception. A good hoe but most of the time, they would be tramps. You had to be a fast talker for that good hoe because she would just sit there and listen to you talk and cling tighter to those dollars. I guess about six weeks had passed and I had only seen Nella a couple of times jumping into a cab or walking out of the lounge door. This particular night, Nella was sitting on a stool in the middle of the bar, the lounge was kind of crowded. She was sitting there by herself and there was an empty stool beside her. Billie Holliday was on the jukebox. Singing:

Maybe I'm a fool but its fun, people said, you rule with a wave of your hand, Darling that's grand they just don't understand, that I'm living for you, It's easy to live when you are in love, and I'm so in love, there's nothing in life but you.

I was trying to make it to that stool where Nella was sitting as I was walking, I didn't see ht Gloria had gotten off a stool in the front of the bar and was coming towards me with her hands stretched out singing Billie Holliday. "Hi baby" she said, "did you miss me?" I was shocked, but at the same time my eyes went to Nella. I could read no kind of emotion in her eyes as my eyes came back to meet Glorias. "Hi, I said. "I got something for you. Come on. Let's sit over here at a table by the jukebox." We sat and for the first time, I knew Nella cared the way she is staring at me through the mirror as if she wanted to cut my throat. Nella observed her giving me two crispy one hundred dollars bills. I kind of let it sit on the table for a minute. "So, what are we going to do with this? "I asked her. "You don't want to have fun with me?" "I can't understand every six-month fun, I think the last time I saw you, you were coming that evening, now here we go through the same routine six months later." She said, "Let's not fight. It's a long story and when a woman likes a man well enough to seek him out and comes to be with him, you should appreciate it." I looked at her and I remembered the conversation that Tommy, Waddell, and Drug Store Bob was having in the restaurant when Tommy asked Drug Store Bob, "Can you believe that the shade of a toothpick, just that little bit of shade beats the hot boiling sun?" I kind of laughed at myself. My pockets were kind of shady. The two hundred dollars could help my pockets. She said, "Come on baby, let's get a bottle and get out of here." Nella was still rolling her eyes at me through the mirrors. I went through the door. I had a pretty nice time with Gloria that night, but I was still pissed off at her. Because I knew in my heart that she was a hoe and maybe I was pissed off that she wasn't hoeing for me. Or maybe I should be mad at myself because at this point, I had to accept the fact that I wasn't strong enough in my game to pull her. After that night, I never saw Gloria again. I often wondered about her, but after a while all the thoughts of her faded away with time.

CHAPTER 48

It was about three weeks later that Nella was sitting in the bar. I had been lucky this week. I had about four hundred dollars in my pocket. I felt pretty good. There were about five people in the bar scattered around. I seated myself next to her to give her a nose full of Old Spice cologne. "I'm getting tired of choosing you and you ignoring me. "I said, "You know I'm in love with you, or have you told you husband yet?" The bartender was in front of me now. We both saw her expression of surprise. Give my wife what she is drinking. Mr. Louis." "Your wife?" he asked, looking questionably. I said, "To be more exact, the woman I'm going to marry." She looked more surprised at me saying that than he did. I said, "Is your husband a shotgun carrier, or does your boyfriend carry a hatchet?" She said, "I have no husband, but my boyfriend might have a hatchet. I just quit him an hour ago." "Well, dies he know you are here?" I kind of backed up off of her. "No, but the last time I saw him, he was on Fifty-Fifth Street." We sat and talked and drank for about two hours. She told me where she lived, and I walked her home. When we got to the front of her house, she said, "All I have in my house is beer, if you want to come in for a beer, you are welcome too." I said "Yeah, I'll have a beer." She had a little small kitchenette with a hot plate on the table, a refrigerator, two chairs, and a bed, and a closet. The shades were pulled down on the window. I had told her where I lived. I had told her that I had been pursuing her for at least two months. I told her how much I liked her. I asked her was she a Filipino or an Indian. “No,” she said, “I’m black, just like you. Everybody gets me mixed up.” I aid, “On account of your hair and complexion and those hairy legs you have. She said, “You don’t like my hair” I said, “I love it.”

I noticed that she had hairs down her back and two or three hairs between her bsreast, the cleavage area. As we sat drinking and talking in a fun-like manner. A loud knock came to the window. “I hear you in there, Nella, open the damn door.” She put her finger up to her lips for me to be quiet. She then led me to the rear door and then let me out. The door closed back as fast as it opened. I quickly walked through the alley and out of view. I remembered the last time I was caught up in someone else’s affairs. I didn’t want any part of this, I thought as I headed for home. A week had gone by when my doorbell rang. I was watching television. I went to the window that was over the vestibule door. I raised the window and looked out. “Hi,” I said. Nella looked up. “Come on down. I want to show you something.” We were walking and almost holding hands. “Al, I know you mean well. Everybody talks sweet, but how much smoke were you blowing up my ass when you told me that you loved me and wanted to marry me?” Well,” I stuttered, “I didn’t mean marriage right now, but I am I love with your hairy-legged ass.” She said, “I know the little game you have been playing with those sluts, ripping them off for their little pennies. I’m not a hoe, Al,” She stopped and looked me in the eyes. “A I told you. I have made one mistake in my life. I have a daughter seven years old who lives with my mother. At this time in my life, I’m tired of the streets and I’m ready to do something for myself. I like you very much, not love, right at the present time, but very interested in you. I’m not going to hoe for you or no man. But I will help my man accomplish anything in life that he thinks he can accomplish, if he’s, my man.

So, if you can agree with this and dig what I'm saying, then I can tell you I have taken the first step to accomplishing our first moves." I said, "I can dig where you are coming from." We were turning the corner of Sixty-Fifth and Cottage Grove going north. She continued talking. "Well, I've been busy since I last saw you. I have gotten a job at the cleaners right there near the grand ballroom on Sixty-Fourth and Cottage Grove across the street from the Mansfield Hotel. And I went a step further and got us our first house at Sixty-Fourth and Maryland. Would you like to see it now?" I said, "Man, man, man, you are a swift young lady." She said, "Yeah, I'm very swift when it comes to things I desire and want."

We were inside of the house now on Sixty-Fourth and Maryland. The room consisted of a closet, a small stove that sat in the corner, a small sink on the south side of the room, a small table with the leaf folded sat in front of the south wall. A window sat on the west side between two buildings. This room was naked on the west side of the room except for the bed that sat in in the middle of the wall. About four feet of empty space and hen the door. She looked at me and said, "Do you like it, baby?" I said, "Yes, and backed her up to the bed and made love on a naked mattress. We had moved in, and I turned over in the bed. It felt good to see Nella fixing breakfast. The small refrigerator we bought sat near the table with the door ajar showing eggs, cheese, butter, milk, etc. She looked at me. She said, "That bacon woke you up, didn't it?" I said, "yes, what time is it?" "It's nine o'clock. Do you know I got to get ready in half an hour for work. I work from eleven to seven. I'll be gone all day. So, you might as get up and get washed up and get ready to eat, Mr. Wynn." Before long, I was in my robe with a towel in my hand going to the bathroom. Nella had bought me a handsome set of pajamas, robe, and house shoes. She gave me a toothbrush, toothpaste, and a towel as I passed her. "Dong forget the crevices," she said.

I didn't think that was too funny. In the bathroom, I thanked God for meeting her. She was twenty-four years old, three years my senior, but she was very cool and level-headed. I, on the other hand, had just made twenty-one, and my job had closed down. I had to make up my mind whether I wanted to get another good hoe or another good job. I thought to myself. I can eat first and then think about it. After all, I had the whole day. I and some of the guys would go slut hunting during the day. We were dressing slick and talking slick out of the side of our mouths. I would hit a gambling joint every now and then. Most of the time, I won a little money. Other times, I would lose. I tried to not to lose my bankroll because it was all I had to keep me going. Sometimes I would meet a decent young lady that I could take over to sue Ross's hoe house where the tricks were eight dollars a throw. She would keep three of the dollars. I've had some girls stay there for at least three days. I would go by to check on my traps, Sue Ross robbing hoe house on Forty-Seventh and Calumet and Frank's hoe house at Forty -Sixth and Vincennes. If I copped the women out south, I would take her to forty-Sixth street. If I copped a woman from Forty-Sixth Street, I would take her out south. Most of the time after the girl works in a hoe house after four of five days, she would just leave because I wasn't spending any time with them. I was really just picking up money. And deep down in my heart I knew that really didn't care for the hoe game. I looked at it like a nasty filthy game. But then I didn't like working either. Keeping it real with myself, I didn't know what he fuck I liked. All I knew was that I liked money. I had my limitations on what I wouldn't do, but most of the things I would.

Six months had passed. I had the same routine. I was partying with hoes so strong that I forgot about the lady Had at home. I was neglecting everything that had to do with my arrangements with Nella. She only saw me after twelve o'clock at night and ten o'clock in the morning when she was going to work. We had moved into the apartment in Aril. Nine months had passed. Nella was getting ready to go to work as I was trying my tie in the mirror. She said, "What time will you be in tonight?" I said, "I don't know, why do you ask?" "Because I have something that I want to talk to you about." I said, "What is it that you want to talk about tonight that you can't tell me this morning" She said, "If you got time." I said, "I got all the time you need." She said, "You know, man, when I first met you, just your mere touch gave me goosebumps. But ain't nothing that you do to me is exciting anymore. Your kiss, your hugs don't do anything for me anymore." I could feel my knees kind of trembling, and tears were swelling in my eyes. She went on talking. "And as soon as you can, I wish you would move." I said, "I've got to go to the bathroom, hold your thought." I rushed in the bathroom in the hallway and looked in the mirror to see the first tear drop on my cheek. I almost started shaking as I reached to get the tissue to wipe the tears from my eyes. I braced myself and thought what the fuck is wrong with me. I was only dealing with another hoe. I wanted to fix my mind to think this way, but something inside of me was telling me that I was dealing with more than just a hoe. I was dealing with my heart, and it had begun to hurt. Her words pierced my heart. I was back in the room now. I was trying to find the words to say, but only the loud, uneducated part of me came out. "Bitch, I yelled out, I'm not leaving going no motherfucking where. I was happy at my mother's house, and you came around there fucking with me. When I find someone that is worthy, I will give you your motherfucking house and everything in it." She said, "I'm not rushing you, Al, the quicker, the better." I got mad at how calmly she said it that I almost slapped her. She left for work.

I had one hoe in a hoe house. I made my way to Sue Ross' hoe house. She said, "I got fifty dollars for you, Al, but your little cut out last night about twelve." I said, "That's alright, Sye, how are things?" She said, "It's slow." I folded the money and pt it in my pocket and left and went to the shoeshine parlor across from the crown Propeller Lounge. The man was beating up on my shoes. I said, "What's your name, man?" He said, "Harold." I said," "How old are you, about fifty?" He said, "Naw, I'm fifty-five." I said, "Look here, my man, I'm going to give you a five-dollar tip. I'm going to ask you a question. And if you answer the question correctly, I'm going to give you the five-dollar tip. Is hat alright with you?" He said, "Shoot with your question." "What does a woman mean when she says, 'there's nothing you can do to suit her, sex and all?" "It's just the way she said it. Either it means that she has another man, or his thang is bigger than yours. When a woman quits you, she mainly got another man." I damned near slapped him with that answer. "Good answer, pop." I gave him the five and stepped off the bench. He took the five dollars and said, I'm not finished." I said, "You are through with me," and walked out of the door.

For the next three days, Nella and I both slept on our sides of the bed, on the edge, not touching each other. Every morning we woke up not speaking to each other. She would go her way, and I would go mine. It was on a Friday when I caught a cab to Twenty-Ningh Street. I had to see Wadell. To my surprise, Henry's restaurant was closed. Eddie had copen ten years in Statesville for shooting some guy. Tommy had got stabbed in a crap game. He was alright, but he had moved to Fifty-fifth Street. Wadell had married a young girl and moved out of the neighborhood to Seventy-fifth and Exchange. Bill was still he bartender at Sam's, and Lee was still running around playing gobble-the goose. Everyone that I knew was happy to see me. I was dressed kind of neatly. I told everybody the damn lie that I had ten women in the streets. I headed back to Sixty-Fifth Street. I began to dread going up the apartment. It had almost been a month that I and Nella didn't speak. My clothes had begun to pile up on my side of the room. She wasn't taking them to the cleaners anymore. In fact, she was not cleaning up the house or making up the bed anymore. The night before, I had made about $250 gambling at Ann Hughes' place. I came and gathered up all my dirty laundry and things, socks and underwear and took them to the laundromat. There weas a cleaner's service also. I got the one-hour service on a suit and shirt. I had only brought five of my suits to Nella's house. The rest of my suits were at my mother's house. When I got home, I dressed to impress in my clean, laundered clothes. I left the washed clothes in the bags. I was going to make up my mind to go back to my mother's or get a hotel room of my own. The tension had gotten too great living her with Nella.

I walked to Ann Hughes' crap house. Only the houseman and the stickman were there betting on each other over craps, at the most two or three dollars. I walked back downstairs to the lounge. I must have played "This Bitter Earth" and "What A Difference A Day Makes" five times by Dinah washing. I loved the part where the record would say, "it's heavenly when you find romance on your menu, what a difference a day makes, and the difference is you." I had made it to the jukebox one more time when some woman busted out crying behind me. I turned to see a woman seated on a stool, head on the counter by my glass crying out loud. I turned and walked back to the counter. I said, "You alright, miss?" She didn't seem to hear me. I touched her on her arm and said, "Can I help you?" the barmaid was standing behind the bar just looking at the woman in a questioning kind of way. She said, "Huh. What?' as she wiped the tears from her eyes with her handkerchief. She looked at me. I said, "Deloris?" She said, "Yes." I said, "Al, form Drake School." She said, "Al, baby, how are you doing?" I said, "Fine, what's all the crying about?" She said, "Let me get my drink first."

She called the barmaid over and asked for a Bloody Mary, and she told he barmaid to give me what I was drinking. The barmaid said, The same?" I said "Yeah, a slow gin fizz." She turned sideways to rest her feet on my stool.

"Baby, I was married to a sixty-year-old guy who gave me everything I thought I wanted," and her voice started crackling again, "and they just gave his sixty years in the penitentiary." She went on crying. "I don't know what I'm going to do now! I mean, I got money and two cars. I live in the Kimbark Apartments, but I'm nothing without him." I said, "Don't feel bad," as I rubbed her back and kind of soothed her. "I'm in just as bad a shape as you are. My old lady just put me out even though we were not married, and it's nothing that I did wrong. It's my street lifestyle that's getting to her. Coming home late at night from hustling. I know I can't stand the misery of being with her any longer. I don't have a job or anything, but I have got to go somewhere. I got to get out of there." "Your worries just stopped, baby. You can come to my home with me. My man just got sixty years. I need company and I have always liked you, Al." "you wouldn't lie to me, would you, Deloris?" "You know I wouldn't lie to you at a time like this, and I have a lot to make up to you for.' "if that's the case, you can pick me up around 9:00 o'clock tonight "She said, "Yes, whatever time you tell me." "Well, come on when we finish with our drinks, I will show you where to pick me up." We stopped in front of my building. I showed her the side window. "That's where I live.," I told her, "If you come back tonight and blow at nine o'clock, I will come down."

It was a crisp, cold January afternoon, and she let the window down to get a better view of my house window. She shivered from the cold draft. "I got you, baby." She spoke. I asked her, "would you drop me off at the grocery store" We drove down to Sixty-Fifth and Cottage Grove. She dropped me off. "Nine o'clock," I said again.

She drove off, shaking her head. I hurried and did my shopping. A pound and a half of calf liver," I told the butcher. I got onions, two cans of Spanish rice, and two cans of spinach. I stopped and got a fifth of gin and some lime juice, and I was off for home. It was five-thirty when I put on the liver and onions. I poured a little water over the spinach to let it cook slowly. I put the Spanish rice in a saucepan and kind of left it on the table. I had changed into denim. And as fast as I could, I cleaned the room, mopped our floors, including the bathroom across the hall. Thre was a bleach odor at first and then when the liver kept cooking, you could smell the liver and onions smell above all others. After I had cleaned the house, the clock said 7:30 pm. In another half an hour, Nella would be coming up those stairs. She got off work at eight. I eased the rice on real low fire. The spinach was done and hot. You could smell that liver and onions a block away. I packed all my clothes in a suitcase. The two or three coats I tied together with a tie. I kept three suits on hangers. They were all folded and laid on top of the suitcase that was in the closet. I went to the bathroom and washed up and changed back into my suit. I turned the Victorian record player on, then in a low vice Nat King Cole was singing,

"Gee ain't it great after staying out late,
Walking my baby back home.
We stopped for a while,
She started to smile she sat with
Her head on my chest."

The record kept going on and on as I heard the downstairs door open, and I looked at the clock and it read 8:15 pm. I walked over to the refrigerator and got an ice tray and dropped he ice into a bowl. I could hear Nella slowly coming up the airs. I cracked the top of the bottle of gin and poured a big shot in a glass. I had picked up the lime juice when she stepped into the room. "Hi," she said, as Nat King Cole went on singing. "Hi," I said back. She said, "My, I see you have cleaned up." I said, "Oh, yes, I feel pretty good today." She said, "Why you got a job or something?" She said, "I see you're not really answering. I see you have cooked, too!" I said, "Yes, you can you do the honor of fixing the plates because the food is ready." I said, "Would you like me to fix you a drink?" She said, "yes.". She fixed the plates, and I ate at the table. She laid her coat on the foot of the bed. She sat on the bed and ate her food while listening to the records. When we were finished eating, I fixed her another drink. She did the dishes and I looked at the clock again, it was saying eight forty-five." I said, "I'm putting your drink over here, do you want me to sit it at the table?" She said, "I don't mind." Kind of smiling at me as if we were about to get it on. We were both sitting when I asked Nella, "You know I love you dearly, if I didn't show you, I'm sorry, but I thought it was understood how much I love you. I'm saying that to say this, that in these nine months that we have been together, I have enjoyed every second that turned into minutes and then hours that I spend with you. I don't know where I messed up with you, but in anyway during those nine months, If I have hurt you, I'm sorry. You know I told you, when you first told me to leave that when I found someone worthy of me, I would leave. I have found someone, and I'm leaving tonight. I packed your suitcase, that was in the closet with my clothes and my sister will bring your suitcase back to you." I was still looking at her now. She was looking down at her drink. I was trying to see a kind of change in her facial expression, but there was one. I went on talking. My friend is supposed to pick me up at nine." We both looked at the clock together. Now the clock said 9:05 pm. I went on talking "Maybe it would have been different with us if you would have let me know where I went wrong or when I hurt your feelings. But whatever it was, if I did something, I'm sorry?" I looked at the clock again, and it was ten after nine. I started to get worried now, supposed Deloris don't show and I would look like the dandyish fool in Chicago, and a bigger fool if I had to drag this shit through the snow. I got up and went to the stack of forty-five records we had on the floor by the table. I picked up the first record on the stack. I took off Nat King Cole, and replaced it wht the record, I'm in the Mood for Love." And he record was saying,

"I'm in the mood for love,
Simply because you're near me,
It's funny but,
When you're near me I'm in the mood for love
Heaven is in your eyes, bright as the stars.
We're under, oh, is it any wonder
that I'm in the mood for love."

I looked back over at Nella. I was just certain that her expression had changed, but she was still drinking down her drink with that same blank expression on her face. I looked back over to the clock. it said twenty-five after nine. I started to say something silly to Nella when I heard the horn blow three times. I rushed to the window. It was her. She was waving. I raised the window a little bit and yelled, "I'll be right down. I let the window down and turned to see Nella standing behind me with big tears rolling down her cheeks and a big butcher knife drawn over her head in the stabbing position. She said, "You better tell that bitch to get the fuck away from here before I kill her motherfucking ass!!" Then with one motion, she dropped the knife and fell to her knees and locked her arms around my legs, "Don't leave me, I love you so much, don't leave me." Why was I so relieved to know that she still cared for me and that knot that I had been carrying in my stomach seemed to melt away. I was myself, and the hurt was gone. "Bitch," I said, in a screaming voice, "why didn't you just say you loved me instead of taking me through all this bullshit. And if you ever pull another knife on me again, I'm going to knock your teeth out." The horn was still blowing, louder and louder as I helped Nella get off the floor. We took two or three steps together, then we both fell across the bed, and she was still saying, "I love you, al, I love you, Al." And I said, "I love you, too, baby." The night was a great thrill as we slipped into total bliss! The next morning when I awakened, Nella was up and dressing and when she noticed I was awakened, she kissed me on my forehead and told me that my breakfast was on the table. I felt better as far as the knot in my stomach, but I was still concerned about where we went wrong. I love her, and she loves me, but we didn't get an understanding past the fact that we loved each other. My mind began to go back to Mr. Buddy's' words about wisdom, "But along with wisdom, there must be understanding." When Nella first brought me to her apartment, she told me that she knew what I did with the sluts. She also stated that she would never hoe for me like the sluts. But it was never discussed how she really felt as far as my lifestyle and Could I still keep that part in my life hustling the hoes. It should have been agreed upon between us, such as certain period of time allowed for me to wrap up my dealings with the hoes. Even with my gambling. Wadell's words came back to me. He said, "shooting craps is good, but it will not support you forever. In the crap game world, something you win, and sometimes you lose." I know now that I love Nella. The real discussion is what am I going to do next. I know now I can't keep going on with the hoes, staying out all night, too tired to make love to Nella, and too tired to do the things that a man in a real relationship should do. Working at the Powder Egg Factory, from nine to five already showed me that I don't like the nine to five kinds of world. It was too confining. I had to find something that I could do legally, which would earn me enough money to maintain myself and sable me to take care of Nella, I had gotten tired of this life. A filthy nasty world, messing with the hoes. Always degrading women, influencing them to sell themselves. I once asked Bob, "What was a pimp?" It has taken me some time to figure it out for myself, what it stands for, and what it was. The highest level that a pimp can go to is a slut eater and a woman beater! If a person my age or younger want to be a shit eater, it is entirely up to them. But I know now that I'm through with the pimp game. I was through with the rawness of it. I was going to find out today what I am all about, what I'm meant to d in life I had always from a young boy who wanted ot be a lawyer or preacher. I don't know why it was just embedded in me. I didn't get enough schooling for either one. But it's never too late. I have a lifetime ahead of me!

Milton Keynes UK
Ingram Content Group UK Ltd.
UKHW020100271124
451585UK00012B/1330

9 798891 902152